# MEGARGEE'S GUIDE TO OBTAINING A PSYCHOLOGY INTERNSHIP

# MEGARGEE'S GUIDE TO OBTAINING A PSYCHOLOGY INTERNSHIP

Fourth Edition

Edwin I. Megargee, Ph.D., A.B.P.P.

Routledge
Taylor & Francis Group
New York London

First published 2011 by Routledge

Published 2017 by Routledge
711 Third Avenue, New York, NY 10017, USA
2 Park Square, Milton Park, Abingdon, Oxon OX14 4RN

First issued in hardback 2017

*Routledge is an imprint of the Taylor & Francis Group, an informa business*

Copyright © 2001 Taylor & Francis.

All rights reserved. No part of this book may be reprinted or reproduced or utilised in any form or by any electronic, mechanical, or other means, now known or hereafter invented, including photocopying and recording, or in any information storage or retrieval system, without permission in writing from the publishers.

Cover design by Joe Dieter

A CIP catalog record for this book is available from the British Library.
 The paper in this publication meets the requirements of the ANSI Standard Z39.48-1984 (Permanence of Paper)

Library of Congress Cataloging-in-Publication Data
Megargee, Edwin Inglee
 [Guide to obtaining a psychological internship]
 Megargee's guide to obtaining a psychology internship / Edwin I. Megargee.-- 4th ed.
 p. cm.
 Includes bibliographical references and index.
 ISBN 1-58391-319-X
 1. Psychology--Study and teaching (Internship) I. Title.

BF77 .M39 2001
150'.79'73--dc21                                                      2001043162

ISBN 13: 978-1-5839-1319-2 (pbk)
ISBN 13: 978-1-1384-6282-3 (hbk)

# CONTENTS

| | |
|---|---|
| Acknowledgments and Dedication | vii |
| Preface | ix |

**1** A Short Course on Predoctoral Internships — 1

**2** Applying for Internship: An Overview — 18

**3** Establishing Your Priorities — 43

**4** Where to Apply? Compiling Your Application List — 68

**5** Preparing Your Resume or CV — 94

**6** Preparing Your Internship Applications — 114

**7** Traveling to Internships: How to Survive and Stay Solvent — 138

**8** The Site Visit and Interview — 155

**9** The Endgame — 173

**10** Dealing With Adversity — 191

Appendix 1: Useful Web Sites for Internship Applicants — 205

**vi** Contents

**Appendix 2: Availability of Internship Positions by Region and State**       207

**Appendix 3: A Sample Curriculum Vitae**       210

**Appendix 4: Questions Interviewers Ask Intern Applicants**       216

**Appendix 5: Questions Applicants Can Ask Interviewers**       221

**References**       224

**Index**       230

# ACKNOWLEDGMENTS AND DEDICATION

I am grateful to the many people who have helped make this book and its three predecessors possible. First and foremost are the many Florida State University graduate students with whom I have shared the internship application process. Their comments, encounters, and reflections on their experiences formed the essence of the first three editions of this book. Next are the internship applicants across the country who have contributed to the Association of Psychology Postdoctorate and Internship Centers (APPIC) intern applicant listserv, especially those candidates who took the time to submit thoughtful critiques of the previous edition of this book. It is they who contributed the interview questions in Appendices 4 and 5 and provided the "war stories" and examples that make this book real.

I am also indebted to the many internship training directors and their staffs whom I have visited and interviewed, from Los Angeles to Boston and from Miami to Seattle, not only for their hospitality but also for their candor and their insights into the internship selection process.

I wish to thank the Board Members of APPIC for their contributions to all four editions and for their efforts to make the internship selection process simpler and fairer for all concerned. Previous editions especially benefited from the advice and counsel of Sanford Pederson, Bernhard Blom, and Robert Klepac. Gregory Keilin and James Stedman were especially helpful in providing information for the present edition.

Sue Cunningham and Marissa Scalla assisted with the library research and with transcribing data from the APPIC *Directories* (Hall & Cantrell, 1996; Hall & Hsu, 1999) into spreadsheets so I could compute the statistics of various types of internships in different parts of the country. A special thanks to Capt. Klaus Dieter Herrgutt, Master Mariner, and the crew of the freighter MV *Superba Bridge* for fabricating the table and providing a spot where I could work on the manuscript and gaze at our wake as we crossed the Atlantic and Mediterranean. Also to my editor, Tim Julet, who worked on the revision while coping with his own serious illness.

vii

viii Acknowledgments and Dedication

Most of all, I wish to acknowledge the contribution of my wife and life's shipmate, Sara Jill Mercer, for her work and support of this and my other writing endeavors. She is my partner and collaborator on this project, as she is on everything worthwhile in my life, and it is to her that this edition, like the three previous ones, is dedicated.

# PREFACE

Since the third edition of this book was published in 1997, there have been important changes in the process of obtaining a predoctoral psychology internship. In many ways the process of applying for internships is easier than ever before. The current rules governing internship selection and the advent of computerized matching of applicants to sites have eliminated most of the duplicity and cheating associated with previous systems and made the system fairer for applicants and training sites alike. Standardized application forms have simplified the application procedure and reduced the paperwork. Electronic communications and the Internet have made it vastly easier to obtain and exchange information.

Offsetting these advances is the "supply-demand" problem. When the first edition of this book was published in 1990, every qualified applicant could be assured of obtaining an internship. It might not be accredited by the American Psychological Association (APA), and it might not be your top choice, but somewhere there would be a slot available. Not any more. Since 1996, there have been substantially more applicants than there are positions. Every year 10% to 15% of the participants fail to get positions. Most of these unsuccessful applicants reapply, adding to the competition the following year. There is no sign that this imbalance will change in the foreseeable future.

Applying for internships has always been exceedingly stressful. Everyone agrees that it involves an inordinate amount of your time, effort, and money. Since the number of applicants has outstripped the number of available positions, students have become even more anxious, and those who remain unmatched are frustrated and often furious. To achieve their career goals, they must have an internship, and somehow, somewhere, someone is obligated to provide them with one.

Unfortunately, that is not how the internship selection process works. It is up to you as an applicant to obtain your internship. Others can help, and this book will assist you, but ultimately it is your responsibility to seek and obtain an internship for yourself. If you are unsuccessful, you must wait a whole year to try again, settle for a career as a master's level psychologist, or abandon professional psychology. Getting angry doesn't

x    Preface

help. Neither does submitting dozens of applications. Instead of working harder, you need to work "smarter."

In today's marketplace, there is no point applying before you are ready. You must make sure you are fully prepared academically, professionally, and personally to succeed in internship. You must learn to assess your qualifications, personal as well as professional, and evaluate them as the Internship Selection Committees will. If you have liabilities, you must determine the best way to overcome them.

When you are ready to apply, you need to be able to select the settings that are best for you, with your special mixture of abilities and goals. You must learn to prepare applications that emphasize your particular talents and skills and to interview Internship Training Directors (ITDs) effectively. As the date to submit rankings draws near, you must evaluate the sites and decide how to rank them. If you fail to obtain an internship on Matching Day, as 15% to 20% of the applicants do, you must be able overcome your disappointment and use the APPIC Clearinghouse effectively to obtain one of the unfilled slots.

Accomplishing all of this while maintaining your obligations to your training program, your job, your significant others, and yourself requires a great deal of specialized knowledge, effective time management, and the ability to cope with stress. It is essential that you understand the implicit as well as the explicit rules of the internship selection game, and learn the agendas and concerns of the other players, especially the ITDs. Your Academic Director of Clinical Training (ADCT) can help you to some extent, but you must realize that your ADCT's primary loyalty is to the overall training program and not to you as an individual. There may be times when what is best for the program may not be what is best for you.

I wrote this book to give you the information and advice you need to succeed. My first goal is to educate you about the internship selection process and why it works the way it does. The second is to advise you how to assess your assets and limitations, skills and abilities, and, in the light of this assessment, how to formulate your priorities for internship, select the sites that best meet your needs, prepare your applications and supporting materials, and interview effectively. The more information you have, the better able you will be to survive the internship selection process successfully with as little damage as possible to your self-esteem, health, relationships, and credit line.

## ☐ Plan for This Volume

There is a lot of game playing that goes on during internship selection. You must understand the rules of the game and the strategies of the players. In addition to you, the applicants, these players include the ITDs and their staffs, the ADCTs and their faculty colleagues, and two organizations, the APA, which sets forth what should be included in internship training, and APPIC, which regulates the internship selection process. While you are new to the game, all these other players have long histories of dealing with internship selection and training. In Chapter 1, I brief you on this history so you can understand where they are coming from. I describe the politics of internship selection and how and why the current rules evolved. Once you understand the concerns and vested interests of the other parties and their power struggles over the years, you will be better prepared to take a hand in the current selection game.

Chapter 2 gives you an overview of the internship selection process. In it, I provide you with a month-by-month timeline of how to prepare by formulating your priorities, selecting the sites that best meet your needs, writing a resume, preparing successful applications, and favorably impressing selection committees. The remaining chapters expand on these points.

Your first two tasks are preparing yourself to go on internship and deciding when and where to apply. Chapter 3, "Establishing Your Priorities," will help you evaluate your strengths and weaknesses and decide what you want in an internship. Chapter 4, "Compiling Your Application List," tells you how to obtain up-to-date and accurate information about the sites that interest you. I also provide you with information about the competitiveness and preferences of internships in various regions of the United States.

The next two chapters deal with the application process. Chapter 5 teaches you how to prepare a resume or curriculum vitae (CV) designed for internship applications, and Appendix 3 provides a sample CV. In Chapter 6, I instruct you on how to obtain and complete the APPIC *Uniform Application Form* and the other documents you must prepare when applying for internships.

Once you have completed and submitted your applications, you should obtain interviews and visit as many of the sites as possible. Chapter 7 gives you practical advice on traveling to internship sites and reducing transportation costs. Chapter 8, "The Site Visit and Interview," tells how to interview effectively and make the most of your site visits. Appendices 4 and 5 provide you with sample questions asked by Selection Committees and the questions you can ask them.

Finally, you must evaluate the information you have obtained and formulate a ranked list of sites to submit to the National Matching Service. Chapter 9 advises you on how to follow up your interviews and rank the internships to which you have applied. Finally, Chapter 10 describes how to cope with various adversities such as not obtaining a position on Matching Day.

As you can see, I have designed this book to help you with all phases of

**xii** Preface

obtaining your internship. Begin by reading the first two chapters to get an understanding of the overall selection process. Next skim the rest of the book, including the Appendices, to give yourself an overview of what you will need to do in the weeks and months to come. Later, reread each chapter more thoroughly when it is time for you to tackle each of the tasks that is described. You can use the timetable included in Chapter 2 to keep on schedule.

Good luck.

Edwin I. Megargee, Ph.D., ABPP
Director of Clinical Training
Florida State University

# A Short Course on Predoctoral Internships

This chapter provides you with the background information you need to understand what predoctoral internships in professional psychology are, what they are supposed to accomplish, and how the rules governing internship selection evolved over the years.

## ☐ Trends in Graduate Education in Clinical Psychology

The American Psychological Association (APA) has accredited doctoral training programs in professional psychology for over 50 years. Ever since the Boulder Conference of 1949, a year-long predoctoral internship, ideally in an APA-accredited program, has been an essential requirement for doctoral degrees in clinical, counseling, and school psychology.

What constitutes an internship? APA, the Association of Psychology Postdoctoral and Internship Centers (APPIC), the American Association of State Psychology Boards (which coordinates licensing), and the National Register of Health Service Providers in Psychology have collaborated on a uniform operational definition of what goes into a satisfactory predoctoral internship training program. These criteria, which are reprinted in the front of the annual APPIC *Directory* (Hall & Hsu, 2000), stipulate that a psychology internship is an organized program of training that goes beyond supervised clinical experience or on-the-job training. Each internship must have a clearly designated, licensed, doctoral-level director

## 2  Megargee's Guide to Obtaining a Psychology Internship

who is on site at least 20 hours weekly and who is responsible for the quality and integrity of the program, as well as at least two full-time, licensed, doctoral-level supervisors (one of whom may also be the director) who provide each intern with at least 2 hours of direct individual supervision each week. An internship must have at least two full-time interns who must work at least 1,500 hours over a 9- to 24-month period, at least 25% of which must be in direct face-to-face service with clients. In addition, at least 2 hours weekly must be spent in didactic training such as case conferences, grand rounds, seminars, and the like. The nature and goals and the quantity and quality of the work expected of the interns, who may also be called residents or fellows, must be written and made available in a brochure.

The 1987 National Conference on Internship Training stated:

> The purpose of the internship is to provide a systematic program of supervised, applied psychological training which extends and is consistent with the prior research, didactic, and applied experience of graduate education and training. Internship training will provide for the integration of scientific, professional, and ethical knowledge, attitudes, and basic skills to professional practice. The internship continues to provide for the professional socialization and development of professional identity. The person who completes the internship training is an individual who has demonstrated the capability to function autonomously and responsibly as a practicing psychologist. (Belar et al., 1987, p. 4)

Predoctoral psychology internships are available in a wide variety of settings. In the United States, the most numerous are university counseling centers (110 sites, 19%), community mental health centers (72 sites, 13%), Veterans Administration (VA) medical centers and clinics (69 sites, 13%), medical schools, (69 sites, 13%), state hospitals (52 sites; 10%), children's facilities (47 sites, 9%), consortia (37 sites, 7%), the psychiatric units of general hospitals (25 sites, 5%), private psychiatric hospitals (24 sites, 5%), correctional facilities (14 sites, 3%), and military internships (9 sites, 2%) (Hall & Hsu, 1999). A few internships can also be found at school districts, health maintenance organizations (HMOs), rehabilitation hospitals, facilities for the developmentally disabled, and pastoral counseling centers.

Although graduating from an APA-accredited degree program is not required for state licensure, for inclusion in the National Register, or for obtaining a diploma issued by the American Board of Examiners in Professional Psychology (ABPP), APA accreditation criteria have become the "gold standard" by which training programs are judged. If your degree is not from an APA-accredited program, you will continually need to convince various credentialing bodies that your program equaled or exceeded APA standards.

## The Origins of Psychology Internships

For the first half of the 20th century, APA had no involvement in professional training. Prior to World War II, APA was a learned society whose primary concerns were promoting and publishing scientific research (Resnick, 1997). In the early years, APA's membership requirements included a Ph.D., an academic teaching position, and a record of published scientific research (Brems, Thevenin, & Routh, 1991). Indeed, in those days there were no formal training programs in applied psychology. Future practitioners earned university degrees in scientific psychology and obtained whatever professional training they could from mentors, reading, or trial and error (Peterson, 1991).

As it did in so many other areas of American life, World War II fostered drastic changes in graduate education in professional psychology. The war created an acute need for mental health personnel to assist the military in screening and classifying troops upon induction into the service and, later, in treating GIs suffering from war-induced traumas. As the war drew to a close, the federal government recognized the need to provide mental health services to the 16 million veterans who were returning to civilian life. Funds for training clinical psychologists were made available through the VA and the National Institute for Mental Health (NIMH; Peterson, 1991).

An educational program of this magnitude created an urgent need for agreed-upon models for graduate training in clinical psychology and for standards that could be used to evaluate the adequacy of training programs and the competency of their graduates. The VA and NIMH asked APA and the American Association for Applied Psychology (AAAP), a professional organization for practitioners, to develop models and standards for graduate training in clinical psychology and to identify university programs that met these criteria. During the 1940s, joint task forces of APA and AAAP met to consider schemes for training and accreditation (Laughlin & Worley, 1991).

In 1945, AAAP merged with APA. The new APA by-laws stipulated that the goals of the organization were to advance psychology as a profession as well as a science and to promote human welfare. Publications and an academic appointment were no longer required for membership, making it easier for practitioners to join.

A new APA Committee on Training in Clinical Psychology headed by David Shakow proposed a model that combined university-based academic training with a year-long clinical internship. The internship would involve supervised, direct clinical experience in inpatient settings combined with indirect experience, such as case conferences, and with administrative experience in which the interns familiarized themselves with the facilities where they worked by participating in staff meetings, main-

**4**    Megargee's Guide to Obtaining a Psychology Internship

taining patient records, and preparing reports. Students were expected to go on internship in their 3rd year of graduate training, after which they would return to their academic settings for their 4th and final year, during which they could integrate their academic and clinical experiences, ideally by conducting a dissertation on a clinical topic (Davies, 1987; Laughlin & Worley, 1991). This model assumed that relatively little direct clinical training would take place in the university setting. It further recommended that APA establish an accreditation program with on-site visits occurring every 5 years (Brems et al., 1991). These recommendations were adopted at an NIMH-funded conference on graduate clinical training held at Boulder, Colorado in 1949. Thus was born the "scientist-professional" or "Boulder model" of clinical training.

## Early Patterns of Clinical Education

Devised largely by academicians, the original Boulder model emphasized the scientific end of the scientist-professional continuum. University faculty members expected Boulder model Ph.D.s to become research producers, not just research consumers. They considered those graduates who went on to do clinical research in academic and medical school settings as successes, but regarded those who never published and went into full-time practice as "hand holders" who had wasted their mentors' time (Peterson, 1991).

During the years when clinical training grants and VA stipends were readily available, graduate education in clinical psychology was controlled by the ADCTs and university faculties. Traditional academic departments were able to retain their scientific values while reaping important practical rewards. By enrolling large numbers of graduate students in clinical psychology, and by winning large clinical training grants, academic departments of psychology were able to generate increased numbers of faculty positions and obtain more space from their universities.

As is so often the case in the internship game, when one player prospers, others become dissatisfied. While the academic departments were, as the late Red Barber would have said, "sitting in the catbird seat," many internship training centers felt as if they were at the bottom of the bird cage. It appeared to them that the universities promoted research training at the expense of preparation for internship. As Peterson (1991, p. 423) noted, "Situated as they were in academic departments, controlled as they were by researchers, the Boulder-style programs all too often neglected training for practice." Summarizing the results of a survey of Internship Training Directors (ITDs), Shemberg and Leventhal (1981, p. 639) reported, "Consistent with previous data, considerable dissatisfaction exists among directors relative to university preparation in clinical skills. Interns are seen by many as not well-prepared in assessment or psycho-

A Short Course on Predoctoral Internships   5

therapeutic activities." In one brief year, the internship center was expected to provide the bulk of the student's clinical training. One ITD and his colleagues warned the academic programs, "In your attempts to mold a scientist-practitioner, beware of over emphasizing the scientist at the expense of the practitioner" (Stedman et al., 1981, p. 419).

## Changing Patterns in Clinical Education

Most university-based training programs have since moved closer to the middle of the scientist-professional continuum. Few graduate students today have to pass foreign language examinations, as my classmates and I did (French, German, Russian—pick two), and today's clinical curriculum provides students with much more clinical instruction and practicum experience than the early Boulder-model programs afforded.

Today's students also differ from those of the 1950s. In those days, graduate students in clinical psychology were typically young men supported by government-financed fellowships, unburdened by student loans, and unfettered by family obligations. It was no great hardship for them to leave their graduate programs for a year and later return to their universities to complete their academic requirements. After the United States Public Health Services (USPHS) fellowship program and clinical training grants were phased out during the Nixon and Ford administrations, it became necessary for most clinical graduate students to earn their stipends in practicum settings, thereby extending the amount of time required to complete a degree. Older students in general, and women in particular, are more likely to have family obligations that make it difficult for them to relocate for a year. As a result, today's students typically complete most, if not all, of their academic requirements before leaving for internship and do not return to their universities.

As a result of the decrease in government-supported clinical training, most internships must now support their interns with agency funds. Many rely heavily on fees generated by the interns and their supervisors to underwrite the cost of training. Indeed, the internship training program may be expected to show a profit (Brickley, 1998; Greenberg, Cradock, Godbole, & Temkin, 1998). In today's marketplace, a 2nd-year student who has received little or no clinical training would find it difficult if not impossible to compete successfully for a fully funded APA-approved internship. Internships now demand a higher level of clinical preparation than the original Boulder model envisioned.

## The Rise of Professional Schools

The Korean war exacerbated the VA's need for mental health practitioners, and the deinstitutionalization of the mentally ill and the prolifera-

6   Megargee's Guide to Obtaining a Psychology Internship

tion of community-based mental health centers in the 1960s increased the demand for clinical psychologists—personnel needs that were not being met by the traditional programs. For example, even though the California State Psychological Association had urged the state's universities to expand their clinical training programs, the entire University of California system turned out less than 20 Ph.D.s in clinical psychology annually (Peterson, 1991).

Although there was a market for practitioners, the decrease in federal support of graduate education in clinical psychology led many universities to reduce the number of graduate students they accepted. Although they welcomed large numbers of undergraduate psychology majors and adopted undergraduate curricula that would prepare these majors for graduate school, only a fraction of those graduating with bachelors degrees in psychology were admitted into their doctoral training programs (Stricker, 1997). University-based scientist-professional training typically followed the scientific tradition in which faculty mentors worked closely with a limited number of graduate students on their research teams. There was insufficient room in their laboratories for all the students seeking graduate education in psychology, especially those whose primary interests were in practice rather than research.

In response to these pressures, various alternatives to the Boulder model were considered in a series of APA-sponsored training conferences at Miami Beach (1958), Princeton (1962), Chicago (1965), Vail (1973), and Salt Lake City (1987). In the 1960s, Psy.D. programs and free-standing schools of professional psychology were initiated. By 1982, there were 44 such practitioner programs in the United States with almost 5,000 students enrolled (Brems et al., 1991).

Unlike traditional academic departments, free-standing professional schools typically rely on the fees paid by students to support their programs. It is to their financial advantage to have large classes. In the past, the traditional academic departments had served as the gatekeepers to professional psychology. My entering class at Berkeley had 25 students, but only 3 of us eventually obtained our doctorates in clinical psychology. With the proliferation of independent professional training programs, the gatekeeping function has now shifted to the internships and the postdoctoral programs. Since 1996, there have been substantially more applicants for predoctoral and postdoctoral positions than there are slots available (Constantine, Keilin, Litwinowicz, & Romanus, 1997; Keilin, 2000; Keilin, Thorne, Rodolfa, Constantine, & Kaslow, 2000; Oehlert & Lopez, 1998).

## Impact of Managed Care

Like the other mental health agencies, most internships have been operating under financial constraints in recent years (Constantine & Gloria,

A Short Course on Predoctoral Internships **7**

1996). Whereas universities and professional schools are in the business of providing education, training is only an ancillary activity at most internship sites. In an era of reduced budgets and "downsizing," some centers are tempted to lower their costs by cutting back or eliminating internship training. In this era of managed health care (MHC), internships, like other mental health providers, have had increasing difficulty billing for the services performed by interns and postdoctoral fellows (Brown, 1996; Constantine & Gloria, 1998). As part of their quality assurance programs, many third-party providers will only pay for services performed by licensed health care providers. If an unlicensed technician carries out a procedure, the licensed provider often must be in the room directly supervising the activity for it to be reimbursable. Reviewing a videotape of a procedure is not sufficient.

This model does not work well for psychologists. Unlike X-ray technicians, nurses, and physicians' assistants, most psychology trainees do not have any sort of license, even though they typically have a master's degree or the equivalent, and it is obviously impractical for an intern's licensed supervisor to be physically present throughout the administration of a lengthy test battery or psychotherapy session. In settings where rules such as this apply, the range of clients that an intern may see can be severely limited if the facility wishes to be reimbursed for the intern's services.

Possible solutions to this dilemma are being discussed (Brown, 1996). Since MHC systems are accustomed to reimbursing for services performed by medical interns or residents, one proposal is that students should defend their dissertations and be awarded their degrees *before* going on internship. This would present a major change, since APA has always insisted that a *pre*doctoral internship is a prerequisite for the doctoral degree in clinical psychology. Still, as we have seen, when money talks, educational programs listen. Another suggestion is to create some sort of limited master's-level license that would permit third-party reimbursements for selected procedures. This would have to be done on a state-by-state basis, and indeed, some states already have master's level-licenses. These discussions are continuing, and their outcome may significantly influence the nature of psychology internships.

Constantine and Gloria's (1996) recent survey of 311 APPIC ITDs suggests that MHC is having a negative impact on internship training; 96 of the 311 ITDs (31%) reported that MHC had affected the number of internship slots, 90 (29%) indicated that MHC had affected the criteria they use in selecting interns, 96 (31%) stated that MHC had affected their ability to fund current internship positions, 87 (28%) reported an adverse effect on the quality of their training, and 142 (46%) responded that MHC had limited the types of services their interns could provide. One implication of these findings is that applicants who have some sort of license or credential may be preferred by some internships, as will stu-

**8**    Megargee's Guide to Obtaining a Psychology Internship

dents with expertise in brief assessments and interventions and those with experience dealing with HMOs (Spruill & Pruitt, 2000). It is no accident that the standard internship application form includes a question asking applicants, "Do you have experience with Managed Care Providers?"

## ☐ APPIC and the Internship Selection Process

As with graduate training, there have been significant changes in the internship application and selection process in the years since the Boulder conference.

### The *Laissez Faire* Period

Before certain internship centers banded together to form APPIC, there were few if any rules governing internship application or selection. Throughout the 1950s and 1960s, the internship selection process was quite simple for most applicants: They went on internship when and where their faculty advisors or ADCTs told them to go. Successful ADCTs established relationships with their favorite training centers, often staffed by former students, which could be relied upon to accept the current students they recommended. In turn, these internships could count on receiving one or more good students each year from these universities.

Imagine yourself as a student in the mid-1960s. If you had a well-connected ADCT or major professor, you attended the internship he (and it typically was a "he") arranged for you. At some point you would be summoned to your Great Mentor's office, advised that next year you would be going on internship, and told which internship you would be attending. With that taken care of, you could go back to the laboratory. As long as you didn't mind being told what to do, these "Old Boy" networks reduced the stress and eliminated the uncertainty of the internship selection process. (By the time this year is over, you may think that was a pretty good system.)

This Old Boy system worked well for the Old Boys and their students, but for those who were not included in these networks, the selection process was chaotic. If you did not have a powerful mentor, you went through an application process similar to the current one except there was no computer matching and no ground rules. Since there was also no APPIC *Directory*, you relied on the brochures sent by the various facilities. (Of course, the brochures did not indicate that some of the positions listed were already allocated through the Old Boy network.)

Let us suppose that after reading the brochures, interviewing at the several sites, and discussing them with faculty and friends, you decided that the best internship site for you was the "Codliver Consortium" and that your second choice was the "Septicemia School of Medicine." In the days before APPIC and Uniform Notification, you might have received a call from the ITD at Septicemia in mid-January offering you an internship for the coming year and giving you 48 hours in which to decide, after which the offer would be withdrawn. You, or your ADCT, would then call the ITD at Codliver and discover that they were operating on a different schedule and were still actively interviewing applicants. While they had been very impressed with you and your credentials and considered you definitely in the running, no offers would be made to anyone before February.

Assuming your ADCT could not cut some deal with the Codliver ITD or get the people at Septicemia to back off, you would be left with two options: (a) you could accept the position at Septicemia and make a binding commitment to attend their program, or (b) you could decline and hope that you would get an offer from Codliver. (Don't even think about the possibility of accepting Septicemia and changing your mind if you subsequently got a Codliver offer. The one rule that has remained constant in the internship game is that accepting an internship is a binding commitment.)

The *laissez faire* system was frustrating not only to the students but also to the ADCTs and ITDs who were not part of the Old Boy networks. By the late 1960s and early 1970s, the "baby boomers" were applying to graduate school. The resulting increase in the number of academic clinical training programs had produced many "New Boys," as well as "New Girls," who were on the outside looking in.

## Uniform Notification

In 1968 a group of ITDs decided to try to bring order to the chaotic system that then prevailed. They banded together to persuade their colleagues to adopt a uniform system of internship selection and notification. The result was The Association of Psychology Internship Centers (APIC), since renamed the Association of Psychology and Postdoctoral Internship Centers (APPIC). (For the sake of simplicity, I shall simply use the acronym APPIC regardless of the year being discussed.) In his history of the Association, Stedman (1989) wrote:

> APIC was organized primarily to deal with a lack of regularity in the intern selection process. . . . [S]tudents of the late '60s complained about deals being made between internship sites and certain select students. . . . [They] . . . complained that their clinical training directors didn't know what to do [and] there was often undue stress on students. (p. 35)

APPIC's first concern was to regularize the then-chaotic selection and notification process. It did so by formulating rules on how the internship

**10**  Megargee's Guide to Obtaining a Psychology Internship

selection process should work and persuading the internship training centers to adopt them (Stedman, 1989). This was a major undertaking. Then, as now, ITDs were reluctant to relinquish their autonomy or surrender their illusion of control.

Older APPIC members remember the early day-to-day struggle to survive. In those days APPIC was a poorly funded, loose confederation that literally lived out of a cardboard box, "a traveling road show, moving from one location to another with each new election" (Stedman, 1989, p. 35). Meetings were held in a Board member's hotel room with participants sitting on the bed and floor. Just producing the *Directory* each year strained its resources, and only recently was APPIC able to establish a professionally staffed central office.

Although it got off to a shaky start, by 1999 APPIC had 567 predoctoral and 66 postdoctoral training centers (Hall & Hsu, 1999). An additional 600 postdoctoral centers have been invited to join (Kaslow, 2000). Members are expected to adhere to APPIC policies and to pay dues; in return, they are listed in the annual APPIC *Directory* and allowed to participate in the computerized matching procedure. While APA sets forth standards for graduate education and accredits university and internship training centers, APPIC has assumed responsibility for formulating the rules governing the internship selection process and, to the best of its ability, persuading all concerned to adhere to them. The once all-powerful university and professional school faculties now have little influence on internship selection and training.

The idea behind APPIC was that internship training centers should agree on a common set of procedures and a uniform selection schedule to eliminate the unfair competition that too often forced students to decide whether to accept offers from their second, third, or lower ranked internships before they had heard from their first choice. Under the "Uniform Notification Day" (UND) policy, the APPIC members agreed among themselves that no ITD could make an offer before an agreed-upon time and that students were to be guaranteed a reasonable amount of time to consider these offers. Moreover, no ITD could make an offer to a student who had already accepted an offer from another institution.

In the interest of fairness to applicants and internship training centers alike, APPIC also stipulated that no training center could make more offers than they had slots available. Once an offer had been made to an applicant on UND, that opening was committed and, until the applicant declined the offer, it could not be offered to anyone else. In short, a student who was holding an offer owned that slot until the selection period ended. An agency with six positions could not make eight offers figuring two people would probably decline. Once its sixth position had been offered, no more offers could be proffered until a student who was holding an offer rejected it.

The ITDs felt that this policy granted students too much power and

A Short Course on Predoctoral Internships    **11**

control over the selection process, especially in the early days when students had several days to decide. Every ITD had horror stories of applicants who held offers for lengthy periods of time, thus tying up the selection process for hours. After UND in 1994, APPIC conducted a survey of 300 internship training centers. One question asked what had been the longest time an applicant held an offer. In 1994, UND lasted from 8:00 AM until 5:00 PM, CST; 51% of the ITDs reported applicant held bids three or more hours, and 17% reported holds of six or more hours (APPIC, 1994).

Why the delays? Some students would put off deciding where they really wanted to go until UND. Others would collect a number of offers and then choose the best one. However, the principle reason students held bids was because they were waiting for an offer from another institution they preferred to attend. A student accepted by her second or third choice would hold that offer hoping to be accepted by her first choice.

In self-defense, internship training sites developed lists of alternate candidates. When a student elected to hold an offer, the ITDs would call the alternates and urge them not to accept another position until the agency had received definite responses of acceptance or rejection to all their outstanding bids. If an alternate agreed to wait until he heard from his first choice, he would naturally hold onto any offer he had already received from lower ranked internships, which in turn asked their alternates not to accept other bids, thus compounding the problem.

Sometimes "gridlocks" occurred (May & Dana, 1990). In a classic gridlock, Adam would have "Halibut Hospital" for his first choice and "Moosehead Medical Center" as his second, while Bettina chose Moosehead as her first choice and Halibut for her second. On UND, Halibut offers a slot to Bettina, while Moosehead selects Adam. Both students decide to hold on to these second-place offers hoping to get accepted at their first-choice institutions. Dr. Almondine Dover-Sole, the ITD at Halibut, then calls Adam, assuring him that he is her "first alternate" and that she will make him an offer as soon as an opening becomes available. Meanwhile, Dr. Buck Muledeer, the ITD at Moosehead, is calling Bettina with the same message. Since internships cannot withdraw offers once made, this deadlock could continue until Adam or Bettina finally caves in and accepts the second-choice offer or until the notification period ends, at which point all bets are off.

Gridlock or no, the longer an applicant held an offer, the more likely it was that an ITD's alternates would accept other offers, leaving the internship with unfilled slots by the end of the UND period. In the days when supply exceeded demand, it might be impossible for the ITD to fill those slots, thus leaving them with empty intern positions for the coming year. Such unfilled slots were a major headache. At best, they indicated that the ITD had failed in the basic task of recruiting interns. At worst, they would leave the internship understaffed and at risk of losing the positions the next time someone was trying to trim the budget.

**12**   Megargee's Guide to Obtaining a Psychology Internship

Over the years, APPIC developed various strategies to cope with this problem. The notification period was steadily decreased from the 5 days allowed at the beginning to 3 days in 1976, 28 hours in 1989, 9 hours in 1991, 7 hours in 1994, and, finally, to 4 hours in 1995. Rules were passed prohibiting candidates from holding more than one offer at a time. Each restriction increased the applicants' anxiety.

It became obvious that the safest strategy for the ITDs was to make offers only to candidates they could be sure would attend. If Dr. Almondine Dover-Sole, the Training Director at Halibut Hospital, knew that Halibut was Adam's first choice while Bettina favored another facility, she could avoid the gridlock by offering her position to Adam. Even though soliciting information about applicants' rankings was against APPIC rules, many programs did their utmost to learn which candidates were most likely to accept their offers. During interviews and, later, as UND approached, applicants discovered that many of the programs to which they had applied tried to determine if they were the applicants' "first-choice site." A few ITDs baldly stated during the interview, "If you want to get an offer from us, you have to tell us we are your first choice." Most were more subtle. Some called candidates to ask if they "needed any more information" in order to reach a decision or to inquire about "how things are going." Others would call the applicants' ADCT or major professor. If a student from Bettina's university was currently interning at Halibut, she might get an unexpected call from him casually asking how the internship selection process was going and which sites she preferred.

These inquiries put students in a dilemma. Should they inform their top-ranked site that it was their first choice, knowing that doing so did not obligate the internship to make them an offer? Would refusing to answer be interpreted as a lack of interest? Some applicants simply assured all the ITDs who asked that they were their first choice. Others stalled when their second, third, or lower choice institution asked for a commitment, meanwhile trying to determine their status at their first-choice setting. Such calls put ethical ITDs into a bind because an APPIC rule stated, "No other information (such as the agency's ranking of the applicant; status as alternate/first-choice, etc.) may be communicated to applicants prior to selection day." Nevertheless, surveys showed that 78% of the students in 1994–1995 (Constantine & Keilin, 1996) and 81% in 1996–1997 (Thorne, 1997) communicated information about their rankings to one or more internships.

At an APA symposium on internship selection, several graduate students asked what they should do when their less preferred internships asked them to reveal their rankings. The then-president of APPIC replied, "Do what everyone else does. Lie!" Some did. On UND many ITDs would make offers to students who had promised they would accept, only to have them rejected or, even worse, held. No wonder one prominent ITD and former APPIC officer referred to UND as a "day of fear and loathing" (Stedman, 1983).

Over the years, APPIC adopted increasingly stringent rules against soliciting ranking information or pressuring students to make first-choice commitments prior to UND. After the 1996–1997 internship selection period, rule violations and inappropriate pressure on students to reveal their choices or commit themselves to their first-choice internships reached an all-time high. As a result, the APPIC Board adopted the following policy statement:

I.  No representative of an APPIC member internship program will solicit, accept or use any ranking-related information from any intern applicant prior to Uniform Notification Day.
II.  No prospective intern applicant will offer information or respond to questions about ranking-related information to any internship site prior to Uniform Notification Day.
III.  No representative of a doctoral training program will offer information or respond to questions about ranking-related information regarding an intern applicant to any internship site prior to Uniform Notification Day. Further, representatives of doctoral training programs will prohibit intern applicants from their doctoral programs from offering information or responding to questions regarding ranking-related information to any internship site. (APPIC, 1997)

This was an extremely strong statement. For the first time, it placed restraints on ADCTs and students as well as internships. The ADCTs are supposed to prohibit students from offering such information to ITDs, and any ITDs receiving such information are pledged not to use it. Internships were required to sign this policy in order to be listed in the *Directory* and to include this statement in their brochures. Applicants finally had an acceptable excuse for refusing to disclose ranking information. However, as long as there was a payoff for cheating, there was still a strong incentive for ITDs to prefer those candidates who indicated they would accept their offers. This incentive was removed with the adoption of computer matching.

## Computer Matching

Both selection strategies I have described had the same basic flaw: sequential decision making that gave one party or the other an unfair advantage. In the *laissez faire* strategy that preceded UND, ITDs had the leverage because they could make an offer and rescind it whenever they chose. With Uniform Notification, the students had an edge because they could hold an offer until a better one came along. Both were like poker games in which some players must reveal their hands before the others.

**14**    Megargee's Guide to Obtaining a Psychology Internship

This disparity created the differences in power and control that led some players to try to equalize the differences by "cheating."

"Computer matching" resolved this problem by allowing the players to make their choices independently and reveal them simultaneously to a neutral third party. The National Matching Service (NMS) examines their selections, seeks the best fits, and advises all the players of the results. As in a real poker game, all the players expose their cards at the same time, and the computer figures out who wins and who loses. There is no advantage in knowing the cards in the other players' hands or how they plan to play them. The best chance for the various players to achieve the results they want is to "call them as they see them," that is, to rank their choices solely on the basis of their desirability. No other strategy can accomplish their goals better (APPIC, 1999c; Keilin, 1998, 2000). Thus there is no realistic incentive for the ITDs to know the applicants' choices, and there is no advantage to the students in "first choicing" one or more internships.

APPIC's "don't ask, don't tell, don't use" rule, in combination with computer matching, has virtually eliminated the pressure tactics and chicanery that were associated with internship selection during the 1980s and 1990s. Few students or their ADCTs report any inappropriate requests for ranking information (APPIC, 1999a, 1999b). The isolated incidents that do occur are typically the fault of peripheral internship personnel who haven't learned that the rules of the game have changed. In short, cheating is no longer a problem.

## Supply and Demand

The *laissez faire* and UND selection policies created considerable anxiety for many applicants. However, when the dust settled after UND, most of the qualified applicants had received offers. A more serious problem was the growing imbalance between the number of applicants and the number of internship positions available (Thorne & Dixon, 1999).

We do not have precise data on supply and demand because record-keeping methods have changed over the years. You can go to the APPIC Web site (www.appic.org) and download a table that will show you APPIC Clearinghouse data from 1986 to date. These data are summarized in Figure 1.1. You can see that supply exceeded demand through 1989. The data are missing for 1990. In 1991, there were 66 more applicants than vacancies. Since 1992 there has been an annual shortfall of approximately 200 to 300 positions.

The APPIC match report for the year 2000 (APPIC, 2000b) indicated that there were 2,713 internship positions available in the United States and Canada. Of these, approximately 80% were fully funded APA-accredited slots. The report revealed that 3,174 applicants had registered for

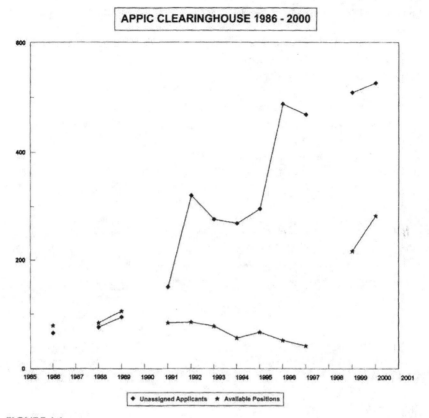

**FIGURE 1.1.**

the match. Of the 2,957 who submitted rankings, 2,429 (82%) were matched with sites on Matching Day, while 528 (18%) were not. Of those that were matched, 1,174 (48%) received their first-ranked site, 465 (19%) their second, 287 (12%) their third, and 180 (7%) their fourth. The remaining 323 (13%) received their fifth choice or higher. For the 528 who were not matched, there were 284 unfilled positions available, indicating a shortfall of about 244 positions.

When the internship shortfall first became apparent, some wrote it off as being limited to poorly prepared applicants from marginal programs. However, surveys of the unplaced applicants in 1996 and 1997 revealed that 83% to 89% were from APA-approved training programs (Keilin, 2000; Keilin et al., 2000).

Certain APA officials suggested that the unplaced applicants had applied unwisely, filing too few applications or limiting themselves to a geographically restricted area (Clay, 1997). This explanation seems to be a classic example of blaming the victim. Poor preparation and ineffective

**16**    Megargee's Guide to Obtaining a Psychology Internship

tactics no doubt influence which applicants will be unsuccessful, but they cannot account for the fact that many students have been left without internships after all the positions have been filled.

Others suggested that budget cutbacks and the impact of managed care had reduced the number of available internships. Comparing the 1996/ 1997 APPIC *Directory* (Hall & Cantrell, 1996) with the 1999/2000 edition (Hall & Hsu, 2000), I determined that 77 programs accounting for 289 positions had closed their doors, but this loss was offset by the addition of 96 new programs with 387 positions for a net gain of 19 programs and 89 slots over the 4-year period. (There was, however, a net loss in the number of APA-accredited programs since it takes several years for a new program to be approved.) Although these data indicate that there has been no decrease in the number of internship agencies and positions, it is also clear that there has not been any noteworthy growth; a net gain of 89 positions over four years works out to an annual growth rate of less than 1%.

In my opinion, the basic cause of the shortfall is an increase in the number of applicants. Chamberlain (2000) recently reported that a National Science Foundation survey indicated that there were more than 53,000 students enrolled in psychology graduate school programs, a 10% increase from 6 years before. Oehlert and Lopez (1998) reported that from 1993 through 1995, from 2,956 to 3,043 students were admitted to clinical, counseling, and school psychology doctoral programs, a figure that closely approximates the number of students applying for internships from 1998 through 2000. This suggests that, unlike my experience in the 1960s, today relatively few graduate students wash out or leave their training programs once admitted.

Before computer matching, there was no way of ascertaining exactly how many students were applying for internship. In the 3rd edition of this book, I used data gleaned from the APPIC Directory and the Clearinghouse to estimate the actual number of students applying for internships. I calculated that there were 2,531 applicants in 1994/1995, 2,837 in 1995/1996, and 2,858 in 1996/1997, an apparent increase of 324 applicants (13%) over the three years.

As noted above, the Year 2000 APPIC matching report indicated that 2,957 applicants completed the matching procedure in 2000. Thus it appears that there were 426 more students applying for internships in 1999/ 2000 than there were in 1994/1995, an increase of 17%. Some of these applicants are candidates who were unsuccessful the previous year who are reapplying. In fact, Keilin et al. (2000) suggested that the annual shortfall can be attributed to unsuccessful applicants from the previous year who are reapplying.

Meanwhile, what do we do about the shortfall problem? Some graduate students, jokingly I hope, have suggested that the backlog of unsuccessful applicants be shot to equalize supply and demand in the future. On a less violent note, Robiner and Crew (2000) noted that while the supply of psychologists increased 44% from 1988 through 1995, the demand for psychological services had decreased due to managed care. They suggested that clinical training programs reduce the size of their entering classes by 20% to 25%. Others have suggested increasing the supply of internships by speeding up the APA and APPIC accreditation processes, developing alternative internships for students planning academic careers, and expanding internships from an exclusive emphasis on health service delivery to areas such as research, primary prevention, community service, public policy, and government (Humphreys, 2000; Oehlert & Lopez, 1998; Pion, Kohout, & Wicherski, 2000). Unfortunately, these are all long-term solutions that will have little impact by the time you apply for an internship.

Fortunately, I don't have to solve the supply and demand problem. My only responsibility is to you, the readers of this book. The odds are in our favor. We shouldn't let our concern over the shortfall blind us to the fact that 85% of the applicants *do* succeed in getting an internship. If my sales data are correct, more than half the applicants do not buy my book, so you already have an edge on most of your competitors. My job now is to reward your investment by helping you be one of the successful 85%. So, let's get on with it.

# Applying for Internship: An Overview

You will soon discover that seeking a predoctoral internship in professional psychology is unlike anything you have previously experienced. At first, the process will resemble applying to college or graduate school. The paperwork required is similar, and your anxieties will be much the same. But you will soon learn that applying for internship is different. When you call programs to inquire about the status of your application or innocently ask how things look, some may respond like CIA agents being interviewed by Mike Wallace, saying that they are not allowed to provide such information. When you request interviews, you may find that some places do not allow interviews and that others interview only those whom they invite and then only on one or two designated days.

The internship application process also differs significantly from applying for employment in the "real world." Ordinary employment interviews in the United States are governed by strict guidelines that prohibit personal questions that are not directly relevant to job performance. However, you may find that some Internship Selection Committees ask you, their future colleagues, personal and probing questions that they would never dream of asking an applicant for a secretarial position. You may be asked about your personal relationships, plans for possible pregnancy, religion, family obligations, and mental or physical health. The most critical difference is that in the real world, if you are turned down for a job this morning, you can apply for another this afternoon. If you don't obtain an internship, however, you must wait a year before you can try again.

## ☐ Politics and Poker

The reason you will find applying for internships unique is that the internship selection process is basically political . . . political in the sense that it involves negotiations, compromises, and a delicate balance of power relationships. As we saw in Chapter 1, the locus of control has shifted over the years as a function of changes in the selection rules and the availability of internships relative to the number of applicants. Under *laissez faire*, the university faculties had the most power. Under UND, once positions were offered, you the students were in charge. With computer matching and more applicants than there are positions, it is the internships and their training directors who are now in command.

This poker game has been going on every year since 1949, the date of the first Boulder conference on professional training in psychology. Before you ante up and take a hand, you should get acquainted with the other players and learn what has been happening in the game so far. To play your hand effectively, you need to understand the other players' goals, what it is they hope to accomplish if they succeed, and what it is they fear will happen if they fail. These hopes and fears are the keys to their game plans and the reason why the internships kept tinkering with the house rules in the hope of shifting the balance of power. The better you understand this game and its players, the more of an edge you will have.

The principal players in this poker game are (a) the ITDs, (b) the ADCTs, and (c) you, the graduate students who are applying for internship. Among the secondary players are the staffs at the internship sites, including the current interns, your major professor and other interested faculty members, your fellow graduate students, some of whom may have a vested interest in whether or not you are accepted at a certain site, and friends or family members whose lives will be affected by your choice of internship. At a tertiary level are the regulatory agencies, APPIC and the APA. Correctly or not, all the principal players perceive this as a high-stakes game in which their careers may be on the line; this perception generates considerable stress and tension for all involved.

### The ADCTs and the Academic Training Centers

The first group of players consists of the ADCT and the other faculty members at the degree-granting institutions. As you well know, this is hardly a monolithic group. Programs differ greatly in the emphasis they place on professional training, and, within each school, individual faculty members often have different attitudes and opinions regarding what you should look for in an internship.

# 20 Megargee's Guide to Obtaining a Psychology Internship

ADCTs typically hope to place all their applicants in settings that will (a) enhance the prestige of their programs, (b) please the applicants' major professors, and (c) provide their students with good training experiences. In addition, ADCTs often try to foster or maintain relationships with settings where their students have received good training in the past. Therefore, your ADCT may urge you to apply to an APA-accredited program with which your university has strong historic ties. Your clinical supervisor might recommend a program with a certain theoretical orientation. Your major professor will probably be more concerned with whether your internship will afford you time to complete your dissertation research.

Nowadays, except for the ADCT, most university faculty members are much less involved in internship applications than they were when the Old Boy networks were more influential. Once university faculty members have written their letters of recommendation, they rarely get actively involved in the internship application process. As travel funds have become increasingly scarce, it has become difficult even for the ADCTs, whose job it is to monitor their students' professional training, to visit the internships where their students are interning.

There are many reasons for the decline in faculty influence, interest, and participation. They include the decrease in the number of academic and research positions available for new Ph.D.s, the phasing out of federally funded clinical training grants, the increasing competition for research grants, the increase in the proportion of professionally trained psychologists seeking positions in applied rather than academic settings, and the entry of large numbers of young "baby boomers" into the profession, all of which have served to dilute the Old Boys' influence.

Although they are less overt now than they were in the past, informal networks still exist. You know from your studies of social psychology that proximity and familiarity are two key elements in interpersonal attraction. These principles apply in internship selection as well. In large metropolitan areas such as Boston, New York, Chicago, San Francisco, and Los Angeles, many of the applicants from local programs have already had practicum placements and are known by the staffs at the internships to which they are applying. I know from experience that certain settings that have accepted our students in the past and been impressed with their training are more likely to accept other Florida State University students in the future than are settings that are unfamiliar with our program.

## The ITDs and the Training Facility Staff

The second major group of players is the ITDs and the training center personnel. The ITD's boss, the Chief Psychologist at the facility, yearns for hardworking, brilliant, congenial interns from the nation's most prestigious universities, stratified to represent all the major ethnic groups and most of the typical genders. She hopes they will go on to achieve great success, which they will attribute to the magnificent training they received at her internship. The Chief also expects them to be highly professional so that they will generate enough billable hours to underwrite the cost of their training and, perhaps, even show a profit. As Greenberg et al. (1998, p. 606) noted, "those sites that are able to attract the most competent and experienced therapists probably have an edge in maximizing cost-effectiveness."

The ITD's obvious objective is to please the Chief and the rest of his colleagues by obtaining the "best" internship class possible, whatever that means. While the ITD would be delighted if the internship class meets most of his Chief's rather grandiose expectations, he will settle for filling all the available slots with candidates who will get the work done and not cause any trouble. They should be ethical, collegial, reasonably competent, free of flagrant psychopathology, and unlikely to precipitate any major lawsuits. As always, it also helps if they are well groomed and physically attractive. Candidates who may be "controversial" are apt to be viewed with suspicion. This includes students who may offend clients or staff by virtue of their atypical political, social, or sexual views, and those who by virtue of physical condition, advanced age (i.e., over 35), or family obligations may not be willing or able to work 60 or more hours a week or be available evenings and weekends.

Both ITDs and ADCTs also have long-term concerns. They play this game every year, so they must establish and maintain good professional working relations with one another. The best ITDs and ADCTs realize that this means being honest with one another and evaluating students and programs fairly and forthrightly.


## The Applicants

The third and most important group is you, the graduate students seeking predoctoral internships. Without you the game cannot continue. As a group, applicants are currently operating at a disadvantage by virtue of the supply and demand problem. As I noted in Chapter 1, every year more than 3,000 applicants compete for approximately 2,700 internship positions, many of which are not APA-accredited and some of which are unpaid. Moreover, the number of applicants is increasing faster than the number of openings.

As an individual applicant, however, your fate is largely in your own hands. Cranking out more applications is not the answer. Data reported at a recent APPIC meeting (Kaslow, 2000) revealed that students who

**22**     Megargee's Guide to Obtaining a Psychology Internship

submitted 25 or more applications had a lower match rate than those who submitted half that many. Painstaking preparation, realistic self-appraisal, and accurate information are your surest keys to obtaining a predoctoral psychology internship.

To maximize your chances for success, you need to evaluate your education, experience, personal characteristics, and skills to decide if you are ready to apply for internship. In general, the further along you are in your program and the more clinical experience you have, the better your chances for success. If you decide to go for it, you must submit thoughtfully prepared, individualized applications to carefully selected internships that are seeking students with your particular qualifications. This requires time, effort, and research. Later you should travel to the sites you have selected, evaluate them for yourself, and, if possible, have interviews with the ITDs and the other members of the internship training staff. This requires more time and, often, considerable expense.

As you can see, the search for an internship is basically a sales campaign. Like any other successful salesperson, you have to know your market and understand your product. Your customers are the ITDs and their Selection Committees. Your product is yourself, with your unique blend of talents and training, aspirations and abilities. If you, as the product, do not meet the needs of the marketplace, you may have to redesign or repackage the product so it is more marketable (Spruill, 1997; Spruill & Pruitt, 2000). Fortunately, different sites have different goals, so your market research should identify settings that are seeking what you have to offer.

You may find that your major professor or ADCT takes a dim view of this advice. University faculty members rightfully deplore the amount of time their graduate students must spend seeking internships. Many also resent the emphasis most internships place on professional preparation as opposed to research. One prominent ADCT recently wrote that he would have grave reservations about any internship that would select students on the basis of the amount of assessment and therapy experience they had accumulated, arguing that the number of publications and conference presentations was a much more relevant criterion. He probably has grave reservations about most settings then, because a survey of 90 internships revealed that ITDs ranked publications and presentations ninth out of nine possible criteria, and that supervised therapy and assessment experience ranked second and third, respectively (Petzel & Berndt, 1980). However, these data do not mean you can ignore your ADCT's advice to publish; letters of recommendation, one of which should be from your ADCT, ranked first in the study.

In this chapter, I will give you an overview of the internship selection process and the steps you should follow to maximize your chances of success. Subsequent chapters will expand upon these topics.

## Applying for Internship: An Overview    **23**

# ☐  Preparing Yourself for Internship

Before you begin the arduous process of applying for an internship, it is essential that you are well prepared personally, academically, and professionally.

## Psychological Preparation

By "psychological preparation" I mean developing the proper mind set. If you have engaged in competitive sports, games, debating or the like, you know the importance of being mentally ready and "putting on your game face." This is also true of applying for internships.

At this stage of your career you have achieved a great deal. By now you have successfully completed several years of graduate training in professional psychology. This is quite an accomplishment. You are probably a person who is used to success. However, this is no time to rest on your laurels. No matter what you have achieved thus far and no matter how wonderful a human being you are, no one owes you a predoctoral internship and no one is going to give you one. To obtain your internship, you have to go out and get it for yourself. If you sit back and wait for one to be handed to you, you may be one of the unmatched people who posts angry and anguished messages the day after Match Day.

My wife and I are both cancer survivors. The most important thing we learned about confronting a challenge like cancer is that getting well was *our* responsibility. It was up to *us* to learn about our diseases, decide what to do, and obtain the best treatment. Blaming doctors or whining about the unfairness of it all was a waste of time, and time was one thing we did not want to waste. So we dealt with it. By the same token, whether or not you approve of the current system of internship selection with its built-in shortfall, it is the only system that you have. It is *your* job to ensure that you will be among the 85% who succeed in February. The sooner you accept the fact that it is your responsibility and no one else's, the more likely it is you will succeed. I will help you, but it is up to you to get the job done. (The good news is that getting an internship is much easier and more enjoyable than coping with cancer.)

## Academic Preparation

Applying for internship is like planning a political campaign or a military operation. It is impossible to begin too soon or prepare too thoroughly. I teach the first course in our clinical curriculum, and I begin by telling our brand new graduate students what they should do to get ready for intern-

## 24 Megargee's Guide to Obtaining a Psychology Internship

ship. The various internship application forms require an unbelievable amount of information. If you begin keeping meticulous records of your academic work and, especially, your clinical activities, you will find it is much easier to complete the forms when the time comes to actually apply. One recent student summed up her advice in three words, "Compulse, compulse, compulse!" Good tip, but at the same time, don't "Obsess, obsess, obsess."

Your academic program will have certain basic requirements that you must fulfill before you can go on internship. One reason to plan ahead is to make sure that you complete the necessary requirements by the time you submit your formal applications. Find out what these requirements are and make sure that you have satisfied them before you start making applications. Your program will probably require that you have (a) completed all your course work, (b) attained at least the minimum number of practicum hours specified by your program, (c) passed your doctoral comprehensive examination, and (d) perhaps defended your dissertation proposal.

On the APPIC "Verification of Eligibility" form that you submit with your application, your ADCT must certify that you will have completed all your program's requirements and will be eligible to go on internship no later than Ranking Day in February. If your ADCT cannot certify this, there is no point in applying. If there is the slightest possibility that you will not be eligible and may have to stay at your university because you failed an examination or because some disaster prevented you from defending your prospectus, your application will probably not be reviewed, much less selected. The bottom line is this: Plan your program so that you will have completed all your formal requirements *before* you apply.

Merely satisfying your university's minimum academic requirements may not be sufficient for many internships. Even if your academic program does not demand that you be advanced to candidacy before you seek an internship, 518 of the 540 American internships (96%) listed in the APPIC *Directory* (Hall & Hsu, 1999) stipulated that applicants must be doctoral candidates.

In fact, many successful internship applicants are considerably farther along than that. A recent survey revealed that by the time they reported to their internships, 25% of the interns had defended their dissertation proposals, another 25% had collected all their data, 6% had completed a first draft of their dissertation, and 14% had defended their completed dissertation (Krieshok, Lopez, Somberg, & Cantrell, 2000). While 78% of those who had defended their proposals made further progress while on internship, with 32% completing their dissertations, 61% of those who had not defended a proposal before beginning their internship had still not defended by the end of the internship year.

The Gainesville conference on internship training sponsored by APPIC concluded that all interns should defend their dissertation proposals before they apply. Indeed, the conferees indicated a strong preference that the dissertation itself be completed before an intern reports for training (Belar et al., 1987, 1989). Another survey indicated that 10% of the students not getting internships in 1997 were rejected because their dissertations were incomplete and 8% because they had clinical training deficits (Thorne, 1997).

There are good practical reasons for favoring more advanced students. Many internships feel they should help their interns find postinternship jobs, and those who still have a dissertation to complete are much harder to place or support. In my experience, students who leave on internship before defending their proposals or collecting their dissertation data are at a much higher risk of not completing their dissertations. Even though they may complete their internships a year earlier, it generally takes them longer to finish their degrees than students who defer going on internship for a year so they can complete their dissertations. For all these reasons, you stand a much better chance of obtaining the internship of your choice if you have defended your proposal and made substantial progress on your dissertation *before* you apply for internship.

## Professional Preparation

Internships typically expect a higher level of professional preparation than university training programs require. For example, academic programs may only require that students complete a minimum of 400 hours of practicum experience, at least 150 hours of which are in direct service and 75 hours of which are in formal scheduled supervision, because these are the accreditation requirements stipulated in the APA's (1986) *Accreditation Handbook*. However, the Gainesville Conference recommended twice this number (Belar et al., 1997). According to my calculations, the average minimum number of hours required by the 540 American predoctoral internships listed in the 1999–2000 *Directory* (Hall & Hsu, 1999) was 732 hours.

Based on their review of the literature and their own surveys, Stedman, Hatch, and Schoenfeld (2000, in press; under review) report widespread dissatisfaction on the part of ITDs with the professional preparation of internship applicants in the areas of psychotherapy and, especially, psychological assessment. Although settings differed on the amount and the nature of the therapy experience expected, it was clear that many ITDs felt that the applicants they were evaluating had seen far fewer clients than the ITDs would have liked. Even more extensive deficits were noted in the area of test-based assessments, especially when it came to writing integrated test-based reports. The ITDs surveyed wanted applicants who could administer, score, interpret, and write up reports of individual intelligence examinations, objective personality tests, and, to a somewhat

**26**    Megargee's Guide to Obtaining a Psychology Internship

lesser extent, projective personality tests. Achievement and neuropsychological testing were deemed less important. They concluded: "Data suggest that the prudent candidate should seek training with intelligence, objective personality, and projective personality instruments because these categories are highly prized by directors of all types of internships" (Stedman et al., under review).

Stedman et al. (under review) and others (Rossini & Moretti, 1997) have also documented what they feel are serious deficiencies in the amount of training in test-based assessment currently afforded in many academic training centers. I had six required semester-long courses on assessment in my graduate program and later did 5 complete work-ups weekly in my full-time work setting. Today's students often take only two or three assessment courses and may do only 5 or 10 complete work-ups a year.

If your academic program does not afford much instruction or experience in assessment, it might behoove you to seek some additional training. Remember to evaluate yourself as a product to be sold to the Internship Selection Committees. If the internships you hope to attend want students who can make a formal diagnosis according to the latest *Diagnostic and Statistical Manual* and who are able to administer, score, and interpret projective techniques such as the Rorschach, you will find it is easier to market yourself if you acquire these skills.

## Strategic Preparation

It is up to you and your advisors to determine when you are ready for internship. In the days when the university faculties played a greater role in the internship selection process and most students were supported by university-based research or training grants, students often went on internship in their 3rd or 4th year of graduate study. By today's standards, the amount of clinical training some students received prior to internship was minimal. When I was at VAMC Palo Alto in 1960–1961, a fellow trainee from a midwestern university had taken courses in test construction and theories of psychotherapy, but had never actually administered a test or counseled a client. There is no way he would be accepted at most internships today.

After the big clinical training grants were phased out during the Nixon and Ford administrations, more graduate students had to support their training by working in clinical settings while at their universities. Practicum agencies insisted on a higher level of clinical competence when they paid their practicum students. As a result, by the time you go on internship, it is likely you will have considerably more clinical experience than the 400 hours your predecessors had 20 years ago. A recent survey of ADCTs indicated that their programs now require on the average 903 practicum hours (Hekner, Fink, Levasseur, & Parker, 1995), and Faverman (2000) recently reported that the average applicant actually accumulated 1,845 hours of practicum experience.[1]

One way to get ready for internship is to keep in touch with more advanced students from your academic program during their internship years and learn from them what skills they were expected to have when they arrived. Their advice may be more salient than that of some faculty members who have not recently been actively involved in clinical work.

Because of family or other personal obligations, some graduate students are forced to apply within a restricted geographical area that has only a few internship settings. If you are in this situation, one ITD recommends that you investigate these internship sites as early as possible in your graduate career. If you can determine what these settings are looking for in a candidate, you can tailor your program to ensure you have the necessary training before you apply there.

## ☐ Preparing to Apply

Since it is never too early to begin, I will first describe long-term preparations you can make. If you are reading this book at the last minute, do not despair. These long-term preparations are highly desirable and will make your job much easier, but if, like most of us, you tend to put things off until the last minute, you can still prepare an effective application. You will simply have to scurry around even more frantically to get everything done. As Casey Jacob (1987, p. 155) noted, "Gradual preparation would have eased the experience for me. Instead, ignorance and lack of preparation determined that 'internship hunting' was a full-time 2-month job." More recent applicants would probably amend this to read "a full-time 3- or 4-month job."

### Long-Term Preparations

Even if you are not planning to apply for internship for a year or so, there are many things you can do to get ready. One of the most important is what you are doing right now, namely, learning about what is involved.

Access the APPIC Web site (www.appic.org) and download the most recent information regarding the rules and procedures for applying for

---

[1]A recent APA/APPIC survey indicated that a number of academic training centers feel that graduate students are spending an excessive amount of time in their practicum and other placements in the belief that the more hours of experience they accumulate, the better their chances for obtaining an internship. They have proposed a "cap" on the number of hours an applicant could report. This would be done by modifying the AAPI so that the most hours an applicant could report would be "750 or more" or, perhaps, "1,000 or more." ITDs, predictably, were not eager to adopt this proposal (Kaslow, 2000).

**28**  Megargee's Guide to Obtaining a Psychology Internship

internship, including the *APPIC Application for Psychology Internship* (AAPI) and the *Academic Program's Verification of Internship Eligibility and Readiness* forms. You should also subscribe to the APPIC Match News and the internship listserv so you will continue to get the latest information as it becomes available. If you do this a year in advance, you can monitor the internship process before you actually have to participate. (Some candidates use the listserv as a chat room and support group; in order to keep from being overwhelmed with messages, I suggest you get the daily digest, which includes all the day's postings in one e-mail message.)

The sooner you obtain a copy of the AAPI the better. Whether you are applying next month or next year, the AAPI indicates the sort of information you will have to provide internships when you apply. If you still have a year or so to go before you start seeking an internship, this will enable you to set up a system for recording and retaining records of your academic and professional education and experience that will help you when you do apply. One student made xerox copies of the relevant AAPI pages for each practicum and used them to keep a running tally of her activities in each setting. When it was time to prepare her applications, she simply merged the data from the various sites over the years.

Whether or not you use her system, you should begin keeping a detailed log in which you record all your practicum and supervision hours, the names and credentials of your supervisors, the number and the nature of the clients you have seen, and the types of treatment in which you have participated, as well as a record of the various assessment devices you have administered, scored, and interpreted. If you enter the basic information onto a spreadsheet program such as Excel or Lotus, you can later sort your cases by type of client, presenting problem, diagnosis, setting, instruments or techniques used, and so forth. A recent successful intern applicant wrote me, "I kept overly detailed client records on a spreadsheet. Just in case, for every patient I saw, I recorded age, gender, race, education, religious affiliation, marital status, sexual orientation, Axis I–V diagnoses, number of sessions, treatments, and setting. Each week I spent maybe five minutes updating this information on my spreadsheet. This fall, when I needed to print out the reports, all the data were there and it was a great time and stress saver."

Most of us are not that well organized. Herschell and McNeil (2000, p. 58) noted that, "The result for those [students] who did not [keep detailed records] has been significant hair-pulling, gnashing of teeth, and compromised accuracy as they desperately try to remember their hours spent at a practicum site 3 or more years ago." Further noting the research evidence on the inaccuracy of retrospective self-reports, they devised user-friendly checklists, paper forms, and software that you can use to record and retrieve practicum data. You can download them free of charge from their Web site at www.as.wvu.edu/psyc.

In anticipation of applying for internship, review the curriculum vitaes

(CVs) of successful intern applicants from your program. How do your qualifications compare with theirs? Are there things you can do to improve your credentials in the year(s) to come that will make your application more competitive? This might be the time to take some elective clinical courses in areas that might catch the eye of ITDs, such as minority mental health, neuropsychological assessment, advanced personality testing, short-term interventions, or geropsychology. Consider taking professional workshops in professional ethics, assessment, psychopathology, or specialized intervention techniques. They will not only enhance your credentials but also indicate your motivation to be well prepared. If the advertised fees are more than you can afford, ask for a student discount or volunteer to help with registration and run errands in exchange for being allowed to sit in on the sessions. (These workshops are also a good place to make contacts and create networks that may prove useful when it is time to apply.) If you have some specialized skill such as a familiarity with a foreign language or American Sign Language, polish it up so you can present yourself as having competency in this area. If you have been meaning to someday publish your master's thesis, this would be a good time to write it up and submit it. In short, while there is time, consider ways you can make your CV stand out as being special when it is compared with those of other applicants.

Earlier, I described the difficulty some internships have getting HMOs to reimburse them for services performed by unlicensed practitioners such as interns. Your state may have licensing available for master's-level psychologists, and it probably also licenses mental health counselors, marriage and family therapists, and other counselors. If you investigate these licensing laws, you may find that your master's degree in psychology goes a long way toward meeting your state's requirements. If you take an examination or a course or two in marital counseling, you may be able to obtain such a license. If so, it might make you very attractive to some internships such as Community Mental Health Centers. You will note that the AAPI has a question that specifically asks you to list licenses or certificates that allow you to practice counseling or psychotherapy in certain states.

If you are in a clinical practicum, you can start preparing a work sample for submission along with your application to those internships that require them. Begin by discussing this with your supervisor. You will need to select a client who will afford you the opportunity to display your clinical skills. Before you begin, you will have to obtain informed consent and a release to allow you to use the materials, suitably disguised, in conjunction with your application. One of my students prepared two work samples, each dealing with a different problem in a different type of setting with a different supervisor so she could demonstrate her range and versatility. (She also hoped that if the internship staff did not care for one, they might like the other.)

**30**    Megargee's Guide to Obtaining a Psychology Internship

You can also begin your preliminary reconnaissance for possible internships, identifying and investigating settings that interest you. If you start doing this a year in advance, you can benefit from the experiences of the people in the class ahead of you while they are applying for internships. They are going to be very busy and rather tense, so they may not want to spend a lot of time educating you. However, if you offer to help them by seeking out and downloading information from the Web, writing for brochures, or assisting in preparing some of their numerous application forms, you will be more welcome. In particular, if you volunteer to help out by taking them to the airport and later meeting their planes when they return from interviews, you will not only be assisting them but also learning about the interview process first hand from seasoned veterans while the experiences are still fresh in their minds. This will be greatly appreciated, since it seems to be an FAA regulation that the only flights intern applicants can take leave before dawn and return after midnight. (If they are scheduled to return at a civilized time, Murphy's Law stipulates that the flight will be delayed.)

In Chapter 4 I recommend attending professional meetings as a cost-effective way to observe and meet personnel from internships that interest you. A number of regional meetings are held in the spring, the APA has its annual meeting in August, and the Association for the Advancement of Behavior Therapy (AABT) meets in the fall. AABT and certain APA divisions sponsor "internship fairs," where students can meet training directors and learn about their programs.

Advance financial planning can also help. Applying for internship can be expensive. Putting aside some funds, paying down the credit cards, taking advantage of tire, luggage, and clothing sales, and getting your car ready for long-distance travel may make it less necessary to float a last-minute loan.

Finally, long before you actually apply, you should discuss your plans with those people who are close to you who will be affected by your plans, such as your spouse or partner, children, parents, and others whose lives may be impacted. Your chances of success will be greatly enhanced if you are free to go wherever you find the best opportunity. This may mean moving hundreds or even thousands of miles. The sooner you start discussing this, the better. If someone is going to move with you, then the prospect of relocating in a year or two can make a difference in their educational, vocational, and personal plans. You should probably think twice about buying a new house, encouraging your widowed mother to move near you, or making plans to adopt a baby if it is likely you will be leaving the following year. If your family cannot relocate, are you prepared to go on your own for the year? How will your family cope during your absence? The sooner these issues can be explored, the better. Once you have actually started applying you will have so much on your mind

Applying for Internship: An Overview **31**

dealing with the application process that it will be more difficult for you to explore major personal issues with your loved ones.

## Short-Term Preparations

While it is never too early to begin planning, the bulk of the effort involved in applying for internship will take place the year you apply. The internship application and selection season begins in the fall semester and runs until the end of February. Although recent applicants strongly advise using the summer to write application essays and CVs and to prepare practicum summaries for the AAPI, most students wait until the fall semester begins to think about internship applications. I once made the mistake of offering an internship application workshop in March; not a single student signed up. In August or September, the crowd typically overflows the room and spills out into the hallway.

In this chapter I will provide you with a schedule of what must be done. I will be idealistic and start in the spring of the year you plan to apply, even though I realize it is unlikely you will actually begin until that fall.

As I noted earlier, you should plan your academic schedule so that you will have satisfied your internship eligibility requirements when the time comes to apply. The spring semester before you plan to apply, make sure you know what all your current requirements are and determine if it will be possible for you to satisfy them by fall. When you have formulated a timetable for meeting these requirements and other goals you may have established, such as beginning your dissertation or completing needed courses, meet with your major professor. Discuss your plans and see if your major professor thinks they are realistic. As an ADCT, I have all my clinical students prepare "time lines" on which they project what they will accomplish each semester. Everyone always overestimates how much they will accomplish and underestimates how long it will take to attain certain goals. Writing and, especially, rewriting major area papers, prospectuses, and dissertations invariably takes much longer than most students anticipate, even without the time-consuming task of preparing internship applications. Complications arise. Maybe that required course you counted on taking in the summer is not going to be offered. Perhaps your major professor plans to be on sabbatical next fall. Now is the time to find out.

Once you have secured the general approval of your major professor, meet with your ADCT to discuss your plans and get advice. When you apply, your ADCT must submit a signed statement certifying that you will have completed all your academic requirements before Matching Day and that you are personally and professionally prepared to go on internship.

**32**   Megargee's Guide to Obtaining a Psychology Internship

(See the APPIC *Academic Program's Verification of Internship Eligibility and Readiness* form, which you downloaded.) If you are not going to complete your academic requirements by the application deadline, wait until next year. Given the current oversupply of internship applicants, legitimate training centers will not risk accepting any interns who may not be able to attend in the fall because they have not fulfilled their academic requirements.

Your ADCT must also complete a series of 5-point Likert scales evaluating your personal and professional readiness for internship. (See Chapter 5.) If your ADCT feels that she is unable to give you a strong positive rating on any of these scales, you need to discuss this with her and with your clinical supervisors. If they feel you need additional supervised training or experience before you are ready to go, it is probably best to wait another year before applying. In this climate, applying without your academic program's full support is probably a waste of your time, effort, and money.

If you get your ADCT's approval to apply, next inspect your academic transcript at the Registrar's office. Check for any "incomplete" grades; if you find any, make sure they are taken care of before you apply. If you have changed your name, make sure the name on your transcript is the same as the name you are going to use when applying. If the transcript has your old name, it may get misfiled at some internships.

## Self-Evaluation

You have now arrived at the first "moment of truth." Is this really the year to apply? Are you actually going to go through with it? Once you have your timetable approved and have made plans to satisfy all your academic goals and requirements, examine your credentials from an Internship Selection Committee's point of view. As we shall see, different internships have vastly different expectations and requirements. Nevertheless, they are all seeking applicants who can hit the ground running, people who can quickly assume a professional role and capably represent the Psychology Department, albeit as a trainee.

Next year, when you actually are an intern, you may be asked to help screen applications. Put yourself in this role now, and ask yourself how you would evaluate your own resume. Is this someone you would recommend? Why? If you can get some input from local practitioners or clinical supervisors, so much the better. Articles on the criteria used by internships to rate prospective applicants may also be helpful; several are contained in the chapter on "Selection" in Dana and May's (1987) book, *Internship Training in Professional Psychology*. See also Stedman et al. (2000). The purpose of this exercise is to identify possible weaknesses or areas that can be improved while there is still time to do something about them.

One student who went through this exercise the summer before he applied decided that he needed more experience in personality assessment with adult inpatients. As ADCT, I was able to arrange for him to obtain supervised experience in such a setting during the fall semester. I also made a point of noting in my letter of recommendation how this student had demonstrated professional maturity and eagerness to learn by taking an unpaid position two afternoons a week to enhance his assessment skills in preparation for internship. Concrete behavior such as this is much more impressive to a Training Director than the banal platitudes often found in most letters of recommendation.

If you applied last year and failed to match, you should diagnose the reason so you will succeed this time. A single mother of three children wrote me that she initially applied only to sites within easy driving distance from her home. After she failed to obtain a match, she decided to sell her house and relocate if necessary. The following year she applied to 16 sites in four states, interviewed at 6, and matched with her first-choice setting. Although her children are unhappy about moving, she is very enthusiastic about her internship site and feels she made the correct decision.

In conducting your self-evaluation, you should be aware that some internships may assess you on the basis of your personal attributes as well as your professional skills. Age is apparently an obstacle for some sites. Some ITDs asked older interns whether they could accept feedback from younger supervisors. Others were concerned that applicants with family obligations might not be able to put in the hours the internship demanded, especially on evenings and weekends. A man with six children was asked about his religion. A lesbian woman applying to a "family oriented clinic" was informed that "homosexuals would not feel comfortable" working there. We all have personal characteristics that might concern some ITDs. You have a better chance of success if you keep these factors in mind when you select sites, prepare applications, and interview.

## Enhancing Your Academic Credentials

Internships differ in the weight they attach to publications. Some say they are irrelevant; others state they are extremely important. One member of the Selection Committee at an internship housed in a major school of medicine remarked that he flips to the back of the CV and counts the publications before deciding whether to read the rest of the application. I hope he was jesting, but it is a fact that all of our students who have been accepted at that internship have had strong publication records.

Fortunately, there are often steps you can take to enhance your CV to make it more competitive. This is a good task for the summer before you apply, but even the fall of your application year is not too late. If you have

# 34 Megargee's Guide to Obtaining a Psychology Internship

been putting off writing up your master's thesis or some other study, now is a good time to prepare it for publication and submit it. You can list it as "under review," and even if it is later rejected it will still enhance your CV while it is being evaluated. Similarly, take the time to prepare proposals for local or regional professional meetings. If you have collaborated on some research with some faculty members who have been dilatory about getting it written up, fuss at them or offer to write it up yourself.

Admissions committees are also favorably impressed by a commitment to the profession. A time-effective way to enhance your CV is to join professional societies and to enroll in some specialized workshops for continuing education credit. If you belong to a graduate student organization at your university or in your state, the next time an opportunity comes to volunteer to head a committee or to stand for office, go ahead and put yourself forward. This will enable your ADCT to comment on the high regard in which your peers hold you and how you have demonstrated leadership. These are little things, to be sure, but they will help differentiate your CV from those of other students who have not engaged in these activities.

## Forming a Support Group

Think of your internship-seeking campaign as you would an important athletic competition such as a tennis tournament. It helps if you have a coach, a cheerleader, a trainer, and practice partners. Your coach should be an experienced person who knows the game and can give you advice. This is the person you ask to look over your essays, advise you on your CV, and help you with your rankings. Your coach might be your ADCT, a faculty member, or a clinical supervisor.

Applying for internship is stressful and it helps to have a cheerleader to get you motivated and help you perform at your best. This is often a significant other or close friend. Some applicants use the APPIC listserv as a cheering section. I prefer a real ally to a cyberfriend. When sending messages to the listserv, remember that ITDs and internship staff may also be monitoring the messages. Don't post anything you would not want the ITD at your favorite internship to read.

Your trainer is the person who takes care of your cuts and bruises and restores you so you can get back in the fray. He or she should be good at stress management counseling. Sometimes your coach or cheerleader can also be your trainer, but often your trainer is someone else, a person to whom you can confide your doubts, worries, fears, and feelings of inadequacy.

Your practice partners are usually your fellow students. They can help by role-playing interviews, and, if they are also applying, you can share impressions of internship sites and personnel. They can also be in your

Applying for Internship: An Overview **35**

cheering section, but if they have their own applications to worry about, you should not expect them to be there for you at all times as your cheerleader will.

## Your Responsibilities

No matter how supportive your program, the responsibility for selecting the internship that best meets *your* needs is *yours*. *You* must make sure that you have met all the requirements. *You* must convince the Internship Selection Committees that *you* are a person they want to have work and study with them for the coming year.

As a psychologist in training, you may have been told that you should not be judgmental. When it comes to selecting an internship, forget it. Making judgments is what the selection process is all about. As you prepare your applications and participate in your interviews, do so in the certain knowledge that you will definitely be judged. At the same time, you must judge yourself and the facilities to determine which is best for *you*. This requires doing your homework and learning everything you can about each internship. If at all possible, you should visit each site and meet the training staff and present interns in person. In every group of internship applicants I have worked with, some students discover that some of the celebrated luminaries they had admired from afar turned out to be jerks, while others who appeared less impressive on paper were dazzling in person. Invariably, after interviewing, some candidates eliminate their former top choices from consideration in favor of other programs they had formerly ranked considerably lower.

## ☐ An Internship Application Timetable

In this section, I will provide you with a month by month countdown of what you should do the year you actually apply for internship. In the chapters that follow, you will find detailed discussions of *how* to accomplish these various tasks. This is simply a list, without much explanation of what each task entails.

## Summer

At the end of last year's internship selection period, I sent a message to all the applicants on the APPIC listserv asking them for their advice for future applicants. I received dozens of responses. The most frequent suggestion by far was to try and get as much of the paperwork as possible done during the summer. Access the APPIC and NMS's Web sites and down-

**36**    Megargee's Guide to Obtaining a Psychology Internship

load the information there. Determine the critical dates for registering with NMS, submitting rankings, and so on, and record them in your planning diary.

Download the AAPI and collect the data you will need to fill it out. Begin preparing your autobiographical statement and essays. When the annual APPIC *Directory* becomes available, begin your reconnaissance.[2] If you attend the annual APA convention in August, use the opportunity to network with present interns and attend any internship fairs or workshops that might be offered.

## September

If you began your preparations 6 months to a year ago, you should be in good shape. If you are like most people who are planning to apply this fall, you are probably just beginning to think about what needs to be done. Get to work; you have a lot to do:

1. Read this entire book as soon as possible. Don't worry about the details; you will come back to them as you do each step. Just get an overall picture of what has to be done between now and February.
2. If, after skimming the book, you are convinced that, given all your other commitments, there is no way you can possibly accomplish everything that must be done in the time you have left, you may be right. If it looks like you will have serious problems meeting some important goal in the time remaining, it may be better to wait and apply next year.

   One year, one of our students who was employed half time and carrying an average course load told me that during the fall semester she planned to (a) complete her major area paper, which in our program is equivalent to the Comprehensive Examination; (b) apply for internship; and (c) arrange her wedding, get married, and go on her honeymoon. I advised her that this seemed to be an overly ambitious schedule and suggested that she cut it back somewhat. However, she was sure she could do it all; for example, she felt her Caribbean honeymoon would afford her ample opportunity to complete her major area paper and fill out her internship applications. By the time the semester had ended, she had actually managed to maintain her employment and her course load and accomplish two of her three goals. I thought this was a triumph, but she was very disappointed. (Sorry, but it is none of your business which two she completed.)
3. If you have not done all the things that I suggested you should do last spring, take care of them now. That is, make sure you will meet all the requirements for going on internship this fall, meet with your major

---

[2]If you order before July 15, you get a discount on the printed *Directory*.

Applying for Internship: An Overview **37**

professor, ADCT, and clinical supervisors, discuss your plans, get feedback, and work out a schedule to accomplish all the necessary tasks in the time allotted.

You should also decide on who you want to write letters of recommendation, contact them, and ask if they will be willing to do so.

4. Read Chapter 3 and prepare your list of priorities. If you have dependents or are involved in relationships with people who will be affected by your decisions, it is time for some serious conversations. Are you willing to relocate? If so, will you go alone, or will one or more people go with you? Either way, their needs will influence your choice of an internship site. Whether or not other people are involved in your decision, some brainstorming with your support group and discussions with former interns and faculty will also help you in establishing priorities.

5. If you have already prepared a resume or CV, update it and do what you can to enhance it in the time that remains. If you have never prepared a CV, read Chapter 4 and start to work on it. As soon as it is complete, give a copy to each of the people writing letters on your behalf.

If you have not already done so, download the application information and forms from the APPIC Web site and start assembling the information you will need to fill out the forms. Also access the NMS Web site (www.natmatch.com/psychint) and download the information on matching procedures. As soon as possible, register with NMS and obtain your matching number. NMS is in Canada, so don't be surprised if it takes 4 or 5 weeks for you to get your number.

6. Start reviewing the APPIC *Directory*. As you identify places in which you are interested, go to their Web sites and download application information. You will discover that many require some information, application forms, or statements in addition to the AAPI. If so, download that material and set up a folder for each site. If the site does not have a Web site, e-mail or write them for brochures and application materials. (Some especially well-organized students ask if they should seek information about specific sites earlier. Since many internships wait until after the APPIC meeting in mid-August to update their materials, I think it is generally best to wait until August or September to download or write for information.)

7. Prepare for travel by joining automobile and airline frequent traveler and hotel discount clubs. Pay down any credit card debt so you have enough reserves to pay for travel expenses. Be alert for fall luggage and clothing sales. If you know you will be traveling to certain cities, start looking for bargain tickets in ads and on the Web. It may be cheaper to book now and later pay a penalty for changing the reservation date than it is to wait until December or January when few discount fares are available.

**38** Megargee's Guide to Obtaining a Psychology Internship

8. Get a flu shot. Airplanes are the world's most efficient virus-transmission devices, especially in the winter. In January, students returning to campus from Christmas break bring with them all the various germs they have collected flying around the country. On most campuses, the flu epidemics begin in mid-January, just when you will be doing most of your interviewing.

## October

In early October, I schedule individual meetings with my intern applicants to discuss their priorities and the various sites that they include on their preliminary lists. They also bring their CVs, AAPIs, and partly completed ADCT verification form to this meeting. We go over them in detail. I make suggestions on how they could be improved and check the hours listed on the AAPI to make sure it agrees with the verification form. These interviews provide the students with feedback, and they give me information that I use in preparing my letters of recommendation. If your program does not have some comparable procedure, I suggest you seek out your ADCT and/or major professor for a similar session.

In any case, whether or not you are going to have such a meeting, by early October and preferably before you should have:

1. Completed your list of personal priorities to be used in evaluating internships.
2. Formulated a preliminary list of possible sites, obtained brochures, and started to evaluate them in the light of your priorities.
3. Completed your CV and autobiographical statement and provided copies of the CV to your recommenders.
4. Completed your AAPI.

After meeting with your ADCT or advisor and revising your list of potential sites, you should:

5. Obtain application materials from each site if you have not already done so.
6. Go to the Registrar's Office and order transcripts to be sent to each place you are considering. (If you have any "Incompletes," get them taken care of first.)
7. Get that flu shot you have been putting off.

## November

At present, each internship has its own individual date by which all materials must be received. They range from late October through early February, with most being due in the 4-week period from November 15

Applying for Internship: An Overview     **39**

through December 15. APPIC is considering adopting a uniform application date for all internships. Until then, the earliest due date drives the overall schedule, since it is easiest and safest to send everything out at once.

Some internships permit you to submit your application materials electronically or by fax. Unless they specifically prohibit this, I suggest that you also send printed paper copies by mail or by overnight courier service. Printed copies are easier for them to duplicate and make a better impression, and e-mail and faxes can go astray. For example, if your word processing software is a more recent version than the internships', they may not be able to read your attachments.

More and more internships are cutting down on their clerical work by having students gather all the materials together, including recommendation letters, and submitting them in a single envelope. If you use the U.S. Post (i.e., "snail mail") you should plan to mail everything by Priority Mail *at the Post Office* at least 5 days before the due date. However, I have heard so many horror stories of posted applications going astray or getting delayed, I recommend that you use a private courier service such as Federal Express or UPS if the deadline is imminent. Send your overnight materials at least two days before they are due. These target dates leave you a couple of days leeway for the various disasters that might occur.

To accomplish this:

1. Provide your major professor, ADCT, and clinical supervisor with copies of your CV, a list of due dates, and instructions on which letters are to be sent directly to the internship and which are to be given to you. Also complete your portion of the APPIC verification form and give it to your ADCT. Remember that your ADCT and other recommenders may have a number of letters to prepare, so allow them as much time as possible.

   For the letters your recommenders are supposed to mail directly, make sure the addresses are complete, as noted in Chapter 6, and do exactly what your program requires with regard to postage and so on.

   For the letters you are supposed to collect and submit, make sure the letter writers follow the internships' instructions with regard to signing and sealing the letter. Ask them to give the sealed letter to you several days before the day you need to mail in materials.[3] You do not want to be chasing all over for letters while the clock is ticking.

2. Complete all your application forms, personal statements, cover letters, and CVs. Add the recommendation letters if you are supposed to, and mail them at least 5 days before the due date.

---

[3]Don't panic if one of your letter writers makes a mistake and sends a letter that you are supposed to submit directly to the site. Internships are accustomed to professors who cannot understand or will not conform to their specific procedures.

**40**    Megargee's Guide to Obtaining a Psychology Internship

3. If your professors are supposed to mail their letters of recommendation directly to the internship, make certain that they have actually been posted. (I have known professors and supervisors who wrote the letters but forgot to mail them.)
4. If you hope to visit internship facilities during Christmas break, you may have to obtain advance purchase tickets during November. Unfortunately, those facilities that interview by invitation only will probably not be ready to decide whom they should invite, so don't be surprised if they put off your request for an appointment. Given all the holiday travel, the sooner you can book air or hotel reservations the better, especially if there is only a modest penalty for changes or cancellations.
5. Make arrangements with your employers to be away during the interviewing period.

## December

A week or 10 days after the due dates, the internships should have received and filed your applications and supporting materials. Some will contact you to tell you your application has been received and whether anything is missing; others will not. Call them and ask if your application has been received and if it is complete. If it is not, send in any missing items as soon as possible.

Now is the time to arrange for interviews and make your travel plans. If you have not already done so, start calling and asking for appointments. Some popular places do not have the time to interview everyone, and late callers may be out of luck. Others will only interview by invitation; if so, let them know you would welcome an opportunity to visit. If you cannot visit in person, arrange for a telephone interview. Before your first internship visit, dress up and do some role-playing with faculty members, clinical supervisors, or the other applicants in your support group, using the questions in Appendices 4 and 5.

You should also check the message you have recorded on your telephone answering machine. Remember that from now until the week after Match Day, ITDs may be calling you. If you have "unique," "amusing," or "entertaining" messages on your machine, ask yourself if this is really how you want to impress your top-choice ITD. Selection staff at internships have told me that one of their greatest frustrations is repeatedly listening to "cute" messages on applicants' answering machines. That aggravation may determine whether or not they call back or decide to try some other applicant. (Some students have told me that this advice alone is worth the price of this book.)

If you have not gotten your flu shot by the end of December, forget it.

Applying for Internship: An Overview **41**

It is too late to do any good. Budget time for being sick when you return, and stock up on tissues and chicken soup.

## January

This is when you will do most of your interviewing. It is also the time when the weather is apt to be poorest for traveling. Follow the advice in Chapters 7 and 8, and be sure to keep in touch with your home base so you can receive e-mails or phone messages from other internships. A cellular phone is very helpful at this stage.

After you have returned from interviewing, compare notes with the other internship applicants, seek the advice of faculty and friends, and rank the places to which you have applied. If you have some remaining questions, now is the time to call and ask. If you were unable to do so during your visit, talking with some of the present interns might help. If you wish to send "thank you" notes to the places you visited, do so. If don't wish to, don't. It will make no difference to your chances of being matched.

Start evaluating the internships to which you have applied and begin to formulate your ranked list.[4]

## February

Read Chapter 10 and rank all those internships you are interested in attending. Do not rank any place you would not be willing to attend; if you are matched, you are required to go there. Make sure you submit your list to NMS before the deadline.

It will be about 3 weeks before you learn the results of the matching. In addition to getting caught up on your work and your life, use that time to prepare extra CVs, AAPIs, generic letters, and other materials you will need to access the Clearinghouse in the event you do not get matched. On the Friday before Match Notification Day you will be told whether or not you obtained a match. If you get a match, use the weekend to celebrate. On Matching Day you will find out where you were placed.

If you did not get matched, notify your ADCT and read over the material on using the Clearinghouse in Chapter 10. Clear your schedule for Monday and Tuesday. Start copying application materials and be prepared to access the Clearinghouse as soon as it opens.

---

[4]If, after interviewing, your list of acceptable places seems too short, consider filing some more applications. Until and unless a uniform application date is adopted by APPIC, there will be some internships with late due dates.

## After Matching Day

Once you are matched, send a formal letter or message of acceptance to the ITD with a copy to your ADCT. You should shortly be receiving a confirmation letter from the internship. If you do not receive one within a reasonable period of time, you or your ADCT should check with the program to make sure there is no problem.

# 3
CHAPTER

# Establishing Your Priorities

You are embarking on one of the most challenging enterprises of your graduate education: seeking a predoctoral psychology internship. For some, applying for internship combines the worst aspects of getting married, applying for graduate school, and taking comprehensive oral exams. On the other hand, obtaining your first full-time professional position can also be challenging, exhilarating, and fulfilling. My goal is to help you minimize the strain and maximize the satisfactions.

Why do so many psychology graduate students find applying for internship so stressful? Some apprehension is justified. Obtaining a good internship is important for your career, and in recent years many candidates have failed to secure a position. An applicant who does not experience some anxiety probably does not understand the situation or is not especially serious about a career in professional psychology.

However, much of your trepidation is unwarranted. Some probably stems from fear of the unknown. You are applying for a professional psychology internship and you do not know what to expect or how to go about it. Relax. By the time you finish reading this book you will have all the information you need. Other worries may be caused by irrational beliefs. In the course of your professional training you have undoubtedly counseled clients to put aside their unrealistic expectations so they can cope more effectively with realistic concerns. It is time you did the same. Let us begin by exorcising some of the demons that haunt many intern applicants.

44    Megargee's Guide to Obtaining a Psychology Internship

# ☐ Some Unrealistic Worries

## Obtaining the Perfect Internship

Many internship applicants seem to have an illusion that somewhere there exists one perfect program that is ideal for them and that their careers will be ruined if they do not procure a position there. Some are even convinced that there is a single special slot or rotation within that ideal internship that they must seek and obtain. This is utter nonsense.

In the course of seeking an internship you will become intimately acquainted with the annual APPIC *Directory* of internships. As you will see, there are approximately 550 predoctoral training centers in the United States and Canada with about 2,500 funded full-time slots, 83% of which are accredited by the APA (Hall & Hsu, 2000). Unless your needs are very unusual, many, probably most, of these sites can meet your basic training needs. At the same time, it is extremely unlikely that any one site can perfectly satisfy all your requirements. So, although your decision is an important one, try not to get too obsessive about it.

## Evaluation Anxiety

Internship selection involves evaluations, and evaluations make some people nervous. As a psychologist, you are going to be making appraisals every day of your professional career. Whenever you make a diagnostic assessment, perform a therapeutic intervention, or consult with another professional, you are constantly evaluating other people, and they in turn are examining you. The same thing happens when you are applying for internship. You will be sizing up the program and staff, and at the same time they will be appraising you. If you think of the internship interview as just another professional assessment, your anxiety should decrease.

## Competition Anxiety

Many students get scared by the numbers. In the most recent year for which total application data are available, there were 43,642 applications filed, an increase of 5,450 (14.7%) from the number I reported in the third edition of this book. During the 1999–2000 selection cycle, the average APA-accredited internship received 77 applications, or about 16 applications for every slot (Hall & Hsu, 2000). Before you panic, you must remember that this is the number of *applications*, not *applicants*. A recent survey of 500 applicants reported in the on-line APPIC Match News on Feb. 28, 2000 reported a mean of 13.8 applications per student, a number very close to my estimate of 13 applications per candidate in the previous edition of this book. Even a "superstar" who gets an offer from every place to which she applies can take only one position; the other dozen positions will go to other applicants.

Moreover, there is great disparity in the numbers of students applying to various facilities. Data that I have extracted from the *Directories* over the years consistently show that 20% of the internship centers receive 40% of the total number of applications. The remaining 80% of the programs are considerably less competitive. And don't forget the nonaccredited internships that only received five applications per slot in the Year 2000. Obviously an APA-accredited position is preferable, but you can still get good training at a nonaccredited facility. Certain parts of the country consistently have a much higher ratio of applications to slots than others. (See Appendix 2.) If you apply to one of these settings, you can improve your chances. So, while there is certainly cause for concern, there is no reason to panic.

## Fear of Rejection

A third irrational fear is that of experiencing rejection. You may as well accept the fact right now that you *will* be rejected. No matter how fabulous you are, it is unlikely that *every* setting you apply to will decide that you belong in their program. I recall one candidate who was a brilliant researcher, a gifted clinician, and fluent in two languages. Most training programs pursued her as if she were the graduate student equivalent of a Heisman Trophy winner. However, even this paragon did not get accepted everywhere. One program turned her down because they felt she was too physically attractive. "The head nurse would have killed me if I brought her in here," the Training Director later confessed. If she could get rejected, so can you. But relax; you will soon discover that you do not like every program you apply to. Some will not meet your needs; others will simply not appeal to you. So why should you expect every program to fancy having you as a trainee? Such rejections, often mutual, are inevitable. Worrying about them is a waste of time.

## ☐ Some Realistic Concerns

Once you stop stewing over the irrational worries that plague many students, you can deal more effectively with the realistic difficulties applying for internship poses. Virtually all of these problems can be anticipated. If you prepare for them, you will be able to cope with them more successfully.

**46**     Megargee's Guide to Obtaining a Psychology Internship

## Applying Is a Hassle

This is a legitimate concern. The dean of a school of professional psychology described the present process as "disruptive to the lives of our students" (Fox, 1991, p. 34) and, indeed, applying for internship will come to dominate your life in the months to come. Identifying the training centers that will best meet your particular needs, filling out application forms, preparing a CV, traveling to the sites, interviewing with training centers—all this will require a lot of time and effort.

## Applying Takes Too Much Time

This is also true, so in planning your schedule for the year you apply, be sure to budget adequate time for the internship application process. "Bob," a recent applicant, sent me a summary of the amount of time he spent seeking an internship. He submitted 14 applications to sites across the country. Not counting travel time, he calculated that he spent over 300 hours on internship-seeking activities. His time estimates are reported in Table 3.1. I advise my students to figure that the internship application process will require at least as much time as the most rigorous graduate course they have ever taken and to modify their academic schedules accordingly.

## Applying Is Expensive

Costs are another realistic consideration. Fox (1991, p. 34) noted, "Going for interviews . . . creates real financial hardships for most students. . . . It

**TABLE 3.1.** Applicant's Report of Direct Time Expenditures

| Task | Hours |
| --- | --- |
| Reading Megargee book and APPIC materials | 9 |
| Reviewing APPIC *Directory* | 14 |
| Obtaining brochures | 3 |
| Reviewing brochures | 50 |
| Requesting transcripts | 2 |
| Compiling practicum data | 50 |
| Preparing summaries for letters & essays | 11 |
| Preparing 14 applications | 104 |
| Time spent in interviews* | 64 |
| Follow-up time | 6 |
| Ranking settings & preparing match form | 2 |
| Total hours | 315 |

*Note: Does not include travel time.

is not unusual for our students to have expenses of $2,000 in interview costs alone." A recent survey of 480 students undertaken for the Council of University Directors of Clinical Psychology (CUDCP) reported a mean expenditure of $1,084 with a wide range of variations (Thorne, 1997). Oehlert and Lopez (1997) surveyed applicants to a midwestern VA medical center. The respondents averaged 6.9 interviews each, and the cost of interviewing, exclusive of child care, clothing, and lost wages, averaged $1,044 (SD = $1,021). They also reported an average cost of $124 (SD = $111) for application expenses such as copying, postage, and the like, for a total mean expenditure of $1,168 to obtain a position paying $17,000.

Bob also sent me a summary of his interviewing expenses. He conducted a nationwide search and spent over $3,000 in direct expenses. This does not include the 3,200 extra miles he put on his car, which the IRS estimates costs 32.5 cents per mile, or the $450 he had to spend for new interview clothes after the airlines lost his suitcase with his interview clothes in it. (See Table 3.2.)

Since he was going to relocate, Bob took his wife with him when possible. Her expenses cost them an additional $850, but they felt it was worth the added expense, especially since she acted as Bob's cheerleader

**TABLE 3.2.** Applicant's Report of Direct and Indirect Expenses

| | |
|---|---|
| **Direct expenses** | |
| **Preparing applications** | |
| 14 transcripts from 2 schools | $140 |
| Materials: Postage, phone, book, etc. | $120 |
| Federal Express | $140 |
| **Personal travel** | |
| Airfare, including change fee | $925 |
| Taxis, tolls | $85 |
| Gasoline | $145 |
| Automobile rental | $140 |
| **Lodging** | |
| Hotels (15 nights @ $60) | $900 |
| Restaurants | $360 |
| **Miscellaneous** | |
| Pet sitters | $100 |
| Gifts for friends who provided lodging | $50 |
| Upgrade of wardrobe | $100 |
| Total direct expenses | $3,205 |
| | |
| **Indirect expenses** | |
| Emergency wardrobe replacement when luggage lost | $450 |
| Spouse's travel and meals | $850 |
| 3,200 miles on personal car | $1,040 |
| 21 days lost at paid placement | ? |
| 13 days lost from spouse's work | ? |

**48**    Megargee's Guide to Obtaining a Psychology Internship

and trainer. Ironically, both fell in love with the first site they visited. Bob estimates that moving there will cost another $3,000.

Obviously, the farther you travel, the more you will spend. You can reduce travel expenses somewhat by developing a list of several places in a particular region instead of applying to internships that are scattered all over the continent. If you follow the advice in this book, you will save hundreds of dollars. (For openers, if you fly, don't check your interview clothes.) Nevertheless, you should be prepared for substantial extra expenditures for travel, lodging, telephone, and wardrobe additions.

## Impact of Your Decision

Another realistic concern is that selecting an internship is an important professional decision that will significantly influence your career. The skills you develop and the techniques you learn will stay with you throughout your career, and the professional relationships you acquire and the contacts you make will have a major influence on your subsequent opportunities. Choosing an internship is indeed an important task that deserves your serious attention.

## Effects on Employment

Unless you are lucky enough to be independently wealthy or have a full fellowship, you probably have a full- or part-time job of some sort. During December and January you will probably have to take a lot of time off for interviewing and travel. You need to discuss this with your employer and make arrangements for others to teach your classes or cover your cases while you are away. If you have to take leave without pay, you need to factor the lost salary into your expense estimate.

## Effects on Family Life

During the 6 months or so that you are applying for internship, you will be under considerable stress. Depending on how you cope with stress, you may be irritable, moody, or preoccupied. You may find it difficult to "be there" for your family or those who depend on you during this time. This can have an adverse effect on your relationships, which is why I recommend discussing these issues with your family and friends early in the game, so they will know what to expect and be more understanding during this period.

## Lack of Control

Feelings of uncertainty and lack of control over the eventual outcome are major sources of anxiety for everyone involved in the internship selection process, ITDs and ADCTs as well as students. No one can predict exactly what will happen, and no one can control the outcome. For applicants, this lack of control is often compounded by not knowing exactly what is involved in the internship selection process. While your university or professional school training program may have provided you with excellent academic training, few prepare you adequately for the process of finding and obtaining an appropriate internship. You can be forgiven if you feel like Alice playing croquet with the Queen of Hearts. Until you understand the process, it is indeed like playing a game on someone else's field with whimsical rules that often appear arbitrary, if indeed they are ever articulated. True, APPIC has published a formal set of explicit regulations, but at times these are incidental to what is actually happening. This book is designed to give you the information you need. You will also find it helpful to read accounts written by previous interns such as Burt (1985), Casey Jacob (1987), Gollaher and Craig (1994), and Kingsley (1985), who have "been there" and successfully coped with the system.

## ☐ Establishing Your Priorities

The first step in applying for an internship is probably the most important. This is establishing your priorities: deciding what it is *you* are looking for in your internship. If you do this honestly and insightfully at the outset, all the remaining steps will be infinitely easier. On the other hand, if you put this step off or fail to determine your real needs, the whole application process will be much more difficult, especially during the final stages in which you must come to some definite decisions.

I cannot overemphasize the importance of analyzing your priorities in the very beginning, *before* you start surveying the APPIC *Directory*, writing for brochures, composing your resume, and preparing your applications. Each person's needs and goals are different; there is no one internship that is best for everyone. Take the time to reflect on what it is *you* want from *your* internship.

You may find it helpful to formalize this process by listing all the features you do and do not want in an internship setting. Weigh the importance of each by indicating whether you regard it as "essential," "important," or "desirable." For examples, see Casey Jacob (1987) and Stewart and Stewart (1996a). After you have refined this checklist and gathered more information, you can use it to help you decide which programs you

**50**   Megargee's Guide to Obtaining a Psychology Internship

will apply to and, later, to help you rank your choices. It is because every person's list is unique that there is no internship that is ideal for everyone.

There are two sets of factors to consider in evaluating internships, professional and personal. The first set has to do with the training you will receive. These include whether a program has APA approval, the nature of the setting, the population(s) you will be exposed to, the rotations available, and the personnel with whom you would be working. The second set has to do with quality of life. It includes such aspects as geography, family ties, and finances. I will discuss a few of the most common considerations below.

## ☐ Professional Considerations

There are many factors to consider in evaluating an internship program. One important consideration is whether a program is approved by the APA. With regard to the nature of the training offered, you need to consider whether you prefer diversity or wish to specialize, if the number or the nature of the rotations available is important to you, and how you value the opportunity to attend didactic presentations and seminars. The training faculty is extremely important. Their expertise, theoretical orientations, supervision styles, accessibility, and commitment to training are all factors you must weigh. The facilities and equipment that are provided and the opportunity to do research will be more critical for some applicants than others; you will have to decide for yourself how you weight these aspects. Less tangible, but still influential, is the atmosphere that prevails; this includes morale, collegiality, and the degree of respect or rivalry that may prevail among different services or disciplines. The prestige of an institution and the degree to which it fits with your perception of your present training needs and your future plans also need to be considered. After it is all over, many report that the single most important factor was an intangible "gut" feeling that this was the best place for them (Stedman, Neff, Donahoe, Kopel, & Hays, 1995).

In the pages that follow, I will comment on some of these factors. While I will offer my recommendations and opinions on these issues, I do so to help you determine your own attitudes. You must decide which aspects are most important for you. For example, since I value internships for the clinical training they provide, I do not weight opportunities for research very high, but for you this might be a vital consideration. If my comments help you diagnose your feelings, they will accomplish their purpose; on the other hand, if you copy them down and say to yourself that certain things are important because Megargee says they are, you will be missing the point.

Establishing Your Priorities **51**

After you have formulated your personal list of priorities, when you start evaluating actual programs, you will soon discover that no place will have everything exactly as you would like it. If it fits your professional goals, it may conflict with your personal needs. Inevitably there will be tradeoffs and compromises. You will have to decide for yourself which aspects are most important for you. By establishing your professional priorities at the outset, before they are intertwined with any specific programs, you will be better able to analyze objectively how important these considerations are for you.

## APA Accreditation

Training programs in professional psychology are accredited by the APA. Each year the accreditation status of predoctoral internship training programs is listed in the December issue of the *American Psychologist*. The printed APPIC *Directory* also notes the APA accreditation status as of June 15, when the *Directory* goes to press. The on-line version may be more up to date.

Of the 567 predoctoral internships in the United States listed in the 2000–2001 *Directory*, 431 (76%) were APA accredited, and they had 2,062 of the 2,489 (82.8%) full-time funded positions. The 136 nonaccredited internship centers had the remaining 427 funded positions (17.2%) as well as 95% of the unfunded slots (Hall & Hsu, 2000).

If your application is "competitive," that is, if you are an advanced student in good standing at an APA-accredited clinical or counseling doctoral program, you should definitely set your sights on a fully funded APA accredited internship program. The fact that a program is not APA accredited does not mean that you cannot receive good training there. Indeed, every accredited program had to train several classes of interns before they could obtain accreditation. A survey of nonaccredited internships revealed that the primary reason they did not seek APA accreditation was the cost involved (Solway et al., 1987). As long as you graduate with a doctoral degree from an APA-accredited doctoral program, it is usually possible to get licensed even if your internship was not APA accredited. It is up to your graduate school to decide whether a nonaccredited internships satisfies your degree program's predoctoral internship requirement.

Why then do I recommend that you concentrate on APA-accredited internships? First, even though it is now possible to obtain a license or other credentials, such as a listing in the *National Register of Health Service Providers in Psychology*, without having attended an APA-accredited internship, this could change. Future legislation might be more stringent. The primary reason, however, is all the hassles it can later lead to. The typical

## 52 Megargee's Guide to Obtaining a Psychology Internship

license application asks if you completed a one-year APA-accredited predoctoral internship. If you did, you simply check "Yes" and skip to the next part of the application. If you check "No," however, you will probably need to describe *and document* all the details of your internship experience so the authorities can judge whether it was equivalent to an APA-accredited program.[5] This may include the number and the nature of the clients you saw, the various rotations on which you served, the number of clock hours of supervision you received, and, as if all this were not enough, you may have to establish all your supervisors' qualifications and credentials. The older you get, the more difficult this becomes. It is far better to concentrate on programs with full accreditation.

Why, then, would anyone attend an internship that is not APA accredited? Solway et al. (1987) surveyed interns at 75 nonaccredited sites listed in the APPIC *Directory*. They reported the most important factor was location. Their respondents indicated that for them attending a setting in a preferred locale outweighed its accreditation status.

In addition, as you might suppose, nonaccredited internships are considerably less competitive. Hall and Hsu (2000) reported that the 136 nonaccredited agencies in the APPIC *Directory* received an average of 18 applications each, or approximately 5 per slot, compared with the 77 applications per agency, or 16 per position, received by the accredited programs. With the current imbalance between supply and demand, more applicants are seriously considering nonaccredited internships.

### Diversity Versus Specialization

Some programs, such as those in pediatric psychology, provide very focused and specialized training. Others feature a variety of more general experiences. Which is better for you?

Other things being equal, I suggest you seek diversity. Your predoctoral internship may be the last chance for you to get such a varied experience. The broader the range of clinical cases, approaches, and settings, the better. In evaluating internships, examine not only the range of cases seen by the internship as a whole, but also the diversity that any given intern such as yourself is likely to encounter. For example, if case selection is driven by the availability of third-party payments, are you, as an unlicensed provider, going to be restricted to cases not covered by an HMO?

I also recommend that you choose a setting that will complement your previous practicum experience. If all your work has been with outpatients, now is the time to get some inpatient experience. If you have been

---

[5]If an unaccredited internship you attend later receives accreditation, you must still list it as being unaccredited unless the APA site visit occurred during the year you were interning.

working at a prison, consider a medical setting, and so on. Look beyond the specific facility and determine what other opportunities exist in the area. Often there will be a number of hospitals or agencies that are geographically contiguous, and one can attend colloquia or Grand Rounds at neighboring facilities or even have a rotation there. Visiting one VA hospital, I discovered it was across the street from a major children's hospital, so that it was possible for the VA interns to do a pediatric rotation even though it was not mentioned in the brochure.

## Number of Rotations Available

While I favor diversity, do not be seduced by the sheer number of rotations that are listed for some internships. An internship is not like a buffet or salad bar where you can have a little bit of everything. Instead, it is like ordering a fixed-price family dinner in a Chinese restaurant: you get one choice from column A, one from column B, and so on. Moreover, just as everyone automatically gets rice and a fortune cookie, you will probably be required to take certain rotations. For example, it is common to require all interns to be involved in both assessment and treatment, to work with both children and adults, and to have both inpatient and outpatient rotations over the course of a year.

There is a finite amount you can experience within a year. You will probably have two, possibly three, major rotations and two or three minor ones. However, you may simply be assigned to one setting for 6 months and another for the remaining 6 months, especially in a consortium in which the various participating institutions are miles apart from one another. In such internships, it is up to the interns and their supervisors to work out a varied array of experiences within each facility.

You may be expected to pick up three or four long-term therapy cases during your first rotation and carry them throughout the year. In addition, there will usually be a standard array of seminars for everyone plus some electives. Given all these obligations, your degrees of freedom are limited.

A vital consideration is who gets to participate in the various rotations. Some internships' brochures display an extraordinary number of rotations. Closer examination may reveal that several are funded from particular sources, such as a specialized hospital within a consortium or a foundation focused on a specific disorder. If so, the interns who receive those stipends may spend the major portion of their time in those settings and have relatively little opportunity to learn about the other settings except over coffee with fellow interns. Moreover, it may be that *only* the interns on those stipends get to work in those areas, especially if highly specialized skills such as administering a neuropsychological assessment

**54**    Megargee's Guide to Obtaining a Psychology Internship

battery are required. It does you no good to have an item on the menu if you can't order it.

Some settings have track-specific selection in which applicants are chosen for particular rotations or programs. Indeed, each track may have its own individual NMS match number. If so, you will apply for that specific program. If it is especially important to you to have a specific rotation or to work with a particular faculty member, you need to find out how interns are selected for these positions. Do you have the qualifications they look for in applicants for this program? In short, before you pass over an internship that has a relatively small selection of rotations in favor of one that appears to have more variety, determine how much of the variety you will actually be able to experience. It may be that you will discover that you would have pretty much the same program in both settings.

## Didactic Training and Seminars

Some internships offer a wealth of didactic training and seminars with top-notch people in their fields. In contrast to the semester-long university courses you are familiar with, these are more apt to be miniseminars, with one to three sessions devoted to a given clinical topic or proseminars with a series of experts discussing their specialties. Grand Rounds and case conferences are another important aspect of internship training.

Since internships vary greatly in their resources and their geography, the opportunities to participate in these additional educational experiences will differ. You must decide for yourself how much weight you will place on this aspect of internship training.

## Personnel

More important than the specific rotations, the populations available, and all the other aspects of the curriculum, are the actual people with whom you will be working. These include the Director of Training, your supervisors, and the other interns.

Good ITDs are sincerely interested in their students and the quality of their educational experience. If necessary, they are ready to do battle with the administration to preserve the quality of their interns' education and prevent them from being exploited. Poor ones are hassled, disinterested, and looking for ways out. If their morale is low, yours will probably suffer as well. How do you discriminate the good from the poor? Tenure in office is no reliable criterion; some who have been directors for many years continue because of their commitment to training, but there are other long-term directors who are obviously burned out and waiting for

Establishing Your Priorities    **55**

retirement. A new director may be excited and filled with ideas to improve training, or resentful over the time that is required. I am always interested in whether the ITD sought out the post or was stuck with it because no one else wanted it. In any event, ask the present interns about the dedication, enthusiasm, and accessibility of the ITD.

Supervisors are also very important. Most of your actual training will take place in one-to-one interactions with individual supervisors. More than any other single factor, a good supervisor can make a rotation, while a poor one can be devastating. You may have to dig a bit to learn about the nature, quality, and quantity of supervision, but it will be one of the single most important aspects of your training.

In evaluating a facility, you may be dazzled by the eminent names listed on the brochure and the chance to work with such people. That is fine, but make sure you establish whether these individuals actually supervise trainees, whether they will be available the year you intern, and whether you have any say over who you get as a supervisor.

Supervisors are not always people on staff. When I was a trainee at the Palo Alto VA, I was assigned a chronic schizophrenic who had been hospitalized for 14 years as my long-term individual psychotherapy case. Not a very promising prospect. However, I also had an outside consultant from Stanford named Albert Bandura as a supervisor who made it an excellent learning experience.

Your fellow interns will be your primary support group during your training. They may become your best friends or your worst enemies. While each class is somewhat different, observing the present interns and their interactions can give you some clues about the types of people selected and whether the institutional atmosphere is divisive or congenial. Are they all Type As or more laid back? Are they doctrinaire and rigid, or tolerant of differing opinions? Are they trustworthy or treacherous?

Sometimes you can pick up important clues when you are given a tour of the interns' offices. I recently visited a children's hospital in which three trainees shared an office they had decorated with numerous snapshots of the three of them with their families socializing together on Halloween, Thanksgiving, and other occasions. A series of charts on the wall, to which they had all contributed, recorded the amusing things their child clients had said (and done) to them during the course of the rotation. Clearly this was a congenial group. I have also visited other settings where the atmosphere was frigid at best and hostile at worst.

## Theoretical Orientations

Settings differ greatly in theoretical orientation. Some places are very formal and authoritarian, expecting everyone to formulate and discuss cases

**56**   Megargee's Guide to Obtaining a Psychology Internship

according to the "official" orientation, whether it be behavioral or dynamic. Other places are more flexible and enjoy a wide range of viewpoints among the students and staff.

Your own theoretical orientation and your degree of commitment to it will be of interest to the internships, as theirs will be to you. Other things being equal, they may prefer students who share their frame of reference. If they do not require that you share their frame of reference, they will expect you to be open to exploring their point of view. Moreover, you should have a sufficient grasp of the basic principles and vocabulary of the prevailing orientation so as to be able to understand what is being said.

I feel that you will probably learn more from a setting with a variety of viewpoints than one with a single party line. One intern I visited had six different supervisors with as many orientations. She learned to shift smoothly from a psychoanalytic to an ego psychology to a cognitive-behavioral to a radical behavioral frame of reference in the course of an afternoon as she went from one supervisor to the next.

This intern's experience brings up another issue with regard to supervisors. Where are they located? In the case of this internship, they were consultants on soft money who were located in their practices around town, and it was necessary for her to travel to them. In other settings, most supervision will occur on the premises, even if the supervisors are not on staff. Not only does this mean they will be more readily available for consults, but also that they are more likely to attend case conferences.

## Service Versus Training

Internships vary in their commitment to training. This is reflected in the numbers of hours allotted for supervision, in the number of seminars offered, and in the number of cases you are expected to process. Are you expected to give minimal batteries and turn out as many reports as possible, or are you encouraged to try various techniques and given an opportunity to read and reflect on a puzzling case? Some interns are expected to "eat what they kill" by generating fees that will reimburse the agency for their stipends and supervision. Some feel they are being exploited and used to provide low-cost service to the facility with minimal educational benefits. Emphasis on service and generating fees seems to be becoming more common as state and federal support for training has diminished and centers have become more dependent on fees for their support.

This issue is best explored through discussions with present interns during your site visit. You can also raise this concern with the training staff as long as you make it clear you are concerned about the quality of the training and not the quantity of work.

## Facilities and Equipment

The facilities that are available can also influence the quality of the educational experience. Some internships have superb equipment; others do not. I recently toured one setting in which each intern had an individual office for seeing clients which was equipped with a complete video recording setup—camera, VCR, and monitor—for taping sessions. Supervisors' offices were similarly equipped. Another internship had two cameras in every therapy room feeding to a central control console worthy of MGM Studios. There, technicians could alternate cameras to catch questions and responses in a dyadic therapy session in one room, while maneuvering the playroom camera angles by remote control to track children as they scurried about. When I read the evaluations of the students interning at these settings, it was obvious that the supervisors closely monitored the actual therapy process and provided the trainees with detailed feedback.

Few places have such superb equipment. However, the availability of audio and video recording equipment, computers, electronic test scoring apparatus, and specialized equipment for neuropsychological assessment, biofeedback, and the like obviously has an impact on what can be done there.

The nature and the amount of space for interns is another consideration. Some interns are provided with individual offices, some with individual desks in a shared office, and some with individual drawers in a shared desk.

## Opportunities for Research

Internships vary greatly in their emphasis on research, ranging from those where there is no research to those that view research as an important aspect of the training program.[6] In the more research-oriented facilities, do not assume that the time allocated for research will necessarily be for your personal research. Some centers like to have all the interns collaborate with faculty members on joint projects that are relevant to the internship, such as a needs assessment of some service or an evaluation of some program being carried out by the facility. The results of such projects benefit the internship, enabling them to carry out studies they could not undertake without the assistance of the interns. Moreover, it provides a mechanism whereby students can work together, which should improve their *esprit de corps*.

---

[6]The Society for a Science of Clinical Psychology issues a directory of clinical psychology internships which reports on the research opportunities available for interns. The current address can be found in an appendix to the APPIC *Directory*.

# 58 Megargee's Guide to Obtaining a Psychology Internship

A few academically oriented internships offer rich opportunities to collaborate with faculty in their ongoing research projects. This may enable you to get shared authorship on several publications. However, it is unlikely you will be able to formulate and carry out a personal research project. Given the amount of time it takes to settle in, observe the opportunities available, write a proposal, and get it approved, it is difficult to do much data collection in the span of a 1-year internship, especially since you will be rotating through a variety of settings. If you plan to stay for 2 years, however, research can often occupy a larger portion of your available time in the 2nd year.

Dissertation research is often problematic. Krieshok et al.'s (2000) study indicates that if you have defended your prospectus before you report for internship, it is likely you will make some progress. If data collection is complete, you might even complete your analysis and write-up. However, working on your dissertation while you are on internship is not easy. Do not count on having much time for personal research regardless of what is stated in the brochures. If you are the sort of person who took a big pile of "important" books home to read over Christmas or summer vacations *and actually read them*, maybe you will be able to accomplish a fair amount on internship, but most interns find there is so much clinical work to do that they quickly lose their academic mindset. After spending 60 to 70 hours seeing clients, attending staffings, writing reports, receiving supervision, and participating in seminars, you will probably have little inclination for crunching numbers or writing technical prose. I personally feel that spending a lot of time on your dissertation can detract from what should be a unique clinical experience. Most major professors will probably disagree.

If you feel you must do a great deal of dissertation work on internship, perhaps you ought to consider waiting another year and applying after you have completed your dissertation. Having a well-advanced or completed dissertation will not only give you an edge on other applicants, but will also make it easier to move smoothly from your internship into a full-time professional or academic position. More and more ITDs are maintaining that a completed dissertation, or at least a defended prospectus, should be *required* before students apply for internship.

## Relations With Other Disciplines

In large multidisciplinary settings, the nature and the quality of interprofessional relations should also be considered. They may be reflected in the formal table of organization that indicates who reports to whom (e.g., does the Chief of Psychology report to the Chief of Psychiatry?) However, it is the personal relationships and mutual respect among professionals from different disciplines that are most important.

Establishing Your Priorities **59**

The tensions between psychology and psychiatry on the national scene can be reflected in the relations between these disciplines in some medical settings. If the psychology interns wear white coats and are called "residents," I usually infer that psychology has a status problem vis à vis psychiatry.

As a psychology intern, you can get caught up in these factional disputes. One of my students was reprimanded by a psychiatric resident because he had the temerity to write a "diagnostic impression" ("patient appears depressed") in a chart, thus usurping the exclusive right of physicians to make medical diagnoses. The resident complained to the Chief of Psychiatry, who complained to the Chief of Psychology. Eventually, a formal hearing was held before it all got worked out. Presumably all of this occurred because everyone wanted to make sure that the patient received the best possible care, but somehow I never learned how the client benefited from all this wrangling. You may enjoy such confrontations, but from my standpoint, with everything else you have to worry about on internship, who needs this sort of bovine residue?

## Politics and Purges

Apart from interdisciplinary harmony, when you visit a program you may hear rumors about high-level political struggles in which administrators resign or are fired. Sometimes these struggles are real, sometimes simply gossip. They are usually conveyed in hushed tones by some interns who are presently at the facility and are eager to display their inside knowledge of programmatic politics. The implication is that you should avoid that setting until the conflicts have been resolved or new people appointed.

An unstable political climate, if in fact it exists, is certainly a factor to consider, but its effects should not be overemphasized. To put the matter in perspective, suppose that as a graduate student you teach introductory psychology to undergraduates at your university. If the Chancellor of the University System fired the President of your school, would it really make any difference in the quality of instruction for the freshmen enrolled in your class? At the intern level, these political battles, unlike the territorial disputes described above, probably have relatively little impact.

## Prestige

Some internships are more prestigious than others. Attending an eminent internship enhances your CV and may open some doors. It also makes your ADCT look good. However, prestige does not necessarily guarantee that the training you will receive is better, or even as good, as it may be at other, less renowned facilities. The famous people whose names add lus-

**60** Megargee's Guide to Obtaining a Psychology Internship

ter to a program's reputation may spend most of their time off doing the things that make them famous instead of working with the trainees. It is up to you to discern how important an institution's prestige is to you and weigh it accordingly.

## Fit With Your Training Needs

In reviewing your readiness for internship, you will no doubt conclude that you are well prepared in certain areas and adequate in others, but that there are some professional skills that need to be enhanced. Unless you plan to be a "Renaissance psychologist," it is unlikely that you want to achieve the highest levels of proficiency in all areas. I am pretty good at using traditional assessment techniques, but I doubt if I ever will have occasion to measure evoked potentials.

In formulating your priorities for internship, you need to establish your personal training goals. What is it you want to accomplish during your internship year? Consult with your faculty advisors and clinical supervisors. What are the areas you most need to work on? With what patient populations and treatment settings should you gain more experience? By asking yourself and your mentors these questions, you should be able to formulate a list of the types of training experiences and rotations you are going to seek on internship, as well as an idea of how much you want to emphasize various areas.

## Fit With Future Plans

Every applicant has different career goals. Consider what you want to be doing 5 and 10 years from now. When evaluating possible programs, keep these objectives in mind and ask yourself how each setting will influence your chances of achieving your ambitions. If, for example, you plan on postdoctoral training in a particular area, will this internship prepare you for the postdoctoral program and enhance your chances of getting accepted? If you are thinking about relocating, you may want to inquire about the licensing laws in the different states you are considering.

Look beyond the professed goals of the training program and examine the actual achievements of its graduates. What kinds of jobs do they get? What are they doing 5 years later? Although some places may profess to prepare you for an academic position, for example, you may discover that virtually all of their former interns enter professional practice.

Some Training Directors and their staffs work very hard at helping their interns find full-time positions at the conclusion of their internship. Obviously this is easiest when the intern has completed the dissertation and the facility is located in the area where the student hopes to locate. Other internships do not regard intern placement as part of their responsibility and do not get involved with this aspect. Such assistance will be more important to some students than to others.

## Balancing Professional Priorities

As we have reviewed some of these professional considerations, it may have seemed that some choices were obvious or trivial. Everyone wants high quality training, dedicated supervisors, congenial colleagues, and a free choice of desirable rotations. What you must do is decide on their *relative* importance to you, because you will find that tradeoffs are inevitable. In order to get that neuropsychological rotation you covet, you may have to go to a place where there is a great deal of interdisciplinary strife. An institution with considerable prestige may emphasize service at the expense of training. If you can decide on the relative importance of these professional issues before they get linked to particular places, you will find it easier to evaluate actual internships.

## Truth In Advertising

Don't believe everything you read on the internship's Web site or in their printed brochures (Grace, 1985). Some rotations may have long since been discontinued; other training experiences may exist only in the vivid imagination of whoever wrote the copy. One recent applicant found that the statements regarding the theoretical orientations of the settings she visited bore little relation to the types of treatment actually being done. Some places that called themselves dynamic were actually more eclectic. One ITD confessed that the paragraph on theoretical orientation was included for historical reasons to please members of the Board of Trustees of the foundation that helped support the internship.

In short, even though APPIC has guidelines for internship brochures, and APA site visitors will examine them every 5 years, it is safest to regard an internship brochure as you would any other piece of advertising, like a circular you might pick up in an auto dealership or real estate office. Maintain a healthy skepticism and check out the claims they make for yourself.

## ☐ Personal and Practical Considerations

In addition to these professional factors, you will have personal preferences and practical concerns. Since you are going to spend at least a year of your life in your internship, it is important that you consider these aspects as well as your professional priorities.

## 62 Megargee's Guide to Obtaining a Psychology Internship

## Family and Personal Relationships

Family ties and relationships often play a vital role in selecting a site. Sometimes it is undesirable, impractical, or just plain impossible for your loved one(s) to relocate. If this is the case, you may decide to intern close to home. This is obviously much easier in some parts of the country than in others. If your region is rich in training resources, interning near your home base may not present much of a problem. If good local training facilities are scarce, however, the decision to stay near home may mean sacrificing some professional goals such as attending a fully accredited training program. When a recent APPIC Board Chairman was asked what was the biggest barrier to obtaining a match, he replied, "When students arbitrarily decide that they will not consider a wide range of geographic locales" (Mellott, Arden, & Cho, 1997).

If you decide to seek an internship in another location, and you have a spouse, partner, or children, the first big decision that must be made is whether they are going to travel with you to the internship. If family members or partners are going to move with you to the internship site, then their needs for employment, education, and so forth will have to be considered along with your training requirements. Having a partner who is unable to find work in a new city can be devastating to a relationship that may already be strained by the stresses induced by the training program.

If you decide to leave your family or friends behind while you go away on internship for a year, accessibility will probably be an important consideration. An internship within driving distance will allow you to come home some weekends. If you must go farther afield, choosing an internship located in a "hub" city will make air travel easier and less expensive.

If you are traveling in tandem with another intern applicant, compromises will be necessary. Some internships make an effort to keep couples together, even when it involves different disciplines such as psychology and social work. Others prefer not to take two people from the same university. This is the sort of issue that can be investigated during the reconnaissance phase.

APPIC provides a couples match to maximize the likelihood of couples finding a mutually satisfactory pair of internships. (For more information, see Chapter 10.) However, the best strategy for couples who wish to remain in proximity is for them to limit their applications to a single geographic area that is rich in opportunities. Other things being equal, metropolitan areas such as Boston, the Greater New York Metropolitan area, the District of Columbia and its environs, Atlanta, Chicago, St. Louis, Houston, Los Angeles, and the San Francisco Bay Area afford couples the best chance to stay together (Stewart & Stewart, 1996b). It is easier to travel by car or train from one major city to another in the Northeast than in other parts of the country.

Establishing Your Priorities    **63**

Caring for children is difficult while on internship, especially in those settings that expect 60- to 70-hour work weeks. Some interns rely on their noninterning spouse or other family members to care for their children during the internship year, especially when circumstances dictate it is best to leave the children behind. Others may have to rely on relatives to provide daycare; if so, they need to select a program located where they have family members who are willing and able to assist them.

Parents lacking family or other childcare resources may seek other alternatives. Commercial daycare for preschool children is one possibility, but internship stipends are limited and most communities do not provide adequate public care, especially for new arrivals. Nor do many training programs provide on-site centers. The solution that is most often discussed is the half-time, 2-year internship that enables parents to complete the APA requirement within 24 months (Blom, 1990, 1991; Ochroch, 1990). Unfortunately, the most recent APPIC *Directory* listed only 77 half-time positions, 33 (43%) of which were unfunded (Hall & Hsu, 2000). This is considerably less than the 123 positions that were available in 1991 (Zimet, 1991).

By and large, ITDs do not seem to care for half-time positions. At a recent meeting one complained that they are not cost-effective because APPIC and APA regulations state that a half-time intern requires the same number of hours of weekly supervision and didactic training as a full-time intern, leaving fewer hours to be spent in direct clinical work. Blom (1991) also noted:

> Political issues also enter the process; for instance, should half-time internships be available to all applicants regardless of parenting status or gender, or should they be exclusively or preferentially provided only for parents of young children or females with young children? Will this open the door for litigation for discriminatory practices? (p. 3)

## Location

In addition to proximity to family members, geography is an important consideration for other reasons. You will make many contacts on internship and no doubt generate some job offers. For this reason, it is sensible to consider a site in the area where you eventually plan to locate. Going to Boston probably will not help you find a job in Southern California.

If you still have your dissertation work to complete, proximity to your university or professional school may be another geographic consideration. If there is a lot of work remaining on your dissertation, you may have to select a site nearby, choose a topic that can be investigated at your new location, or decide to postpone applying for internship.

Of course, geographic considerations need not always be practical. If you would like to spend a year in Hawaii or there is some other place you

**64**  Megargee's Guide to Obtaining a Psychology Internship

have always wanted to visit, put that down and give it an appropriate weight. Quality of life, rural versus urban environment, climate, proximity to a beach, and similar factors are also worth considering.

## Financial Considerations

Finances are another factor. Among the funded positions, stipends vary greatly, ranging from $2,300 to $54,000 with a mean of $17,800 (Hall & Hsu, 1999). Given the shortfall in the number of positions, some students whose financial resources permit it opt for an unfunded position in preference to waiting a year or accepting a funded position at a less preferred site. I have never favored this strategy. Funded or unfunded, an internship will expect the same workload. I feel that unpaid interns who are working the same hours as the other trainees sooner or later will begin feeling exploited, although some disagree (Carlin, 1982). However, in certain situations, this may be the only way to get the experience you wish. For example, various regulations limit the types of stipends available for students who are not American citizens. Certainly an unfunded position is preferable to those now being offered by some professional schools, where *you* pay *them* for the internship experience.

Fringe benefits also vary greatly. They range from none at all to some settings with very generous benefits including health care for the trainee and his or her family, housing and subsistence allowances, commissary privileges, and paid attendance at workshops and professional meetings. Ironically, the latter are also those with the highest stipends, namely the internships offered by the military.

Pay particular attention to whether medical benefits are provided, especially if you have a family and/or health problems. While you are at it, check and see if your university provides health benefits to students who are not in residence and, if so, what fees you must pay to keep your university health plan active. You may discover that the availability of health insurance makes an enormous difference in the actual value of a stipend.

To people accustomed to the usual graduate school deprivation schedule, a stipend of $18,000 or so may seem quite adequate. However, you may find that your expenses are significantly higher on internship. Additions to and maintenance of your wardrobe, transportation expenses, and rent will often be higher. If you re-register your car, you may have to pay an impact fee. You may have to budget travel back to your university, and, if you are separated from a loved one, you can count on the phone bill being higher.

If your graduate school is in a relatively rural region and your internship is in a metropolitan area, you can expect the cost of living, especially rents, to be substantially higher. If your stipend is modest, you may have

Establishing Your Priorities **65**

to live at some distance from the site to find housing that is more nearly affordable; this increases the time and money spent commuting and decreases the time spent at the facility. Consortiums may require you to travel back and forth from one facility to another, which has the same effect. No one is going to get rich on internship, but if the stipend is so low and/or the living expenses so high that you must take a second job to survive, you will get less out of the experience.

Evaluate the local cost of living by asking other interns and by checking the rents in the classified ads when you visit. If possible, inspect the areas with the rents you will be able to afford on your stipend. Is the neighborhood so bad that you will have to budget $100 a month for ammunition and emergency room expenses? You can ask your insurance agent for the auto liability and theft rates at possible sites. In addition to their impact on your budget, the rates might be a good, unobtrusive index of the relative safety of various locales.

I recently visited one of our interns at a prestigious setting in the Northeast. He was unable to meet me at the train station because his car had been stolen from his driveway. What astonished him was that none of the staff members at the training center were surprised because all of them at some time had had their cars stolen or boosted. Needless to say, no one had informed him of this probability when he had interviewed at the internship.

You might also want to check your insurance coverage; my intern's car was recovered in another city, but by the time the police notified him, the daily storage charges had accumulated to the point where they exceeded the value of his automobile. Partly because he had relocated in another state without informing them, his insurance company refused to reimburse him, and he was forced to abandon his car.

## Quality of Life

One aspect of an internship that is not readily apparent from the brochures is the pace and the amount of stress placed on interns. Some are frenetic: The interns all carry beepers and rarely complete a meal or a trip to the bathroom without being summoned to a phone. Others are more leisurely and laid back. Some places require interns to work 60 hours or more and put in 6- or 7-day weeks to keep abreast of their duties; others expect no more than the standard 40-hour, 5-day work week. What you choose is up to you, but a Type B personality can be miserable in a Type A setting and vice versa.

How rotations are assigned is another important factor influencing intern morale. If the trainees feel that assignments are distributed honestly and fairly, morale is generally good, but any perceived favoritism is corrosive. The worst morale I ever observed was at a program where the train-

**66**  Megargee's Guide to Obtaining a Psychology Internship

ees had been assembled on the first Saturday, placed in a room together, given a list of the rotations that had to be covered each quarter, and told to decide among themselves how they were to be distributed. Hours later, the most powerful individuals emerged with all their preferred placements; the rest got what was left over as well as a bitter attitude that poisoned the rest of the year for all concerned.

Another potential stressor is the type of clients you will be treating. Psychopaths and sex offenders pose special problems, and a pediatric AIDs or oncology ward requires extraordinary emotional stamina. You need to evaluate yourself on these dimensions and select accordingly, especially if you are applying for specialized programs such as the VA's gerontology slots.

Amenities will vary greatly from one site to the next. I have visited interns ensconced in brand new, beautifully furnished private offices that I would kill for and others that had to share a battered desk in a room crowded with other trainees. Some sites, usually VA facilities, have magnificent, well-maintained grounds with ocean views, tennis courts, and golf courses; others are in inner-city ghettos where staff wear Kevlar vests and venture outside only in groups. Availability of secretarial help, the adequacy of the library, the accessibility of parking, and even the quality of the cafeteria can all influence morale.

## ☐ Negative Items

In addition to all the things you are seeking from your internship, there are undoubtedly some other things you do not want. Casey Jacob (1987), for example, did not want an inpatient psychiatry rotation and negatively weighed those internships that had such a requirement. The more inpatient psychiatric time that was required, the more it detracted from the overall score on her "decision grid." Some of my Florida State trainees try to avoid any settings where they may encounter snow or ice.

You may feel so strongly about some things that they constitute "veto items." These would cause you to not go to a program under any circumstances, no matter how desirable it was in other respects. These items may be professional or personal, rational or irrational. Most students will not consider an unfunded position, and many will not attend an internship that is not APA accredited. Others will not apply to an internship that does not offer a particular rotation or experience they consider essential. Some may rule out settings with a strong theoretical orientation that is alien to their own. On the personal side, a setting that does not offer health benefits or does not have adequate job opportunities for a spouse or partner may be considered out of the question.

Whatever these veto items are, you should note them down and make

Establishing Your Priorities **67**

them explicit. By eliminating any settings that have this negative characteristic, you will save yourself a great deal of time. Of course, if you have so many veto items on your list that you are left with only a handful of potential internships that do not fit well with your qualifications or needs, perhaps you should reconsider your veto items and be more flexible.

All of these considerations, professional and personal, positive and negative, are unique to each individual. This is why there is no one internship that is best for everyone. Once you have formulated your list and weighted the various aspects in the abstract, you should use it to evaluate possible programs and identify those you wish to investigate further. These lists will also guide you to the information you need to gather about each setting. Later, when it is time to make your rankings, you can use them to score programs on the factors that you have decided are most important for you.

CHAPTER 4

# Where to Apply? Compiling Your Application List

Once you have established your personal priorities, you need to compile a list of possible internships that you are interested in investigating. Although students spend hours downloading and studying internship materials, this is probably the easiest part of the process. Since you have already established your priorities, you know what it is you are looking for.

## ☐ Preliminary Reconnaissance

Some preliminary explorations can take place early in your academic career. You probably already have some internships that you are interested in. Perhaps you have heard about them from faculty or students who interned there. Maybe they are in a part of the country that has always appealed to you. If it is convenient, you might find it helpful to make a preliminary informal visit to such sites just to get a feel for them and to see what they look like. If it is a real "turn off," you will save yourself the trouble of applying. However, keep a low profile; most ITDs have more than enough to do without feeling obliged to entertain casual visitors who might someday apply for internship.

If someone on your faculty interned at one of these sites, or if fellow graduate students are presently enrolled there, solicit their opinions. Often current interns return during the course of the year for committee meetings and other academic chores. Ask their major professors when they are likely to be in town, and see if you can schedule some time with them. If they are located at an internship that is not too far away, you might be able to arrange for an informal visit. Failing this, you may send them an e-mail, write a letter, or phone them at home.

Another cost-effective way of reconnoitering is to identify personnel connected with the training sites in which you are interested and observe or make contact with them at regional or national professional meetings such as APA or AABT. If you are really interested, you might write or call in advance to see if they are free for coffee or a chat. Otherwise, attend one of their presentations and introduce yourself afterwards. This will not only give you a chance to study the person during the presentation, but may also be advantageous later if you apply. When you interview, you won't be just another nameless applicant but someone the interviewer has previously met at a professional meeting.

However, unless you are one of those superorganized people who always mail all their Christmas cards the day after Thanksgiving, you are probably reading this in the fall of the year you plan to apply and you have not taken any of the above steps. Given the fact that you will soon have to begin filling out applications, how do you develop a list of places and check them out?

## ☐ Using the APPIC *Directory*

Begin by gathering information on a number of internship facilities. Although your ADCT probably has a file of brochures distributed by various clinical training programs, your best source of comprehensive, recent information is the *Directory of Internship Programs in Professional Psychology* which is available in both on-line and printed versions. If your training program is an APPIC subscriber, a printed copy will be sent to your ADCT in August or September. If you wish, you can also purchase your own personal copy; as noted earlier there is a discount if you order in early July.

You will probably find the on-line version of the *Directory* more useful because it has a search engine that enables you to specify the factors you are seeking in an internship. These include location by state or by nine metropolitan areas (Boston, Chicago, Denver, Los Angeles, Miami, New York City, San Diego, San Francisco, and Washington, DC). You can also specify the training opportunities you are seeking with respect to client populations, treatment modalities, and specialty areas. The on-line *Directory* is updated every July. Your NMS registration fee includes use of the *Directory*, but you do not have to wait until you register to access it.

Both the on-line and printed versions of the APPIC *Directory* include a wealth of valuable information on each facility. They list the names and credentials of the Chief Psychologist and Training Director, as well as the

# 70 Megargee's Guide to Obtaining a Psychology Internship

number of full- and part-time licensed, doctoral-level psychologists employed. They specify the agency's current APA and CPA (Canadian Psychological Association) accreditation status. They provide the training program's complete postal and e-mail addresses, phone and fax numbers, and the date applications are due. They indicate the number of full- and part-time funded and unfunded internship slots expected. They stipulate what requirements you must meet with regard to citizenship, number of practicum hours completed, and progress toward your degree, as well as their preferences regarding the types of training programs from which they welcome applications. They list the major and minor rotations available, the stipend level and fringe benefits afforded, and, finally, how many completed applications they received the previous year. This last item, in conjunction with the number of stipends available, is very helpful in determining how competitive a program is. Much of this information is not available in any other source, including the internships' brochures or Web sites.

Because the printed version of the *Directory* is limited to what can be fitted on the one page allotted to each site, the on-line version contains considerably more information. It specifies in greater detail what requirements you are expected to meet with regard to progress toward your doctoral degree and hours spent in practicum training. If the internship has chosen to provide it, it may even contain a profile of the current intern class, indicating the number and the range of patient contact and practicum hours they reported on their AAPIs and, a key question, how many integrated assessment reports they wrote. It can also specify how many came from clinical, counseling, and school programs. These data should help you decide whether you are the sort of applicant they are seeking. Finally, the on-line listing often contains the responses to a detailed questionnaire the internship is asked to fill out reporting what happens to their interns after they complete the program. Not all ITDs complete this questionnaire, but when they do, it can help you decide how well the program dovetails with your aspirations.

## Organization and Contents of the *Directory*

### *Statistical Summaries*

The printed *Directory* provides aggregate data listing the total number of agencies, funded and unfunded vacancies, and numbers of applications received by all APPIC members the previous year. It also furnishes you with overall information regarding the average stipend levels and the average number of applications received for each funded slot. In addition, it breaks out these data separately for APA-accredited and nonaccredited internships and provides subtotals for 11 different types of internship settings.

## Eligibility

Each listing in the *Directory* has a section entitled "Applicant Requirements/Restrictions" indicating who is eligible to apply. The first variable is citizenship. Some internships in the United States require applicants to be U.S. citizens, and some in Canada are limited to Canadians. Usually these are internships run by government agencies such as the VA and the military. If you are not a citizen, you can inquire if someone with your particular immigration status is eligible, but you will probably find that they cannot legally appoint you.

Four items indicate eligibility as a function of your academic progress: (a) the minimum number of years of graduate training required, (b) whether you must have passed your comprehensive examination, (c) whether your dissertation proposal must be approved, and (d) whether your dissertation must have been defended. Two items indicate the program's requirements with regard to practicum experience: (a) the minimum number of clock hours of direct practicum, and (b) the minimum number of clock hours of indirect practicum. Programs vary greatly with regard to these criteria. You should be sure to check the requirements for each program to determine your eligibility. If you fall short or are unsure whether you meet a criterion, you should check with the program before going to the trouble of filling out an application.

## Internships' Preferences

In addition to requirements, the *Directory* also indicates each setting's preferences. For each program, there is a section with the heading, "Applicants welcome from what programs?" There are six academic program categories:

1. Clinical, APA accredited;
2. Clinical, nonaccredited;
3. Counseling, APA accredited;
4. Counseling, nonaccredited;
5. School, APA accredited; and
6. School, nonaccredited.

ITDs from various settings indicate whether they welcome applications from each type of program by rating them as "Only," "Preferred," "Acceptable," or "Not Welcome." In Table 4.1, I have summarized these rankings for all the American internships listed in the 1999–2000 *Directory*. As you can see, applicants from APA-accredited clinical, and, to a

# 72 Megargee's Guide to Obtaining a Psychology Internship

**TABLE 4.1.** Programs from which applicants are welcomed by APPIC internships

| | APA accredited | | | Not APA accredited | | |
|---|---|---|---|---|---|---|
| | Clinical | Counseling | School | Clinical | Counseling | School |
| Only | 179 | 149 | 15 | 1 | 0 | 2 |
| | 33% | 28% | 3% | 0% | 0% | 0% |
| Preferred | 311 | 189 | 42 | 9 | 2 | 2 |
| | 58% | 35% | 8% | 2% | 0% | 0% |
| Acceptable | 41 | 131 | 69 | 245 | 196 | 48 |
| | 8% | 24% | 13% | 45% | 36% | 9% |
| Not welcome | 9 | 71 | 414 | 285 | 342 | 488 |
| | 2% | 13% | 77% | 53% | 63% | 90% |

lesser extent, counseling, programs were the most desired applicants. Within the clinical category, Stedman et al. (1989, p. 36) suggested that internships prefer candidates from traditional university-based Ph.D. programs rather than professional Psy.D. granting institutions.

The few settings that did not welcome candidates from APA-accredited clinical programs were typically school-based internships, which, naturally, preferred candidates from APA-accredited school psychology programs. Although applicants from nonaccredited clinical programs were deemed acceptable by 45% of the internships, those from school psychology programs and nonaccredited counseling programs were generally not welcomed. As you might suppose, the nonaccredited internships are more likely to welcome applicants from nonaccredited academic programs.

Pay close attention to this section when you are reviewing the *Directory*. Unless your individual credentials are outstanding, you may be wasting your time applying to an internship that indicates in its listing that it does "not welcome" applicants from programs such as yours. Check the on-line *Directory* and see if any of the current interns were from your type of program. If so, you might give it a try. Or, you could follow the example of a recent counseling student who contacted the ITD of a program that stated they only accepted clinical students. She described her qualifications and asked if she should apply. He encouraged her to do so, and she ended up being matched there.

If you are not enrolled in an APA-accredited clinical or counseling program, you have a smaller pool of potential places to which you can apply with a reasonable chance of success. This means you should do everything you can to build up your individual qualifications and credentials. Even if you are not in a clinical program, you may be able to take clinical courses and practica that show you are capable of doing clinical work. Perhaps a year at an unaccredited clinical internship will prepare you for a second year at an accredited facility. In short, you will probably have to

## Where to Apply? Compiling Your Application List    73

work harder and do more to demonstrate to the Selection Committees that you are as good as or better than the applicants from the preferred programs. You will also probably have to submit more applications and include a greater proportion of less competitive internships on your list.

If you are fortunate enough to be enrolled in a preferred program, don't think you can rest on your laurels. Remember that most of the applicants who were not matched were from APA-accredited clinical programs.

## Requirements

Another section is entitled "Applicant Requirements/Restrictions." It indicates the minimum basic requirements an applicant must satisfy to be considered for an appointment. Exceptions may be made for some requirements, such as the minimum number of practicum hours, but others, such as being a U.S. citizen, are typically inflexible. If you fail to meet some requirement, it is best to describe your qualifications and ask the ITD if you are eligible before you go to the trouble of completing an application.

## Types of Settings

The *Directory* may not appear very user friendly when you encounter it for the first time. It is hard to assimilate all the different types of settings, rotations, and other information included. If you are just starting your search, you may not have given much thought to the type of setting in which you want to do your internship. To get you started, I have compiled some basic information about the characteristics of the various kinds of internship agencies listed in the *Directory*.

There are about a dozen different types of settings listed in the *Directory*, and they differ in a number of ways. Table 4.2 summarizes the types of applicants each setting indicated it preferred. The best sources of information about these different types of internships are, of course, their individual listings in the *Directory* as well as their Web sites and brochures. However, I will provide some descriptive comments based on my analysis of the U.S.-based internships listed in the 1999–2000 *Directory* to help you decide which settings most interest you.

In addition, I will summarize the findings of two surveys contrasting the preferences of ITDs in various settings. Stedman et al. (2000) inquired regarding the level of preinternship training in testing and psychotherapy that applicants were expected to have. Specifically, with regard to assessment, they asked ITDs how many (a) integrated test reports, (b) integrated neuropsychological (N.P.) test reports, and (c) integrated test reports including either the Rorschach or Thematic Apperception Test (TAT)

74    Megargee's Guide to Obtaining a Psychology Internship

**TABLE 4.2.** Agencies' preferences for applicants from six types of academic programs

| Internship setting | Preference | Clinical APA accredited | | Counseling APA accredited | | School APA accredited | |
|---|---|---|---|---|---|---|---|
| | | Yes | No | Yes | No | Yes | No |
| Children's facilities | "Only" or "prefer" | 94 | 2 | 40 | 0 | 38 | 0 |
| | "Acceptable" | 4 | 51 | 45 | 34 | 32 | 15 |
| | "Not acceptable" | 2 | 47 | 15 | 66 | 30 | 85 |
| Community mental health centers | "Only" or "prefer" | 82 | 3 | 45 | 0 | 0 | 0 |
| | "Acceptable" | 15 | 60 | 36 | 44 | 18 | 8 |
| | "Not acceptable" | 3 | 37 | 19 | 56 | 82 | 92 |
| Consortiums | "Only" or "prefer" | 92 | 0 | 65 | 0 | 5 | 0 |
| | "Acceptable" | 8 | 43 | 24 | 41 | 8 | 8 |
| | "Not acceptable" | 0 | 57 | 11 | 59 | 87 | 92 |
| Correctional | "Only" or "prefer" | 100 | 0 | 86 | 0 | 7 | 7 |
| | "Acceptable" | 0 | 50 | 0 | 36 | 0 | 0 |
| | "Not acceptable" | 0 | 50 | 14 | 64 | 93 | 93 |
| Medical schools | "Only" or "prefer" | 99 | 0 | 30 | 0 | 9 | 0 |
| | "Acceptable" | 1 | 26 | 33 | 16 | 21 | 9 |
| | "Not acceptable" | 0 | 74 | 37 | 84 | 70 | 91 |
| Military hospitals | "Only" or "prefer" | 100 | 0 | 89 | 0 | 0 | 0 |
| | "Acceptable" | 0 | 33 | 11 | 33 | 0 | 0 |
| | "Not acceptable" | 0 | 67 | 0 | 67 | 100 | 100 |
| Private general hospitals | "Only" or "prefer" | 92 | 4 | 44 | 0 | 16 | 0 |
| | "Acceptable" | 8 | 72 | 48 | 48 | 16 | 20 |
| | "Not acceptable" | 0 | 24 | 8 | 52 | 68 | 80 |
| Private psychiatric hospitals | "Only" or "prefer" | 100 | 8 | 45 | 0 | 13 | 4 |
| | "Acceptable" | 0 | 67 | 38 | 50 | 13 | 4 |
| | "Not acceptable" | 0 | 25 | 17 | 50 | 74 | 92 |
| Schools | "Only" or "prefer" | 14 | 0 | 29 | 0 | 100 | 29 |
| | "Acceptable" | 43 | 57 | 42 | 57 | 0 | 57 |
| | "Not acceptable" | 43 | 43 | 29 | 43 | 0 | 14 |
| State hospitals | "Only" or "prefer" | 100 | 6 | 52 | 0 | 10 | 0 |
| | "Acceptable" | 0 | 54 | 35 | 37 | 17 | 8 |
| | "Not acceptable" | 0 | 40 | 13 | 63 | 73 | 92 |
| University counseling centers | "Only" or "prefer" | 88 | 1 | 94 | 2 | 1 | 0 |
| | "Acceptable" | 11 | 59 | 5 | 58 | 4 | 3 |
| | "Not acceptable" | 1 | 40 | 1 | 40 | 95 | 97 |
| Veterans administration centers | "Only" or "prefer" | 100 | 0 | 97 | 0 | 0 | 0 |
| | "Acceptable" | 0 | 1 | 0 | 0 | 0 | 0 |
| | "Not acceptable" | 0 | 99 | 3 | 100 | 100 | 100 |

Where to Apply? Compiling Your Application List **75**

they felt applicants should have completed. For each category they reported the median (med.) and semi-interquartile ranges[7] (SIR) for each of the 11 different types of settings. With regard to treatment they asked ITDs in the 11 settings how many clients applicants should have seen in each of eight different treatment modalities, (a) long-term psychodynamic, (b) short-term psychodynamic, (c) cognitive-behavioral (the top choice in all settings), (d) group, (e) marital, (f) family, (g) interpersonal, and (h) play therapy. For each modality they reported the median number of clients ITDs would have liked their applicants to have treated and the SIRs.

Tipton, Watkins, and Ritz (1991) used 7-point Likert scales on which ITDs from eight different types of settings evaluated the importance they placed on the following seven prerequisite skills they considered in selecting interns: (a) psychological assessment, (b) vocational counseling, (c) behavioral approaches, (d) therapeutic skills, (e) academic career skills, (f) understanding psychological processes, and (g) psychodiagnosis. A rating of 7 indicated that they felt the skill was "extremely important" and 1 was designated as "extremely unimportant." For each skill they reported the mean rating and the standard deviation.

## Children's Facilities

Children's hospitals and other child-oriented internships are, naturally, most attractive to students in child-clinical training programs. Clients tend to be children, adolescents, and their families. They include children with medical as well as mental health problems, and young people with acting out and conduct disorders, substance abuse problems, and neurological disorders. Most include both inpatient and outpatient psychiatric services. Compared with other settings, there is less opportunity to work with adults.

There were 47 children's facilities listed in the 1999–2000 *Directory*, 34 (72%) of which were APA accredited. They reported having 188 funded full-time positions, 3 funded part-time positions, and 4 unfunded slots. The minimum number of hours of practicum experience they required ranged from 200 hours to 1,500 hours, with a mean of 867. Their stipends ranged from $6,000 to $21,000, with a mean of $15,900. As can be seen from Table 4.2, children's facilities were the most eclectic with regard to the types of applicants they welcomed. Although students from APA-accredited clinical programs were preferred, students enrolled in APA-accredited school and counseling psychology programs were acceptable, and some settings indicated that they also accepted applicants from non-accredited training programs. On the average, children's facilities reported

---

[7]The semi-interquartile range delineates the 25th and the 75th percentiles and indicates the middle 50% of the overall range of responses.

76     Megargee's Guide to Obtaining a Psychology Internship

receiving 76 applications each, and the mean number of applications per funded slot was 18.4.

Stedman et al. (2000) reported that the ITDs at children's facilities would like their applicants to have completed a median of 20 integrated test reports (SIR 11 to 30), 10 including the Rorschach (SIR = 4 to 17) and 11 including the TAT (SIR = 9 to 20). There was no desire for them to have neuropsychiatric (NP) testing experience. With regard to therapy, the preferred modes were cognitive-behavioral, family, group, and play therapy. Indeed, the child facilities ranked significantly higher than most of the other settings in their desire to recruit applicants with family and play therapy experience.

Tipton et al. (1991) reported that the most valued prerequisite skill was understanding psychological processes, followed by psychological assessment. Behavioral approaches, psychodiagnosis, and therapeutic skills were virtually tied for third position.

## Community Mental Health Centers and Nonprofit Outpatient Clinics

Comprehensive community mental health centers (CMHCs) and other nonprofit outpatient clinics deal with clients of all ages. Some deal exclusively with outpatient treatment, while others also treat inpatients at short-term, county-run, acute mental health units and in alcohol and drug abuse rehabilitation programs. Clients may include patients discharged into the community after a period of inpatient treatment at a state hospital.

There were 72 CMHCs, 45 (62%) of which were accredited. They had 284 full-time and 16 part-time funded positions, as well as 3 unfunded slots. They required anywhere from 300 hours to 2,000 hours of practicum experience, with a mean of 798 hours. Stipends ranged from $10,000 to $25,000, with a mean of $18,000. Virtually all welcomed applicants from APA-accredited clinical and counseling programs. Applicants from non-accredited clinical, and, to a lesser extent, counseling programs were generally acceptable. The number of applications averaged 55 per agency, with a mean of 13.8 per slot.

According to Stedman et al. (2000), the median number of integrated test reports preferred by ITDs was 20 (SIR = 12 to 24), 12 including the Rorschach (SIR = 5 to 20) and 10 including the TAT (SIR = 5 to 15). They would also like applicants to have conducted 2 NP assessments (SIR = 0 to 6). With regard to treatment, the ITDs preferred candidates who had treated a median of 11 clients with cognitive behavior therapy (SIR = 7 to 26), 6 with long-term psychodynamic therapy (SIR = 0 to 11), and 5 with short-term dynamic treatment (SIR = 2 to 5).

Tipton et al. (1991) found that understanding psychological processes and psychological assessment were virtually tied as the most desirable prerequisite skills, followed by psychodiagnosis.

Where to Apply? Compiling Your Application List    77

## Consortiums

Consortiums are groups of mental health facilities that band together to create a joint internship training program. They often include CMHCs, state hospitals, and VA medical centers as well as other settings. The exact nature of the rotations available depends on the types of facilities in the consortium, but typically both inpatient and outpatient mental health settings serving a wide range of clients are included. In some, "rotations" consist of spending a day or two each week in two or three different settings; in others, interns spend several months in a single setting and then rotate to a different facility. If the facilities are located in different communities, some commuting may be required and interns may not have much opportunity to interact with one another. Typically, one afternoon a week all the interns gather at a central location for training meetings, case conferences, and didactic training experiences.

The *Directory* listed 37 consortiums, 26 (78%) of which were accredited. They had 258 full-time and 5 part-time funded positions, as well as 2 that were unfunded. Practicum experience required ranged from 400 hours to 1,200 hours, with a mean of 700 hours. Stipends ranged from $6,000 to $31,000, with a mean of $16,000. There was a clear preference for applicants from accredited clinical and counseling programs, and 13% also welcomed candidates from accredited school programs. Candidates from nonaccredited programs were generally not welcomed. The mean number of applications was 93 per internship, and there was an average of 12.9 applications per vacancy.

According to Stedman et al. (2000), consortiums placed the highest premium on integrated tests reports, wanting applicants with a median of 25 (SIR = 15 to 31). They did not especially care whether the integrated test reports included the Rorschach (med. = 3) or TAT (med. = 1), and they were not seeking candidates experienced in NP assessment (median = 1).

Cognitive-behavioral therapy was by far the most preferred mode of treatment. Consortiums wanted their applicants to have treated more cognitive-behavioral clients than any of the other settings, with a median of 13 (SIR = 9 to 21). The next highest modalities, group and short-term dynamic, lagged far behind with medians of 3 clients each.

Tipton et al. (1991) did not include consortiums in their survey.

## Correctional

There were 14 internships at correctional agencies, 10 of which were at institutions run by the Federal Bureau of Prisons; 10 (71%) were accredited. Altogether they had 46 funded full-time positions, as well as 3 that were unfunded. As a general rule, the range of clients seen in a prison setting is more limited than at most internships; the clientele is generally

78    Megargee's Guide to Obtaining a Psychology Internship

limited to adults, and typically only one gender is represented at any given institution. However, within these limits, prison populations can be surprisingly heterogeneous with regard to psychopathology. In recent years, substance abuse programs have been increasingly prominent. A correctional setting is good for someone interested in seeing multicultural clients or for a student interested in forensic psychology. Unlike some other settings, correctional institutions are not fee driven, so interns may be able to administer a broader array of assessment techniques or engage in longer term as well as short-term interventions.

The number of practicum hours expected by the correctional agencies listed in the *Directory* ranged from 300 hours to 1,000 hours, with a mean of 700 hours. Stipends were higher than in most settings, ranging from $13,500 to $29,000, with a mean of $22,000, and good fringe benefits are common. Applicants typically must undergo a background and security check. As can be seen from Table 4.2, applicants from APA-accredited clinical and counseling programs were definitely preferred, although half the facilities accepted applicants from nonaccredited clinical programs. School psychology applicants were almost never sought. The mean number of applications received was 61, and there was a mean of 17.4 applications per vacancy.

The correctional sites in Stedman et al.'s (2000) study preferred applicants who had completed a median of 20 integrated test reports (SIR = 10 to 21), with 4 including the Rorschach and 4 the TAT. There was no expectation of any NP testing. The ITDs at the correctional facilities would have liked their applicants to have seen 11 clients in cognitive-behavioral treatment (SIR = 9 to 16), 5 in short-term dynamic (SIR = 2 to 10), and 4 groups (SIR = 3 to 9).

Tipton et al. (1991) did not investigate patterns at correctional facilities.

## *Medical Schools*

Medical schools are one of the most popular internships. They typically afford trainees a wide variety of experiences and clients, and there is often more emphasis on research than is found in other settings. Obviously such "medical" specialties as behavioral medicine and neuropsychological assessment are more likely to be found in these internships. The work load and the pace in medical schools are apt to be higher than at most settings, and there may be turf wars with psychiatry and other medical specialties.

The *Directory* listed 69 internships based in medical schools, 65 (94%) of which were APA accredited. They reported having 299 full-time and 4 part-time funded positions, and 4 unfunded slots. Practicum experience expected ranged from 300 hours to 2,000 hours, with a mean of 869 hours. Stipends ranged from $10,000 to $19,000, with a mean of $15,000.

Where to Apply? Compiling Your Application List    79

There was a clear preference for candidates from APA-accredited clinical training programs, some tolerance for those from APA-accredited counseling programs, and little or no interest in school psychology candidates or students from nonaccredited training programs. There was a mean of 12.2 applications received per internship and 20.0 applications per slot.

Stedman et al.'s (2000) survey showed that medical schools set their sights high with regard to previous assessment experience. The ITDs preferred applicants who had a median of 25 integrated test reports (SIR = 15 to 31); if they had their way, 8 of those reports would include a Rorschach (SIR = 0 to 18) and 8 a TAT (SIR = 0 to 14). They also placed more emphasis on prior neuropsychological assessment experience, preferring applicants with a median of 5 integrated NP reports (SIR = 0 to 18). The preferred mode of treatment was cognitive-behavioral (median = 10 clients, SIR = 8 to 20); group, family, and marital therapy were tied for second, with a median of 2 clients each.

Tipton et al. (1991) reported that understanding psychological processes and psychological assessment were the two most preferred skills, followed by therapeutic skills.

## Military Internships

The nine military internships, all of which were accredited, are unique in many respects. Applicants who are accepted are commissioned as officers and are expected to serve on active duty for 3 years after completion of the internship. To be considered, they must be U.S. citizens, 18 to 33 years old, and able to pass a rigorous preinduction physical examination. Since interns go directly from the internship to active duty, their dissertations should be completed by the time they finish their internships. As military officers, they receive much higher pay and allowances than any other group of interns. However, like any other service personnel on active duty, they go where they are sent and do what they are ordered to do. If they choose to continue in the military after their payback period, there are good opportunities for travel and for early retirement. The clients served by military interns are service men and women and their families, typically at military hospitals, so there is opportunity to work with a wide variety of cases in the younger age ranges in both inpatient and outpatient settings.

The nine military internships had 57 funded full-time slots. The practicum hours required ranged from 500 hours to 1,000 hours, with a mean of 625 hours. The stipends are by far the highest of any type of internship, ranging from $37,000 to $43,000, with a mean of $40,000; 20% to 25% of the salary is considered a housing allotment and is therefore tax exempt, and there are generous fringe benefits. All nine settings indicated they preferred candidates from APA-accredited clinical or coun-

**80** Megargee's Guide to Obtaining a Psychology Internship

seling programs, although three stated they would also consider applicants from nonaccredited clinical or counseling programs. None were interested in school psychology applicants. The mean number of applications received by the military internships was 52, and there was an average of 8.2 completed applications per slot.

Neither Stedman et al. (2000) nor Tipton et al. (1991) included military internships in their surveys.

## Private General Hospitals

Private general hospitals treat a full range of medical problems, in contrast to private psychiatric hospitals, which are strictly mental health facilities. Interns can be involved in medical psychology and behavioral medicine as well as traditional mental health services with both inpatients and outpatients and their families. Most have inpatient psychiatric units geared toward short-term hospitalizations.

There were 25 private general hospitals listed, 14 (56%) of which were APA accredited. They reported 119 full-time and 11 part-time funded positions. The practicum hours expected ranged from 300 hours to 1,400 hours, with a mean of 675 hours. Stipends ranged from $2,000 to $20,000, with a mean of $14,000, the lowest of any setting category. Perhaps because of the relatively high rate of unaccredited facilities, these internships are less restrictive with regard to the applicants they will consider. As usual, APA-accredited clinical and counseling students were preferred; 72% accepted students from nonaccredited clinical programs, and 48% would take students from nonaccredited counseling programs. About a third also considered students from accredited school programs. The mean number of applications these facilities reported receiving was 84, and the mean number of applications per slot was 15.6.

The ITDs of private general hospitals indicated that they preferred applicants who had written a median of 21 integrated test reports (SIR = 8 to 30). Ideally, they liked the Rorschach to be included on a median of 11 (SIR = 8 to 20) and the TAT on 14 (SIR = 8 to 20). Of all the settings, private general hospitals placed the highest value on integrated neuropsychological reports, preferring candidates with a median of 6 reports and a SIR of 3 to 13 reports.

Cognitive-behavioral treatment was most preferred with ITDs, who hoped applicants had treated a median of 11 CB clients (SIR = 6 to 14). Short-term dynamic treatment was the next most preferred (med. = 5; SIR = 0 to 11), with family therapy and long-term dynamic tied for third (med. = 3).

Tipton et al.'s (1991) survey indicated that understanding psychological processes was the most preferred skill, followed by psychological assessment and therapeutic skills.

## Private Psychiatric Hospitals

Private psychiatric hospitals are primarily mental health facilities treating both inpatients and outpatients for various mental disorders and substance abuse problems. Interns are more likely to see seriously mentally ill patients in these hospitals than in general hospitals or community settings. Patient fees and third-party payments are typically significant sources of revenue.

The *Directory* listed 24 private psychiatric hospitals, 10 (42%) of which were accredited. They reported having 90 funded full-time positions and 14 unfunded full-time positions. They required applicants to have completed 180 to 2,500 hours of practicum, with a mean of 979 hours. Stipends ranged from $12,000 to $19,800, with a mean of $15,000. They had a clear preference for students from APA-accredited clinical and counseling psychology programs; 60% would also accept students from nonaccredited clinical programs, but there was little interest in students from nonaccredited counseling programs or any sort of school program. The mean number of applications received was 57 per setting, and the mean number of applications per slot was 13.2.

Private psychiatric hospitals were second only to consortiums in the assessment experience they sought, preferring applicants who had prepared a median of 25 integrated test reports (SIR = 19 to 30). They ranked first in their desire for projective test experience, preferring a median of 20 integrated reports including the Rorschach (SIR = 15 to 30) and 21 including the TAT (SIR = 8 to 30). They placed less emphasis on NP testing, preferring applicants with a median of 3 NP test reports (SIR = 0 to 6).

Compared with the other settings, private hospitals sought the least therapy experience, preferring applicants who had treated a median of 9 clients with cognitive-behavioral therapy (SIR 6 to 15). The next most preferred treatment modalities were long-term psychodynamic (med. = 4; SIR = 2 to 14) and short-term psychodynamic (med. = 4, SIR 3 to 5).

Tipton et al.'s (1991) survey indicated that private psychiatric hospitals placed the greatest emphasis of all the settings on understanding psychological processes, giving it a mean rating of 6.3 on a 7-point scale. Next highest was psychodiagnosis and psychological assessment.

## Schools

Although school psychologists are in increasing demand (DeAngelis, 2000) and APA is urging Congress to provide more mental health resources to schools (Rabasca, 2000), there are few schools or school district–based internships in APPIC. Although the traditional role of the school psychologist was assessment of cognitive functioning and achievement level to assist in class placement, school psychologists increasingly find them-

82    Megargee's Guide to Obtaining a Psychology Internship

selves in the role of mental health consultants to educators and school systems concerned with crisis intervention, early identification of troubled and potentially violent children, and dealing with students using both legally prescribed and illicit drugs.

The *Directory* listed seven school-based internships, four (57%) of which were APA accredited. Interestingly, four were in Texas and two in Tennessee, suggesting there is considerable opportunity for expansion in other states. The seven internships had 30 funded full-time slots. They expected applicants to have from 350 to 800 hours of practicum study with a mean of 480 hours. Stipends ranged from $10,000 to $33,000, with a mean of $19,000. As one would expect, applicants from APA-accredited school psychology programs were preferred by all the settings, followed by students from unaccredited school programs and accredited counseling programs. Students from clinical programs were deemed acceptable by more than half of the settings. The mean number of applications per setting was 31, with a mean ratio of applications to sites of 7:1.

Neither Stedman et al. (2000) nor Tipton et al. (1991) included school-based internships in their surveys.

## State Hospitals

In contrast to private psychiatric hospitals, state facilities get more patients from the lower end of the socioeconomic spectrum, including long-term, chronically mentally ill patients, a number of whom are involuntarily committed because they are considered a threat to themselves or others, and individuals with problems relating to substance abuse. Many state hospitals also treat forensic cases in which the state has an interest, such as clients referred by the courts for competency and legal sanity evaluations, people remanded for treatment under mentally disordered sex offender acts, and, in some states, mentally ill state prisoners. Although some children and adolescents are evaluated or treated, most of the clients are adult men and women, including geriatric cases with various forms of dementia.

There were 52 state facilities listed, 37 (71%) of which were accredited. They had 221 full-time and 1 part-time funded slots, as well as 6 unfunded full-time positions. The number of practicum hours expected ranged from 250 hours to 1,200 hours, with a mean of 707 hours, and stipends ranged from $12,000 to $29,000, with a mean of $18,000. Like most of the internships, the state facilities preferred APA-accredited clinical and counseling program students and would also accept nonaccredited clinical students. Nonaccredited counseling and all school candidates were generally not accepted. On average, the state hospitals reported receiving 76 applications each, with a mean of 17 applications for each funded slot.

Where to Apply? Compiling Your Application List    **83**

ITDs at state hospitals demand less in the way of assessment experience from their applicants, seeking candidates with a median of only 10 integrated test-based reports (SIR = 10 to 20), 10 of which should include the Rorschach (SIR = 6 to 15) and 6 the TAT (SIR = 5 to 15). They would like a median of 2 integrated neuropsychological reports (SIR = 0 to 5; Stedman et al., 2000).

Cognitive-behavioral was the preferred mode of treatment, with applicants expected to have treated a median of 10 clients (SIR = 5 to 15), followed by short-term dynamic (med. = 5 clients; SIR = 1 to 10) and group therapy (med. = 3 groups, SIR = 3 to 7).

Tipton et al.'s (1991) data indicated that psychological assessment was tied with understanding psychological processes as the most preferred skill, with therapeutic skills and psychodiagnosis virtually tied for second.

## *University Counseling Centers*

University counseling centers (UCCs) are the single most numerous type of internship. (See Figure 4.1.) They are also the most popular, averaging 21 applications per site. Interning at a UCC enables students to complete their internship requirement while remaining in an academic setting, complete with a research library and access to a college or university faculty, colloquia, and cultural resources. Although I am not familiar with any data on the subject, it would be reasonable to suppose that UCCs would be one of the settings most supportive of their interns' research activities.

UCCs typically serve the university community, with all its multicultural diversity. They specialize in the outpatient treatment and counseling of students and other adult clients who may present with a wide variety of problems.

The *Directory* listed 100 UCCs, 77 (77%) of which were accredited. They had 339 full-time and 6 half-time funded positions, as well as 6 unfunded slots. They expected applicants to have from 150 hours to 1,000 hours of practicum, with a mean of 621 hours. Stipends ranged from $8,000 to $21,000 with a mean of $16,000. As one would expect, applicants from APA-accredited counseling psychology programs were most preferred, closely followed by those from accredited clinical programs. Students from nonaccredited counseling and clinical programs were also deemed acceptable by approximately 60% of the UCCs, but they were not interested in school students regardless of whether or not their programs were accredited. The mean number of applications received by the UCCs was 74, and, as noted above, they had a mean of 21 applications per site, making the UCCs the most competitive of these settings.

Stedman et al.'s (2000) survey showed that UCCs differed from most other settings in the experiences and skills they expected their applicants

**84**    Megargee's Guide to Obtaining a Psychology Internship

to bring to the internship. There was considerably less emphasis placed on assessment experience. The UCC ITDs sought applicants who had completed a median of 10 integrated test reports (SIR = 4 to 15), which was significantly less than most of the other settings, and they did not care especially if these reports included the Rorschach (med. = 1, SIR = 0 to 7) or TAT (med. = 3, SIR = 0 to 7). Being campus based, perhaps many of the ITDs share in academia's widespread distaste for projectives. They also did not value neuropsychological testing experience (med. = 0, SIR = 0 to 2).

With regard to treatment, cognitive-behavioral approaches were tied with short-term dynamic interventions, the ITDs indicating that they would like applicants to have seen a median of 10 clients in each (SIR = 5 to 11). The third most favored was interpersonal approaches, with a median of 5 clients (SIR = 0 to 10; Stedman et al., 2000).

Tipton et al. (1991) reported UCCs most preferred therapeutic skills, closely followed by understanding psychological processes. Uniquely, vocational counseling was in third place.

## VA Medical Centers

As we saw in Chapter 1, the VA took the lead in training clinical psychologists after World War II, and despite some shrinkage in recent years, the VA programs are still vigorous. Before women were admitted into the services in significant numbers, the VA clientele used to be almost exclusively male, but many more female veterans are now being seen in VA facilities.

As the World War II and Korean veterans have aged, the VA has increasingly emphasized geriatric psychology and the treatment of elders along with its traditional focus on adult inpatients and outpatients. Substance abuse and posttraumatic stress disorder (PTSD)-related problems are well represented. As in the medical schools, the comprehensive VA medical centers afford opportunities to practice medical psychology and behavioral medicine and deal with neuropsychological disorders.

Zeiss (2000) recently reported that the VA is reviewing its priorities for psychology internship training. She noted, "The new system will specifically emphasize training in areas of high clinical priority for the VA, particularly primary care, mental health, rehabilitation, and geriatric settings" (p. 310).

There were 70 VA internship centers listed in the *Directory*, 69 (99%) of which were APA accredited. They had 326 funded full-time positions and expected applicants to have completed from 300 hours to 1,500 hours of practicum with a mean of 851 hours. The stipends ranged from $17,000 to $20,000, with a mean of $18,000. Only students who are U.S. citizens and who are enrolled in APA-accredited clinical or counseling psychol-

Where to Apply? Compiling Your Application List **85**

ogy programs are eligible. The average VA medical center received 83 applications, and the mean number of applications per position was 17.5.

Stedman et al. (2000) reported that VA ITDs preferred applicants who had a median of 15 integrated test reports (SIR = 10 to 21), including 5 with Rorschachs (SIR = 2 to 10 ) and 3 with TATs (SIR = 0 to 7). They would also like applicants to have 4 integrated neuropsychological test reports (SIR = 2 to 10).

With regard to therapy, the VA prefers an applicant who has seen a median of 11 clients in cognitive-behavioral treatment (SIR = 5 to 11), 5 in short-term dynamic treatment (SIR = 2 to 10), and a median of 4 groups (SIR = 2 to 5).

Tipton et al. (1991) reported that psychological assessment and understanding psychological processes were virtually tied for the most preferred prerequisite skills, followed by therapeutic skills.

## Other Settings

In addition to the 12 categories discussed above, the *Directory* also listed facilities for the developmentally disabled, rehabilitation hospitals, pastoral counseling centers, and facilities run by HMOs.

## Regional Differences

A glib explanation for the recent shortfalls has been that students are applying to the "wrong places," concentrating on the large metropolitan areas on the two coasts and neglecting facilities in the middle of the country (Clay, 1997). To investigate this hypothesis, I aggregated the *Directory* listings for each state, calculating the total number of internship training centers, both accredited and nonaccredited, the number of funded full- and part-time positions, the mean stipends, and the mean number of applications per position available. Based on these data, I have divided the country into six regions, based partly on geographical contiguity and partly on competitiveness as indicated by the mean number of applications per position reported in the 1999–2000 *Directory*. The data for the states in each region are reported in Appendix 2. The overall findings for each region are summarized here.

### Region 1: East Coast, Northern Section

Proceeding from North to South, this region consists of the states of Maine, New Hampshire, Vermont, Massachusetts, Rhode Island, Connecticut, New York, New Jersey, Pennsylvania, and Delaware. With the exception of Vermont, all are on the Atlantic and highly competitive. This region has

86 Megargee's Guide to Obtaining a Psychology Internship

135 internship centers, 117 (87%) of which are accredited, with 664 full-time and 16 part-time funded positions as well as 2 unfunded slots, thus making it the largest of my six regions. The mean stipends of the states in Region 1 range from $14,000 to $19,119, with an overall mean of $16,530. Except for Vermont, which averaged only 9.7 applications per position, the states in Region 1 had from 14.8 to 27.3 applications per slot, with an overall mean of 18.2.

## Region 2: East Coast, Southern Section

The Southern Section of the East Coast is the most competitive in the country based on its average application-to-slot ratios. The region includes Maryland, the District of Columbia, Virginia, North Carolina, South Carolina, and Georgia, but not Florida. This region has 59 internship settings, 53 (90%) of which are APA accredited, with 249 funded and 7 unfunded positions. Region 2 has the nation's highest proportion of accredited internships and also the nation's highest mean stipends, ranging from $17,330 to $21,200, with a regional mean of $19,409. The mean number of applications per position in these six states ranged from 16.2 to 26.8, with an overall mean of 20.7 applications per position.

## Region 3: Eastern Central

From North to South, this region includes Michigan, Ohio, West Virginia, Tennessee, Alabama, Mississippi, and Florida. These seven states are all less competitive than those on the East Coast and those in the Northern Central region. They have 86 internships, 57 (66%) of which are APA accredited, with 382 full-time and 7 part-time funded positions as well as 30 unfunded slots, 27 of which are in Florida. Stipends in this region range from $13,800 to $18,200, with a mean of $15,480. The average number of applications per funded slot for the states in this region are almost all lower than those in Regions 1 and 2, ranging from 9.1 to 16.8 applications per slot, with an overall regional mean of 13.3.

## Region 4: Northern Central

This region consists of five states, Minnesota, Wisconsin, Illinois, Indiana, and Kentucky, which share a higher application-to-position ratio than those that surround them. They have 89 internships, 61 (69%) of which are APA accredited, and 330 funded as well as 8 unfunded positions. Stipends range from $15,400 to $19,800, with a mean of $16,138. The mean number of applications per position for the states in Region 4 range from 15.9 to 22, with an overall mean of 18.9 applications per position.

### Region 5: Western Central

From North to South, this region includes nine states lying between the Mississippi River and the Rocky Mountains: South Dakota, Nebraska, Iowa, Kansas, Missouri, Oklahoma, Arkansas, Texas, and Louisiana. (North Dakota has no APPIC members.) Like the Eastern Central states, these are among the less competitive sites for internships. Region 5 has 56 internship centers, 46 (82%) of which are APA accredited, and 283 full-time and 2 part-time funded positions as well as 4 unfunded slots. Stipends range from $14,900 to $22,600, with a mean of $18,653. The mean number of applications per position in Region 5 range from 5.6 to 20.3, with an overall mean of 12.7. Although they have 11.7% of the nation's internship positions, they receive only 7.5% of the applications.

### Region 6: West Coast and Mountain

This region, which is the largest in area, includes the states of Washington, Montana, Oregon, Wyoming, California, Nevada, Utah, Colorado, Arizona, and New Mexico plus Hawaii. (Idaho and Alaska have no APPIC members.) Altogether these 11 states have 90 internship centers, 73 (81%) of which are APA accredited, with a total of 475 full-time and 21 part-time funded positions as well as 30 unfunded slots. The vast majority of the unfunded and part-time positions are in California. Stipends range from $14,700 to $23,700, with a mean of $16,800. There is wide variability in competitiveness, the application ratio ranging from 9.4 to 23.3, with an overall mean of 16. The ratios in Hawaii (9.8), Utah (10.8), and Oregon (12.7) are the lowest for the region, while those for Arizona (22.8) and Montana (23.3) are the highest.

## ☐ Other Sources of Information

The APPIC *Directory* is not the only source of internship information. A number of societies and APA divisions have compiled their own directories listing internships that provide training in their particular areas of interest, including behavioral and empirically validated treatment techniques, behavioral medicine, clinical child and pediatric psychology, geropsychology, and neuropsychology and clinical neuropsychology. A list of these directories and where to obtain them can be found in an appendix to the printed version of the APPIC *Directory*.

Many students use the APPIC internship listserv to exchange information about programs, especially when they are interested in training opportunities that are not discussed in the *Directory*. During September and early October, numerous inquiries are posted asking which internships

88 Megargee's Guide to Obtaining a Psychology Internship

provide training in specialized areas such as pastoral counseling, neuropsychological assessment, or sports psychology, or experience working with populations such as ethnic minorites. Others ask which settings or sites may be more or less receptive to applications from lesbian, gay, or bisexual students. The listserv connects you with many fellow students, but, as with any Web-based information, remember that it comes with no guarantees of accuracy. Also keep in mind that anyone, including ITDs, can be lurking, so be discreet.

Your faculty is another good source of information, although some of their knowledge may be dated. Discuss programs with faculty members who interned at places that interest you or who share your particular clinical interests. In the course of these discussions, you may discover that certain faculty members are personally acquainted with members of the training staff at one or more of the institutions that interest you. If you decide to apply there, it may help to ask these faculty members to send reference letters or call their friends on your behalf. Recommendations from friends and people with whom we are personally acquainted always carry greater weight than those from strangers.

Most graduate programs have a staff member who keeps track of students and former students. This individual can probably provide you with addresses of students from your school who have recently gone on predoctoral internships. This information helps you in two ways. First, you can analyze the acceptance and attendance patterns at your school and find out which internships prefer your school's applicants. If your colleagues have consistently gone to certain training centers and done well, their achievements should enhance your chances of being accepted at those placements. As a general rule, applicants from my program have always had a much higher rate of success applying to internships that have had previous students from our university than they have applying to settings where we are relatively unknown. Second, you can use this list to contact previous students directly and get their opinions about the internships they attended.

## ☐ Assembling Your Initial List

As you know, Maslow's motivational hierarchy distinguishes survival needs from those that are centered on fulfillment or self-actualization. You need to consider both in compiling a list of places to which you might apply. In setting forth your personal priorities in Chapter 3, you were probably thinking in terms of self-actualization. You probably tried to describe internships that would enable you to develop to your fullest in a congenial setting. That is good, but you also have to consider the survival aspects, because you won't get fulfilled if you don't get admitted.

Experienced photographers calculate the optimal camera settings to ensure a perfect photograph; they take most of their pictures using that combination, but to be on the safe side, they customarily make some additional exposures above and below that setting. In applying for internships, you need to do likewise. Most of the programs you apply to should be ones that appear to be "just right" for a person with your needs, skills, and abilities. But you should also add some that are more competitive in case you have underestimated your marketability, and others that appear easier to get into in the event that the competition is tougher than you expected. You should investigate enough so that, by the time you have finished interviewing and have discarded those that you did not like or where you got little encouragement, you have a list of about 13 places, with 2 that you think may be out of reach, 8 that are just right, and 3 in your safety net.

Making these sorts of estimates involves two sets of calculations. The first is assessing how difficult it is to get accepted into a given program. The second is estimating how strong a candidate you are.

## Assessing the Programs

How do you determine a setting's competitiveness? Unlike college admissions, there are no published guides to internships rating the difficulty of securing admission. However, there are data available that permit you to make some educated estimates. The index I have used is the ratio of applications received to positions available. If someday APPIC reveals how many applicants actually ranked a setting, this information would give a more precise estimate.

Other things being equal, programs where students from your school have done well in the past and where you or your faculty mentors have strong ties are those most likely to be favorably disposed toward your application. The reverse is also true. If you decide to apply to places where no one from your program has preceded you, you may find it more difficult to get accepted. To compensate, you might need to submit more applications and apply to more places that appear less competitive. If it is also impossible for you to visit these places personally, so that you will have to rely on telephone interviews, your task will be even more difficult. All of the things that enhance and detract from the strength of your application at various places must be considered when you are formulating your list.

Some programs attract more applications than others. Typically, more applicants are interested in working with children than with geriatric patients. If you are interested in geropsychology, consider the VA and other settings that have specific geropsychology slots. If you have special skills,

**90** Megargee's Guide to Obtaining a Psychology Internship

such as fluency in Spanish, consider internships located in cities or states with a large Hispanic population, where your language skills will be an asset. In other words, do your homework and identify internships where your particular combination of skills, training, and contacts give you an edge.

## Assessing Your Chances

For each program you are interested in, pay close attention to the preferences listed in the *Directory*. You have an edge at internships that rate programs such as yours "O" (Only) or "P" (Preferred). Internships that are academically oriented and that pride themselves on their research may favor Ph.D. candidates from traditional university departments. Psy.D. candidates, especially those from free-standing professional schools, might do better at internships that are more practitioner oriented. Keilin et al. (2000) reported that 85% of the applicants in Ph.D. training programs, 79% of those in Psy.D. programs, and 58% of those in Ed.D. programs obtained matches on Match Day, as did 83% of the clinical and school applicants and 80% of the counseling students.

You should also assess the match between your theoretical orientation and that of the internships you are considering. The two need not be perfectly congruent, but the greater the disparity, the more open you should be to points of view that differ from your own.

Your past training and experience should match the program you are seeking. If you have had no experience working with children, you will be at a disadvantage in competing for a position at a children's facility. Submit some applications for more generalized training programs for which you are better qualified as well.

A number of surveys have analyzed the characteristics of successful and unsuccessful internship applicants. The one factor that has consistently emerged is that the more successful applicants were those who did whatever was necessary to obtain an internship. They were the ones who were willing to consider internships in a variety of locales, who spent the extra time and trouble to individualize their applications, and who studied the characteristics of the internships to which they applied so they could discuss them intelligently with the selection staff.

Consider the Gainesville conference and its prototype of the ideal intern: a student who has had considerably more clinical experience than the APA minimum and who is on the verge of completing or has already completed his or her dissertation. The closer you match this template, the better your chances. Conversely, the farther you are from finishing your degree and the less supervised clinical experience you have, the more difficult it will be to find a placement.

# Where to Apply? Compiling Your Application List **91**

## ☐ Investigating Possible Programs

After you complete your reconnaissance, you should have an initial list of about 20 to 30 internships that interest you, ranging from some that are quite competitive to others where you feel reasonably sure you can gain admittance. These internships should all be ones that you think you might like to attend, but at this stage you know too little about them to be sure. Your next task is to investigate them more closely so you can select about 13 +/– 2 to which you will submit actual applications.

There are two basic sources of more detailed information than is available in the APPIC *Directory*. The first is the Web. Psychology internships have been rather slow to develop Web sites, but I expect the number having sites to increase in the years to come. The best way to access their Web sites is through the on-line *Directory*, which has the Web addresses and, sometimes, a link to the Web site.

Some Web sites give you specific information about psychology internship training. Others, which are aimed at potential patients, people making referrals, and other members of the public at large, provide more generalized information.

In addition to accessing the Web site, you should also write to the internship requesting information. You will often obtain vital information that is not included in the *Directory* or on the Web page, such as changes in the due date of applications and the fact that the internship requires extra forms in addition to the AAPI. It is best to wait until late August or September to write to make sure you get the most recent forms and information; any earlier, and you may get a packet left over from the previous year.

Whenever you post mail to an internship program, whether you are asking for information or actually applying, it is essential you include *all* the information on the address you obtained from the APPIC *Directory*. Many students send their inquiries or applications to the training center without indicating the specific person or the program for whom it is intended. With thousands of patients and hundreds of staff members from dozens of disciplines passing through a major training center in the course of a year, hospital mail rooms have little time or inclination to deduce whom you wanted to contact. A common mistake is for applicants to write to the "Internship Program." As Belar and Orgel (1980, p. 672) pointed out, a major consortium may have a number of internship programs in a dozen different disciplines scattered over several hospitals.

As with other aspects of the application process, sending for brochures is easier if you have a support group to divide up the work. When you get the brochures and materials, stamp the date on them. Then try to ascertain when they were published. Be wary of brochures that do not have the current year printed on them. Some programs leave their materials undated so they can use the same brochure year after year. If so, some of the information, such as staff rosters or application deadlines, may be out of date.

Remember that the purpose of the brochure, like any other piece of advertising, is to sell you on the internship so you will apply there. Without a pool of applicants, an internship will go out of business. Every year I was surprised when a large number of students expressed enthusiasm for some program that previous classes had disregarded. When I checked the files, I often found that the program in question had just issued a slick new brochure or developed a sexy new Web site. Be wary about judging a program on the basis of its circulars. As Grace (1985, p. 475) gloomily noted, "The prospective intern should not accept on faith that the internship will meet his or her needs or even that it is primarily designed to do so. Nor should one assume that all information in written and verbal descriptions is accurate. Programs change and misrepresentation is not unheard of." Grace's warning takes on added weight by virtue of the fact that he himself was an ITD when he wrote his article.

Once you have received your materials, it is time to narrow your list and investigate the most appealing programs in greater depth. Discuss them with faculty and supervisors, especially those who may have interned or visited the site in which you are interested. When possible, talk with fellow students or recent alumni who may have interned there recently.

After doing all your homework, you may have some specific questions that will be critical to your application decision. Perhaps you are not sure whether applicants must be U.S. citizens, or you really want a neuropsychological rotation but it is not clear from the brochure whether one will be available this year. By all means, call or e-mail the program and ask. The sites' preferred method of being contacted—post, phone, or e-mail—are listed in the *Directory*. When you complete this information gathering, you should have narrowed your list down to about 12 to 15 possible programs.

Some universities require that you get clearance from your ADCT or from the clinical faculty before you may submit any applications. Others may have rules about where you may apply; for example, one university-based program reduces interstudent competition by having each student select one first choice and forbidding other students to apply there. Whatever the ground rules, make sure you get your list approved and verify that you have your program's permission to apply to the internships you have selected.

Once you have been cleared to apply and your list has been approved, you are ready to begin the application process. Take your list of sites, *with complete addresses*, to the Registrar's office and arrange for transcripts to be sent.[8] This is a very low priority item with most Registrars. It can take

---

[8] If you have changed your name, make sure the name on your transcript matches the name you will be using when you apply.

them forever to mail out your transcripts, so order them as soon as possible. Some applicants worry that the transcript may get lost if it arrives before the formal application; others fret that they may change their minds and not apply. Relax; this is the least of your worries. Internship Selection Committees are well aware that some materials arrive before a formal application is received, and they have drawers labeled "Incomplete Folders" set aside for that purpose. If you later decide not to apply, so the rest of your materials never arrive; they are also skilled at emptying the "Incomplete Folders" drawer into the recycling bin after Match Day.

After you have ordered your transcripts and paid whatever fee is required, it is time to prepare your resume or CV. This process is described in detail in Chapter 5. And, of course, you will need to prepare your applications. This is discussed in Chapter 6.

**5**

CHAPTER

# Preparing Your Resume or CV

Your first step in actually applying for a predoctoral internship in psychology is preparing and submitting an application. At a bare minimum your application should include an application form, which almost invariably is the AAPI, a CV (sometimes referred to as a "Vitae"), and a transcript of your graduate course work.[9] You may also be asked to complete additional forms and essays and to submit one or more work samples. Supporting documents will include your ADCT's verification of your eligibility and letters of recommendation.

Until you interview at a site, your application materials are all the Internship Selection Committee has to evaluate you. In effect, your application *is* you. Given the overabundance of applicants, if your application does not set you apart from all the others and indicate that you are especially well suited for that setting, you may not even be granted an interview.

## ☐ What Internships Say They Want

Applicants often ask what internships are looking for in an applicant. ITDs' opinions have remained remarkably consistent over the last quar-

---

[9]Some ITDs maintain that an application form is all that is needed. I disagree. One reason I like to see an applicant's CV is that it is a personal document that is a work sample as well as a collection of information. It gives you a chance to expand on the bare facts and to explain items that might otherwise be ambiguous. It is important for you to differentiate yourself from the other applicants, and that is difficult on any uniform document. So, my advice is always to include a CV.

ter century. In 1976, Spitzform and Hamilton surveyed 100 of the then-116 APA-approved internships regarding their selection criteria. Those internships that interviewed applicants placed the most weight on the personal interview, especially when the internship had a psychodynamic orientation. Other important criteria were recommendations and practicum experience (which were cited by all 100 sites), personal and professional goals (92 sites), where the applicant trained (88), and prior work experience (87). Ranking considerably lower were honors and awards (mentioned by 62 sites), research in progress (55 sites), publications and presentations (54), professional memberships (24), and the state in which the applicant resided (10).

Petzel and Berndt's survey (1980) got responses from 90 of the 120 internships then in APPIC. They asked the ITDs to rank-order nine different possible selection criteria. The rankings with their means were:

1. Letters of recommendation (3.01). The ITDs stated that the ADCT's letter was especially important and that ADCTs should work hard at drafting a thorough and comprehensive letter, although many of them did not.
2. Supervised therapy experience (3.25).
3. Supervised diagnostic experience (3.97).
4. Personal interview (4.41).
5. Personal statement and biography (5.21).
6. Academic course work (5.82). The ITDs stated that courses in assessment and in psychotherapy were especially important.
7. Prestige of the applicant's university (6.26).
8. Graduate grade point average (7.02).
9. Publications and presentations (7.95).

Although APA required only 400 hours of practicum experience, Petzel and Berndt (1980) reported that the ITDs they surveyed preferred applicants with 1,000 hours or more.

Drummond, Rodolfa, and Smith (1981) compared the preferences of sites that were APA accredited with those that were not. The APA-approved sites ranked letters first, followed by practicum experience and personal and professional goals, while the non–APA accredited sites placed practicum experience first. Letters and structured assessments were tied for second, and personal and professional goals were third.

Durand, Blanchard, and Mindell (1988) surveyed academic departments and internship training centers listed in the *American Psychologist* with regard to their attitudes toward and emphasis on projective testing. Not surprisingly, they found the internships placed more importance on projectives than the academic departments did; whereas 65% of the ITDs stated that projective testing was as important as ever, less than 49% of the ADCTs agreed. The ITDs felt that their interns were not getting suffi-

**96**   Megargee's Guide to Obtaining a Psychology Internship

cient training in projectives and noted that 60% required remedial training in projective testing.[10]

More recently, Lopez, Oehlert, and Moberly (1996) surveyed 115 ITDs at APA-accredited training sites. They reported that the highest ranking criteria were clinical experience, interviews, letters, strength of graduate coursework, and the applicants' fit with specialty areas. Least important were GPA, minority status, prestige of the applicant's training program, and whether or not the dissertation prospectus had been approved. As in previous studies, the ITDs noted that assessment experience was most applicants' biggest deficiency, especially with regard to projectives. They concluded:

> Although there is no objective formula to offer applicants to ensure selection, the most attractive candidate would appear to be an individual who has well-documented clinical experience, documentation of adequate assessment experience, an interview manner that communicates interest and poise, and strong letters of recommendation. (p. 520)

When asked what internships are looking for, one ITD recently responded with the following list, which I have paraphrased:

1. How well does the applicant's interests, training, and experience match with our program's rotations and overall philosophy?
2. Do the applicant's stated goals match his or her past training and experience?
3. How strong are letters from the applicant's clinical supervisors? (This ITD noted, "We prefer to see most of the letters from clinical supervisors as opposed to academic/dissertation letters.")
4. How does the applicant present in interview? Is this someone we could work well with and who would relate well to our patient population?
5. Good grades (As and Bs) do not mean much, but we pay close attention to poor grades (Cs).

Throughout this book, I emphasize that there is no one training program that is perfect for everyone. There is also no prototypical applicant that will suit every internship. Internships differ greatly from one another, and applicants who are an excellent match for some settings may not even be asked to interview at others.

---

[10]If anything, the gulf between the academy and the internships regarding projectives has widened since this survey. In 1997, after viewing the 47 tests listed on the first version of the AAPI, a senior academic psychologist wrote, "The APPIC form asks students to report on their experiences with an incredible array of psychological tests and assessment procedures, almost none of which has any substantial evidence of validity or utility. For many of them, if the student listed any experience at all, the training program of origin should be censured and the student should be put through corrective exercises to get rid of this contamination."

## ☐ Preparing Your CV

The purpose of this chapter is to help you write a successful resume for applying for internship. I use the term "resume" deliberately, because even though you will probably call your resume a "Curriculum Vitae," the document you will prepare for applying to internship will differ in certain respects from an academic CV. Your academic CV will focus almost exclusively on scholarship (i.e., your educational history, research experience, professional memberships, and publications), whereas the resume you prepare for internship applications should also include a detailed account of your clinical and professional training, experience, and skills. In addition to listing your previous clinical positions, it should contain a brief description of your duties, the types of patients you saw, the nature and extent of the supervision you received, and your experience with various interventions and psychometric instruments—items that would be inappropriate in an academic CV. With the understanding that I am not referring to an academic CV, I will use the terms "CV" and "resume" interchangeably in this chapter. (A sample CV is presented in Appendix 3.)

The purpose of your CV or resume is to present a complete and accurate account of all your qualifications in an attractive format that will help you compete successfully with other applicants. This is not the time to be modest. Include *all* your credentials and relevant experiences. As an ADCT, I interview all our internship applicants and go over their CVs with them. Every student's CV that I have examined has omitted some salient bit(s) of information that would impress some ITDs. Among the most common omissions were professional workshops they may have attended (or even presented), undergraduate accomplishments such as graduating with honors, and special skills such as fluency in a foreign language or experience with some empirically supported treatment technique.

While you should not be overly modest, you should not "pad" your CV by listing the same item several times, by including trivia, or by overstating your accomplishments or qualifications. For example, do not list your master's thesis under "education" and again under "publications," or claim expert status on the Rorschach based on five administrations.

You will also need to fill out the APPIC's AAPI form as well as any other forms required by the various internships to which you apply. The data included in a CV and the AAPI overlap to some extent, so I suggest that you begin by assembling all the data you will need for both your resume and your application forms.

In preparing a CV, especially their first CV, many students get so overwhelmed by stylistic questions that they tend to forget the more substan-

**98**    Megargee's Guide to Obtaining a Psychology Internship

tive ones. What font(s) should I use? Should I put my name in the middle or at the side, in regular type or boldface? Should I have it professionally printed? What color paper should I use?

I suggest that you divide the process into four steps and deal with them one at a time:

1. Gather together all the information you will need to complete the CV and the various application forms.
2. From the collected data, select the information you wish to include in your resume.
3. Decide the best way to organize the information you choose to include (i.e., the sequence of topics and what will be listed under each).
4. Present the information in a clear and attractive format. (This is when you decide the stylistic questions.)

## Step 1: Assembling the Information

Writing your first resume is like filing your income tax . . . the biggest problem is amassing all the data you may need. In this section, I will provide you with a comprehensive list of all the information you should ever need for writing your CV and filling out your application forms.

Your first step is to go to the APPIC Web site and download the current AAPI. (If you are not connected, you can obtain it by writing the APPIC central office.) It is important to get the current edition because it changes somewhat from year to year.

Although I will concentrate on the information you need to assemble for internship applications, as long as you are going to all the trouble of gathering these data, it makes sense to collect and preserve other records you might need later when applying for employment, licensing, or obtaining a National Register listing or Diplomate status. Information that seems trivial now may be essential at some future date, but as the years go by and you move from place to place these data will become increasingly difficult to obtain.[11]

As you build up this data bank, don't worry about how to present or display material. That will come later. Just obtain and record the information in whatever manner you find most convenient. I suggest you use a system that will make it easy to add and subtract items such as a multipocket file folder or loose-leaf notebook. Most multipurpose computer software packages include an information storage and retrieval sys-

---

[11]When I became a consultant to the U.S. Secret Service, I had to obtain a "top secret" security clearance. I had to complete a form that asked for many pages of information including every job I had ever held and the exact street address and apartment number of every residence I had occupied for my entire life.

tem that will allow you to transfer the information to your word processing program. If you elect to store your data on a computer, make sure you back it up on a floppy disk and with hard copy. Preserve these data, whether computerized or not, in a place that is not only safe but also secure.

The list of information that I propose you collect is designed to be overly comprehensive; there will be many items included that you will not choose to put in your CV. Nevertheless, it will be helpful for you to have these data available. Since I am trying to think of everything that anyone might have, there will undoubtedly be many items that do not apply to most readers; do not let this give you a feeling of inferiority.

## Personal Information and Identifying Data

This information is designed to tell the person who reads your resume who you are and where you can be found. Although you have considerable discretion about how much personal information you wish to disclose, and equal employment opportunity laws place severe restrictions on the information employers can require, for the purpose of assembling a database I have listed everything I can think of that you may want or need to include.

- *Name(s).* List your complete legal name, including any suffixes such as "Jr." or "III"; any nicknames or former names, especially if you have used them professionally; and any name changes you anticipate between now and Matching Day.
- *NMS registration number.* This is the code number that you obtain from the NMS that uniquely identifies your applications for the NMS match. If your name is "Jim Smith," it distinguishes you from all the other "Jim Smiths" who are applying. Internships must use this number to rank you on the form they submit to NMS.
- *Addresses.* Record your home and work addresses as well as the address of your academic training program and the address of someone who will always know how to locate you. Note any anticipated address changes.
- *Communication numbers.* List all your phone and fax numbers and e-mail addresses, the days and times (including your time zone), when you can be reached at each, as well as any special information that would be helpful in reaching you, such as "ring 12 times to activate the answering machine."
- *Social and demographic information.* Include your date and place of birth, Social Security number, marital status, names and birth dates of children and other dependents, your ethnic, racial, or minority status, and your gender if it is not obvious to American readers from your name. If you are not a U.S. citizen, record your citizenship, passport number,

**100**   Megargee's Guide to Obtaining a Psychology Internship

current visa status, and other relevant data, such as whether you are married to a U.S. citizen.

- *Military status.* If you have served in the armed forces, record the branch of the service, your dates of service, rank, medals and honors, discharge status, military serial number, service-connected disabilities and/or Purple Heart, and if you are eligible for a veteran's preference. This information may be especially important if you apply for a VA placement.
- *Legal status.* List any arrests, convictions, probation, parole, or imprisonments, indicating whether they were for misdemeanors or felonies. Prepare explanations of each, as well as of any ethical charges or complaints that might have been filed against you with any licensing boards or professional associations.
- *Health.* Note any conditions that might have an impact on your ability to perform the duties of your position (e.g., need for a wheelchair-accessible workplace).

## Education

By and large, for your CV you will only need to list your undergraduate and graduate education, noting the degrees and majors, but some applications call for lists of courses and dates, so you should get copies of your transcripts and have them available. The more general the application form, the more likely it is to ask for things such as the number of semester hours or credits you had in your major or minor.

Internships do not usually ask for GRE scores, but you should keep a record of them in case you someday apply for admission for further graduate education.

- *High School or GED.* Make a record of schools you attended with addresses, dates attended, and so forth. You will not use this in your CV, but some applications may call for it.
- *Undergraduate education.* List every institution of higher learning you attended, noting for each the name of the institution, its address, the dates you attended, your major and minor, any degree you received and the date, and any honors or awards (cum laude, Phi Beta Kappa, etc.). Note any scholarships, awards, achievements, memberships in organizations, extracurricular activities, service on university committees, student government, and volunteer activities. Instead of using initials, use the full name of organizations or clubs. If you received an award that is specific to that school (e.g., the "Phineas P. Phollansby Senior Trophy"), record what it is for; other readers won't know and after a couple of decades you will forget. If you completed an honors project, record the name of your major professor or advisor and the title of your honor's thesis.

- *Graduate education.* For each program attended, list the same basic data as above. Have available a transcript for those applications that inquire about specific courses or numbers of hours. Also include the specific degree program (e.g., "APA-approved Ph.D. program in Clinical Psychology"); the title of your master's thesis, major area paper, and dissertation; the name of your major professor(s); and your current status (e.g., completed doctoral comprehensive examination, candidate for Ph.D.). Record the dates or anticipated dates of all significant milestones, such as completion of your master's degree, doctoral coursework, doctoral comprehensive examination, defense of dissertation prospectus, completion of data collection, and defense of your dissertation.

Note any major gaps in your chronology, that is, any periods when you were not enrolled in school or were unemployed, and be prepared to account for them (e.g., raising small children, doing missionary work, in prison, and so on).

## Other Educational Experiences

- List professional workshops you have attended, including the person who presented, the date, place, and number of continuing education hours for each.
- Technical or professional courses such as computer seminars, software "short courses," and the like. Don't forget any relevant specialized training you may have received if you served in the military.
- Conferences you may have attended, especially if they had an impact on your professional development or help depict the sort of psychologist you are.
- Personal therapy or training analysis.

## Special Skills

Include knowledge or skills that might be useful in some internship settings.

- List any foreign languages you know and your proficiency level in reading, writing, speaking, and understanding.
- Special computer skills.
- Ability to operate relevant equipment such as biofeedback apparatus.
- First aid or CPR training.
- American Sign Language for the hearing impaired.

## Professional Credentials

List any relevant professional licenses or certificates, including those from allied professions such as nursing. Include the state, the license number, and the date awarded.

## Memberships in Professional Organizations

List the various professional organizations to which you now belong, or have belonged, with the dates of membership and the level of membership (i.e., student, associate, member, fellow). Include any committees on which you served and any offices you may have held, such as program chair or nominating committee. Do not use initials to identify organizations.

### Honors and Awards

List any honors and awards you may have received in college and elsewhere. Later you can decide what details to include. Also record exceptional high school awards such as Girl's State Governor or a Presidential Scholar award, as well as awards from civic or professional organizations (e.g., Lou Brock Leadership Award or APA outstanding first paper award). Don't forget any athletic trophies or honors you may have earned or other contests you may have won. If you were an Olympic medalist or Miss America runner-up, everyone will want to interview you. If the nature of the honor or award is not obvious, note the name of the organization that presented it and why you received it. If there was a citation, record it verbatim.

Record election to honorary societies such as Sigma Xi, any degrees with honors, and any fellowships or grants. Note offices you have held, both elective and appointed, such as Graduate Student Member on Clinical Training Committee, President of Psi Chi. (When it comes to organizing your actual CV, you can decide whether to list the college awards such as Phi Beta Kappa separately or under "Education"; at this stage redundancy is acceptable.)

### Previous Employment

In a resume you give a complete employment history, whereas in a CV you typically list only professionally relevant experience. For your internship applications, you will probably strike a balance, including all the positions of a strictly psychological nature as well as others that may be seen as tangentially related, such as a weight-loss counselor, sleep lab technician, or computer consultant, but omitting other jobs, like being a bartender, that you may have taken to get through school.

On some application forms you may have to list all the jobs you have ever had in chronological order, beginning with your current position and working backward. This usually includes part-time as well as full-time positions. Don't forget to include military service, especially if your military experience was psychological in nature. At this stage it is a good

Preparing Your Resume or CV **103**

idea to gather together all the data you will need for your CV, the AAPI, and other application forms.

Preparing a complete employment history is always difficult, especially the first time you do it. Unfortunately, you generally need to submit one for a federal or state position. If you maintain a list of jobs held and update it as you move from position to position, the task is easier. Starting with your present position and working backward toward the dawn of time for *each and every* job you have ever held, to the best of your ability list: (a) the name and address of your employer, (b) the dates you began and ended your employment, (c) the average number of hours you worked per week, (d) your starting and ending salary, (e) the name of your immediate supervisor, (f) the nature of the business, (g) the exact title of your job, (h) a description of the work you performed, (i) your specific duties and the percent of time doing each; and (j) your reason for leaving. If you can't recall all the details of the nonrelevant jobs you held, don't worry about it. It probably isn't worth the time and effort required to track them down. However, you should try to assemble these data for all the various psychological positions you have held.

## Professional Training and Experience

On a CV, in contrast to an employment application, you only include those jobs that are relevant to the position for which you are applying, namely a psychology internship. Many students find it convenient to maintain separate records for their clinical, research, and teaching positions, and to list them separately on their CVs.

- *Clinical experience.* For your CV, you first need to compile a list of all the clinical positions you have held, both practicum and nonpracticum, as well as any that you may have held prior to entering your training program. For those positions, in addition to the information listed above, record the names, titles, and credentials of the Chief Psychologist, the Training Director, and your immediate supervisor(s) (e.g., "Barry Cuda, Ph.D., ABPP, Chief Psychologist [Licensed East Idabama]"), your specific title (e.g., "Clinical Psychology Trainee"), the nature of the setting (e.g., community mental health center), and your specific duties and the percent of time spent doing each (e.g., "Outpatient-based assessment [50%] and therapy with adult, adolescent, and child populations [50%]. Client population includes a variety of developmental, anxiety, mood, personality, and organic disorders. Complete assessments performed for learning disabilities, neuropsychological, attention deficit hyperactivity, and personality disorders. Therapy experience included group, family, conjoint, and individual using an eclectic approach"). The above is a general description such as you would include on your CV. The AAPI requires much more detailed information. For each clinical setting in which you worked, you will have to report the number of "clock hours" you spent in various activities such as therapy, support activities, supervision, and "other" activities.[12] You will also need to record the characteristics of the clients you saw in each setting, including their ages, gender, ethnicity, disabilities, and whether or not they qualify as being "multiculturally diverse." I suggest you also keep a record of their formal diagnoses. With regard to therapy, you need to determine the number of clock hours you spent administering various types of treatment, such as individual or group, to each of several different types of clients, such as adults, adolescents, or children. Similarly, you need to compile the number of clock hours you spent in support and in other activities such as psychodiagnostic test administration, neuropsychological assessment, intake interviews, and a number of other specific activities. With regard to testing, you need to be able to report how many times you have administered and scored each of the adult and children's tests the AAPI lists, as well as any others you may have used, and the number of integrated testing reports you have written based on each. As Stedman et al. (2000) pointed out, this is a key selection criterion for many ITDs. Moreover, even though they may not be considered tests in the strictest sense, you should nonetheless keep a record of other assessment techniques you have used, such as structured diagnostic interviews. These can be included in the "Other Tests" category on the AAPI. You will also need to document the number of hours spent in various types of supervision.

Although the AAPI focuses on your practicum placements, you should also record data regarding the other nonpracticum clinical settings in which you may have gained experience. Don't forget any settings in which you may have acquired experience before entering your current doctoral training program. One of my students had worked several years as a master's-level licensed school psychologist before enrolling in our doctoral program in clinical psychology. By including information regarding her experience in that setting, she made her application more attractive to the child-clinical settings to which she applied. This information can be reported on your CV and in the section of the AAPI labeled "Other Clinical Experiences."

If you have maintained systematic records of your clinical experience using a system such as that devised by Herschell and McNeil

---

[12]The term "clock hours" is a key element. These are not course hours, or semester hours, or the number of hours you were assigned to a placement, e.g., 20 hours a week. It consists of the actual number of minutes or hours you spent in each specified activity. The only exception is that a 50-minute therapy session counts as a clock hour.

Preparing Your Resume or CV **105**

(2000),[13] you should have all the data you need. Even so, compiling the data can be quite a chore, which is why I recommend that you do it the summer before you apply.

If you do not have complete data, you will have to reconstruct the information as best you can from whatever records you have available. Look through your old appointment books. Go back and consult the files at the practicum and other agencies where you worked. Perhaps your clinical supervisors or the person in charge of assigning practicums may be able to assist. Don't have a panic attack if you cannot recall every last detail or account for every minute. All any internship expects is a good faith effort on your part to convey a reasonably accurate summary of your previous clinical experience.

- *Teaching.* Many graduate students accumulate a significant amount of teaching experience. This, too, should be documented. In recording your teaching experience, you should indicate the name, number, and date of each course, its subject matter (e.g., "abnormal psychology"), the type of course taught (e.g., "large lecture"), the number and the level of students (e.g., "150 undergraduates, mostly freshmen and sophomores"), and what your role was. Did you have primary responsibility for the course, did you handle only the labs or sections, or were you limited to proctoring and grading the exams? Record all this information for every course in which you have been involved at your present and any previous universities.

In addition to classroom teaching or assisting in formal courses, you should also record other presentations, such as colloquia presented to groups of scholars, guest lectures in other people's courses, workshops, and staff training presentations at your workplace. A brief course description, which can often be copied from the catalog of courses, is also useful. Remember that at this stage you are simply collecting any and all data relevant to your professional experience. Later we will sort out what goes into your CV, the AAPI, and other forms.

- *Research.* You should also record the nature and extent of your research activities. For your personal research, briefly note the details of each study. For research you may have done for others, perhaps as a paid research assistant, indicate the name of the project, the principal investigator, and the overall nature of the investigation. Specify when you worked on the project, who your supervisor was, the nature of the

---

[13]Herschell and McNeil's (2000) code form uses categories taken directly from the AAPI. It enables you to record data efficiently and succinctly for later entry into a computerized data retrieval system or a spreadsheet. An advantage of their system is that it feeds directly into a computerized database using the Microsoft Access system, which is part of the MS Office package. As noted earlier, computerized and hard copies of their forms and system are available free at their Web site, www.as.wvu.edu./psyc.

**106**     Megargee's Guide to Obtaining a Psychology Internship

project, and your title or role as well as your specific responsibilities (e.g., running subjects, analyzing data, etc.). Note any publications or presentations resulting from the project, especially if you are listed as a coauthor or your contribution is specifically acknowledged. Also record the specific skills you needed and the techniques you used (e.g., administered SCID interviews to 100 state hospital patients). Record your unpaid as well as paid research experience, and include undergraduate as well as graduate experience. Remember, you are preparing a *comprehensive* summary.

## Publications and Presentations

This is the section that is the core of an academic CV. Most internships will be duly appreciative of your scholarly credentials, as long as they are convinced you can pull your weight clinically. As in previous sections, put everything you can think of into this inventory, then later pick and choose what you will include on your CV. List all items according to the style in the current APA *Publication Manual*. In this section include:

- Articles in refereed journals, including articles already published, those "in press," those being revised for resubmission, and those under review.
- Papers presented at scholarly meetings, posters, symposium contributions, etc. in which there is a review for quality. Include those presentations already made and those that are under review.
- Chapters or contributions to books or monographs that have been published or accepted for publication.
- Reviews, notes, and comments such as published book reviews and published letters to the APA *Monitor* or the newsletters of learned societies, etc.
- Unpublished writings, such as your thesis, dissertation, or major area paper, technical reports prepared for granting agencies, as well as training manuals or other internal documents published by your department or employer.

## Other Evidence of Scholarly Activity

In addition to publications and presentations, you should also keep a record of any other scholarly activities in which you have engaged. (These are in addition to the research positions you have held that are included above.) You should record:

- Editorial activities, such as reviewing submissions for a journal or a scholarly meeting or being involved in the editing of a publication such as a journal, a newsletter, etc.

- Grants and fellowships applied for or received. Include intramural and local grants such as dissertation awards as well as extramural funding.
- Consulting activities of a scholarly nature.
- A summary of current research and plans for future research.
- Anything else of a scholarly nature you can think of, such as writing software programs, creative writing, and film, TV, or other media presentations.

### *Miscellaneous*

Note any accomplishments or activities not included above that might enhance your resume or help the reader get to know you. Include recreational activities, sports or hobbies, civic service, and nonprofessional honors, awards, or recognitions such as winning a prize in an art show, being elected to office in a civic organization, or being awarded a sports trophy. One intern applicant in her 50s who felt she was being regarded as too old and feeble for the rigors of internship pointed to the fact that she was a marathon runner and professional ski instructor.

## Step 2: Selecting What to Include

Having assembled all the material you can possibly use, plus a lot more, you must now select what information you wish to present in your resume. Since your CV is your creation, there are no formal or explicit rules about what you may and may not include. However, there is a large body of custom, and people will generally look askance at those who deviate from the generally agreed upon format.

The basic goal of your CV is to get you interviews. As the number of applicants and applications has increased, getting interviews has become more difficult. In selecting material for your CV, you want it to include things that will interest internships and exclude material that might turn them off.

One way to steer between the Scylla of appearing to overstate your qualifications or pad your CV with trivial items and the Charybdis of omitting potentially helpful information is to label items clearly. For example, whereas it is not appropriate to include unrefereed items like grant reports or training manuals under "Publications," you can include them as "Technical reports (unrefereed)" or "Training manuals." That way they get on the record, but no one can accuse you of misrepresenting these items as refereed publications.

As you examine the material you have assembled, deciding what to put in your CV, you may also note other items that are not appropriate for inclusion in your resume that you will wish to include in a personal statement or cover letter.

**108**    Megargee's Guide to Obtaining a Psychology Internship

## *Personal Information*

Personal information is just that, personal, and it is entirely up to you what to include under "personal" material. You obviously need to list your name, NMS number, address, and communication numbers. Other than that, it is up to you.

Some people list their birthdate or age on their CV. If you are still in your 20s, I recommend that you do so. If you are elderly or a senior citizen, i.e., in your mid-30s or older, I would think twice about including your age. I personally have mentored graduate students in their 40s and well into their 50s; I actually preferred such students because they were typically highly motivated and brought maturity and a wealth of life experiences with them. However, a recent APA survey showed about 28% to 30% of the applicants over 40 failed to match in the Year 2000, compared with only 10% to 18% of those under 40 (Guerrero, 2000). Moreover, a number of older applicants reported that age became an issue in their interviews. For example, a 36-year-old man was asked if he would be able to relate to the other interns who would all be much younger than him.[14]

Information about your marital status, relationships, and dependents is optional. Some internships seem to prefer younger, unattached applicants who "don't have a life" outside of the internship and are therefore willing to put in 10- to 12-hour days, 6 or 7 days a week. If you fit this category, I suggest that you indicate that you are single and unfettered by family obligations. If not, then I suggest that you simply omit these details from your CV because they may make it more difficult to get interviews. Once you obtain your interviews, you may have to deal with these issues, but by then you have your foot in the door and can convince the Selection Committee that your personal life will not interfere with your professional performance. (I will discuss dealing with intrusive questions about personal matters in Chapter 8 on interviewing.)

If you qualify as a minority, I would include this information, since there are some stipends that are reserved for minority applicants. If you are not a U.S. citizen, you may be ineligible for some positions, so it is best to make this known in advance rather than after you have invested a lot of time and effort in interviewing.

I would not include health or legal status in your CV, but if there are problems, be prepared to deal with them in the interview or on an appli-

---

[14]Although you may elect not to include your age on your CV, the individual application forms currently being used by some internships do ask for your birthdate and also your Social Security number. Some applicants have asked the APPIC Board to prohibit this practice in the future. Until they do, you must choose whether to comply or risk alienating the internship by refusing to supply the information.

cation form. Concealing relevant information or lying on an application form can not only cost you a job, but could subject you to prosecution.

## Education and Special Skills

Turning to education, do not include high school data on your CV and do not list the college or graduate school courses you have taken. Save that for the application form or your transcript. Do list all the degrees you have received along with the dates and any honors, such as "Magna Cum Laude" as well as your current status in your graduate program. Also include the workshops and continuing education seminars you may have attended, but under a separate heading, as shown in Appendix 3.

If you are fluent in a foreign language or in American Sign Language, I would note that under the heading "Special skills" in your CV. Other special skills, such as being able to design Web sites, do not generally go in a CV. They can be included in your AAPI or mentioned in your cover letter. Do, however, list all your current professional organizations, along with offices held and honors received, and any professionally relevant licenses or credentials you may have.

When it comes to honors and awards, some discretion is in order. You definitively want to include the important ones, especially those of a clearly professional nature, but do not include others such as being "Hilton employee of the month" or the fact that you won the local pub's wet T-shirt contest. High school awards can be included if they are truly exceptional; the more they relate to professional activities, the better, such as winning a major science fair competition.

## Previous Experience

Under previous experience and employment, include all your relevant professional experience in your CV, but do not put in all the various other jobs you have held. In the section "Step 3: Organizing your CV," I suggest that you subdivide your experience into homogeneous categories such as "research," "clinical," and so on. You do not need to limit this to paid positions; for example, you might wish to include a research apprenticeship, even though it was unpaid, under "research experience." With regard to other activities such as volunteer work, you should decide for yourself how significant this activity is and whether it enhances or detracts from your CV. It may be better to allude to it in your personal statement or in your discussion of goals.

In describing your experience, write clearly and directly, stating what it was that you accomplished. Be forceful; avoid weak, passive, or "wimpy" constructions. One university's guide to preparing resumes advises, "Concentrate on the positive and use active verbs in the past tense when stat-

110 Megargee's Guide to Obtaining a Psychology Internship

ing what you did. To say that you planned, organized, supervised, coordinated, implemented, or designed is far better than saying you were 'involved in' or 'participated in,'" (Stanford University Career Planning and Placement Center, 1988, p. 2). While this advice is aimed at bachelor's-level business applicants, you get the idea.

## Scholarship and Publications

Under "Scholarship," definitely include all your peer-reviewed publications and presentations and label them as such. Also include your thesis and, if you have prepared one, your major area paper, but I suggest you list them under "Education" rather than as publications. It is appropriate to list items that are under review, but do not put the name of the journal to which they have been submitted. Do not list articles that are "in preparation" under publications. You may refer to them in describing your future research plans.

In my CV, I have two sections labeled "Notes, reviews, and comments" and "Technical reports," in which I include items that have not been refereed. You may wish to include such materials somewhere on your CV as well, but do so in a way that makes it clear you are not trying to pass these items off as refereed publications. If you have publications in other areas, such as poetry or short stories, include them in your CV, but list them in a separate section from your psychological writings.

Opinions differ on including sports, hobbies, and other nonprofessional activities. While it may be frowned upon in an academic CV, I do not have any problems with it in a CV designed for internship applications, especially if it enables you to list an outstanding achievement not included elsewhere (e.g., Gold medal in Decathlon, 2000 Summer Olympics). While some activities, such as being a software designer, might enhance the perception of your skills, I think the chief value of such material is that it can help the interview get started or assist you in finding some common ground with the interviewer.

## Step 3: Organizing Your CV

Your CV should be organized so that readers can easily find the information they are seeking. A well-organized CV gives the impression that you are a well-organized person. The sample CV in Appendix 3 will give you some ideas as to organization.

One key is consistency. If you start with your most recent positions and work backwards in the employment section, then you should do likewise in the education section.

I favor putting all the identifying material up front, including demographics, organizations, and credentials. Once this is taken care of, I find

Preparing Your Resume or CV **111**

it useful to arrange a CV used for internship applications topically. Begin with the section on education, and put all the information relating to this topic together. Lead off with your current graduate student status, and then add the information relating to your dissertation (including the title, prospectus date, and major professor) first, followed by your major area paper, followed by your master's. Include dates to the left. (If you chose to list your master's thesis under "Publications," do not list it here as well. However, I think it best to put it here.)

Next, summarize your undergraduate education. Include any educational honors you have received, unless you have chosen to list them separately under "Honors." (Do not include them twice, although if you graduated with honors you should list your bachelor's as "A.B., *summa cum laude*" or whatever.)

In a separate subsection under education, list other educational items such as continuing education workshops you have taken. I would also include relevant special skills under this same general heading.

Next, present your professional experience. Rather than putting everything chronologically, thereby mixing different types of experience, I prefer to use homogeneous subtopics such as "research," "teaching," and "clinical." The order is up to you and is one way you can choose what it is you want to emphasize.

Within each section, list the positions you have held in reverse chronological order, beginning with the most recent in that topic area. As noted above, include your title, the dates, the number of hours worked weekly, your supervisor and his or her credentials, a description of your duties, and, perhaps, the proportion of time spent on each. Do not include beginning and ending salaries or reasons for leaving in a CV.

Although you may want to put them in a separate section, I suggest that you list your publications immediately after your various research positions. That way everything relating to research is in one section. Combine any sections that are too small (i.e., if you have one refereed publication and two presentations, put them together as "publications and presentations").

At the end of the CV, you may include a list of the names, titles, addresses, phone numbers, and e-mail addresses of all those you have asked to write letters on your behalf.

## Step 4: Style and Esthetics

Now that we have dealt with substance, let us turn to style. The most important stylistic criterion, overriding all other concerns, is that your resume should be neat, legible, accurate, and easy to read.

Your CV will probably be duplicated for distribution to raters and interviewers at the internship, so use dark, high-contrast typography; do not

## 112 Megargee's Guide to Obtaining a Psychology Internship

use multiple colors. Prepare your CV on a word processing system and print it using the highest quality laser or ink jet printer available. Spend the extra money to purchase high-quality, high-contrast paper that is specifically designed for the printer you plan to employ.

Present your data in such a way that the reader can easily follow the sequence and locate things. Use headings, subheadings, and hanging paragraphs to show what belongs with what. Boldface type or different fonts, used judiciously, can also help, but keep it in good taste.

A common mistake on computer-produced CVs is having an entry carry over a page break. Do not put a heading at the bottom of a page and then have the subordinated material begin on the next page, and try not to allow a page break to split a job description or reference. If you cannot get the complete entry all on one page, it is better to begin the new entry on the next page. Having generous borders and wide margins is not only attractive, but it also gives the reader a place to make notes.

While you may elect to employ a copying firm, stay away from the outfits that prepare jazzy resumes for vinyl siding salesmen. The use of different colored inks, "bullets," raised type and other devices utilized by professional resume firms are fine if you are seeking a sales position, but they are a "turn off" when used in a professional resume or CV. Similarly, it is not customary to include a photograph on a CV.

No matter how many times you have gone over it, before you take your CV or any other material to be copied, check for typographical and spelling errors. Use a computerized spell-checking program, but do not rely on it. Computers do not understand the differences among words such as "for," "fore," and "four." Check everything again when you get it back from the copying firm; do not accept it if there are dark spots or slanted pages. Make sure you check every copy. It is a Fundamental Law of Nature that the copy you do not check will be the one with the blank page. One applicant wrote me that he had to resubmit his applications to eight internships after he discovered his printer was skipping pages. Better to check your application before you send it off.

This may seem very basic, but all of these mistakes have been made in the past. Even one error or botched page can give a negative impression. I recently read an application for a faculty position in which the candidate misspelled the name of his home state. The fact that the applicant had obviously not bothered to check a document as important as a job application for accuracy made me wonder if he could be trusted to analyze data or prepare research articles correctly.

Mistakes are especially likely to happen when you rely on others to prepare or copy your materials. I speak from experience; before we submitted the manuscript for the first edition of this book, four different people had proofed it in its entirety. However, the cover was prepared by the publishing company. When I received my copies from the printer, I looked at the cover and saw that my name had been spelled incorrectly!

The books had all been printed and it was too late to correct it. However, it certainly was an effective illustration of my point that no matter how careful you are, mistakes happen. Let's hope that the publisher gets my name right in this edition, and that you get your CVs right before you submit them to the internships.

# 6

CHAPTER

# Preparing Your Internship
# Applications

Once you have formulated your priorities, compiled your list of possible internships, and prepared your CV, it is time to fill out your applications. Allow plenty of time. The one thing that all internship applicants agree on is that preparing applications took much more time and effort than they had anticipated. Mellott, Arden, and Cho (1997, p. 193) advised, "The application process can be extremely time consuming, and it requires good organization and effective planning in order to successfully meet the required deadlines."

The first step is ensuring that you have the full support of your training program, specifically that of your ADCT and your major professor. Download the most recent APPIC *Academic Program's Verification of Internship Eligibility and Readiness* form. After filling in the information specified in the directions, go over the form with your Training Director and determine whether he or she has any reservations about certifying that you are ready for internship and strongly endorsing your candidacy. Without your ADCT's support, applying is probably a waste of time, so resolve any problems with your ADCT before you do anything else.

Let us assume that you have gotten your program's approval and discussed your choices with your advisors. It is now late September or early October and you should have:

1. Compiled a list of places where you plan to apply.
2. Downloaded the latest *APPIC Application for Psychology Internship* (AAPI) and verification forms from the APPIC Web site. (Make sure you obtain the most recent forms, because they change somewhat each year.)
3. Contacted the sites where you intend to apply, obtained any addi-

**114**

Preparing Your Internship Applications **115**

tional application forms they require, and verified the deadlines in the *Directory* or Web site. (A recent APPIC survey showed that 37% of the sites require additional documents or essays.)

4. Collected and collated all the information you need to complete the application forms.
5. Prepared a CV or resume and had it laser printed and duplicated.
6. Had transcripts sent to all the places where you might conceivably apply.
7. Contacted the people you want to write letters of recommendation on your behalf, secured their agreement to do so, provided each with a copy of your CV, and asked them to get all their letters to you or in the mail at least a week before they are due at the internship.

Some students worry that transcripts and letters that arrive at the internship before their formal application materials may go astray. This is probably a needless concern. Every year at this time internship training centers all over the country start receiving application materials. As soon as an item comes in, they check their database to see if they already have a listing for that applicant. If so, the material is added to the file; if not, a file is opened and subsequent material is inserted as it arrives. However, to be on the safe side, you may choose to follow Gollaher and Craig's (1994) advice to send a letter, post card, or e-mail advising your selected internships that you plan to apply and asking them to open a file for materials that will soon be arriving. If you do so, make sure you put your complete name, Social Security number, and NMS match number on the card, especially if you have a relatively common name such as "Jim Smith" or have had a recent name change that might not be reflected in your transcript.

Although there is some sentiment within APPIC to adopt a uniform application date, different training centers currently have different due dates, ranging from late October until early February. If you are pressed for time, prepare those with the earliest due dates first, submitting each application as soon as it is ready. However, since most of your references will send the same basic letter to all your sites, it is best to give them your complete list all at once so they can mass-produce their letters.

## ☐ Deciding Where to Apply

You have now arrived at the second "moment of truth." The first moment of truth was when you decided that you are actually going to apply for an internship this year. The second is when you decide where you are going to apply and how many applications you will submit. As I indicated earlier, your application list should include settings that range in competitiveness. By all means apply to those places you are really enthusiastic about,

**116** Megargee's Guide to Obtaining a Psychology Internship

but if they are very competitive, also apply to some other places that are less popular. Your final selection should include facilities that range from being highly competitive to relatively noncompetitive. However, every site on your list should be one that you would be willing to attend based on the information you have collected thus far.

While you are deciding on the internships that should be on your final list, identify some others for what I call your "lifeboat list." These are programs with late due dates that you would be willing to attend but which do not appeal to you as much as the ones on your "A" list. As the name implies, the lifeboat list is for emergencies. You use your lifeboat list if something goes wrong midway through the application process. This is the backup list you turn to if some disaster strikes. One of my students actually had his primary sites shut down by an earthquake. A more likely scenario is that you haven't gotten enough interviews or you have been informed by some of your choices that you are no longer under consideration. If you have a lifeboat list you can quickly submit some additional applications to settings with late deadlines. (Of course, if APPIC does adopt a uniform application date, this strategy will no longer be possible.)

Internships that have separate programs such as child, substance abuse, or gerontology, may separate the applications for their different tracks and review them independently. If so, your application must make it clear which program or programs you are applying for. Although other internships may not have track-specific selection, they may need to ensure that all their major rotations are covered. The interests expressed by the applicants may be an important selection criterion. Thus, you should be sure your preferences are clearly indicated.

Do not make frivolous applications. This is no time to indulge in ego trips. Do not apply to famous places you have no intention of attending simply to see if you can get interviews. You may interfere with the chances of other students who are seriously considering the site in question. Also, do not apply to nearby facilities "for practice" so you can use them to hone your interviewing skills even though you have no plans to attend. This will give all applicants from your institution a bad name and may interfere with the chances of your fellow students who must stay in the area and who may be very interested in those sites. The bottom line is: Do not apply to any place you are not willing to attend. It wastes your time and the internship's, and in my opinion it is dishonest.

Survey data consistently show that the students who fail to obtain matches are often those who submitted only a few applications in a geographically circumscribed locale (Clay, 1997; Thorne, 1997; Keilin et al., 2000). An APPIC survey of participants in the 1999 match showed:

> A total of 29.3% of applicants reported that they had applied only to internships within a single geographic area, defined for the study as all sites being located within 200 miles (322 km) of each other. These applicants

reported applying to significantly ($p < .001$) fewer slots ($M = 9.4$) than did applicants who were not so geographically restricted ($M = 15.8$) and were matched at a significantly lower rate (79.6% vs. 90.0%), $p < .01$. (Keilin et al., 2000, p. 291)

There are good reasons why geographically circumscribed searches are less successful. Matching your experience and qualifications with different internships' preferences is difficult. If you apply within a limited area, especially one with relatively few programs, it is unlikely that you will find as many programs that fit well with your goals and talents as you would if you conducted a broader search. If you do not fit as well with a program as the other applicants, you will probably be ranked lower.

If you come from a large program with many applicants, you may also find yourself competing with other students from your program if you limit yourself to settings within a day's drive of your university. Since most internships seek variety in each class of trainees, you are further handicapping yourself if you adopt this strategy.

Whether or not your program requires it, you should try to coordinate your applications with those of your fellow applicants. Some internships resent getting too many applications from the same school (Belar & Orgel, 1980). One ITD told me she had received a carton containing two dozen applications from a single professional school. Apparently, identical cartons had been sent to a number of major training centers, with no attempt to match the individual applications to the resources of the facilities. The ITD sent the carton back by return mail with instructions for the ADCT to select and submit the best application for her internship.

There is nothing wrong with several people from a single university applying to the same internship. It is not uncommon for some internships to accept two candidates from the same program, although most would balk at three. Moreover, after interviewing, it is likely that each of you will end up with a different first choice. Still, other things being equal, you stand a better chance at settings where you are not competing with other students from your training program.

## How Many Applications Should You Submit?

Plan to submit a reasonable, but not an excessive, number of applications. There is no point submitting more applications than you can manage. If you submit two or three dozen applications, you will probably do your chances more harm than good, as well as adding to your expenses. You can't interview well at that many sites or negotiate effectively with that many ITDs. This is confirmed by a recent APPIC survey that showed a lower match rate among students who submitted 25 or more applications.

Well, then, how many applications should you prepare and submit?

**118**    Megargee's Guide to Obtaining a Psychology Internship

The number varies with the competitiveness of the internships to which you are applying, the reputation of your training program, the number of your fellow students applying to the same internships, the impressiveness of your credentials, and whether you are applying in tandem with someone else.

Perhaps you are enrolled in one of the "less preferred" training programs discussed in Chapter 4, such as a Counseling Psychology program that is not APA accredited. If so, you will need to submit more applications than someone from a more preferred program, and you will have to target them to centers that are more receptive to Counseling Psychology applicants. If you are an average student, you should apply to more places than if you are the class superstar, especially if you are applying to the same places as the superstar.

Hugely popular internships that receive hundreds of applications are always risky, no matter how strong a candidate's credentials. I never sleep well when my students apply to such programs, even though we have a good record with some. If one or more of these programs is at the top of your list, you should back them up with some smaller or less competitive settings. You usually will have a better chance applying to training centers with which your university has strong traditional ties than one that has never before taken a student from your school. Within internships, child and psychotherapy tracks seem to draw more applications than rotations such as chemical dependency or gerontology.

"Personal baggage" is another important consideration. Given the shortfall in the number of positions relative to the number of applicants, internships are enjoying a seller's market. They can afford to be more selective without worrying that they may not fill all their positions. If they prefer energetic young bachelors who will work 12 hours a day, 6 or 7 days a week, they can pass over older applicants and those who have family obligations. If ITDs do not wish to risk offending their clients, they might not rank applicants who appear controversial, people like the recent applicant who was told he had failed to match for the second time because he came across as being "too San Francisco."[15] If you have personal baggage because of your family situation, gender orientation, health, legal status, or other factors, you will probably need to submit more applications to a broader range of internships to find a good match than will someone who is not similarly encumbered.

In deciding how many applications to submit, be prepared to delete a couple of possibilities after you visit, because you will probably find one

---

[15]"Too San Francisco" referred to the fact that this applicant was an openly gay Jewish man who sported nose and ear rings, tattoos, and a pony tail. That might have been OK if his personal essay had not been devoted to an account of his political activism on behalf of "LGBTQ" and Zionist causes in the various clinical settings where he had worked. Nevertheless, he eventually matched.

Preparing Your Internship Applications **119**

or more of them unattractive or even unacceptable for some reason. For example, one of our students, who had obviously not done his homework very well, submitted an application to a VA hospital that did not even have a psychology internship training program! If circumstances will prevent you from interviewing in person, submit more applications than you would otherwise. Even though they may say telephone interviews are acceptable, most programs favor candidates they have actually seen. As noted above, you should apply to some less competitive as well as some more competitive internships, and it is a good idea to have a lifeboat list tucked away in case it suddenly becomes necessary to submit some additional applications at the last minute.

In terms of actual numbers, I have had students who submitted only one application and others who submitted as many as 26. Your goal should be to have about 10 viable choices after you have completed your interviews, so I recommend submitting 13 +/- 2 applications, a number that is close to the estimated national average (APPIC, 1999b). This is two more than I recommended in the first edition of this book, because it seems to me that the competition is getting tougher. However, an intern participating in a symposium at the 1989 APA Convention stated that she had been one of 40 students applying from a free-standing Psy.D. program and that she and her classmates had averaged 22 applications each! This is more than the number I recommend, but we have far fewer students applying each year, and our program is one of those that is considered "preferred" since it is a traditional university-based APA-approved Ph.D. program in Clinical Psychology. The APA Graduate Student Association's Internship Task Force recommends that you apply to no more than 20 programs (Lopez & Draper, 1997). Ultimately, you must decide what is the best number for *you* to submit; for many applicants, deadlines and fatigue are the final determinants.

## ☐ Completing the Paperwork

There is an unbelievable amount of paperwork involved in filling out internship applications. You have already taken care of getting transcripts sent, and you have prepared and duplicated your resume. Now the real paperwork begins.

### AAPIC Application for a Psychology Internship

Although they are not required to do so, the vast majority of the APPIC internships have adopted the uniform AAPI form. The good news is that this makes applying simpler than it was when each site had its own unique

**120**   Megargee's Guide to Obtaining a Psychology Internship

form. The bad news is that the AAPI is longer and more complicated than many of the pre-AAPI application forms were.

The current AAPI is a synthesis and integration of a number of forms that were in use in the mid-1990s. An APPIC committee collected 81 different application forms being used at various sites around the country and recorded all the questions they asked; the mean number of questions was 41 per application and the range was from 5 to 235 (Holaday & McPherson, 1996). After eliminating redundancies and overlap, they developed a 72-question prototype that went through three revisions before it was sent to a sample of 100 ITDs for review and comments. The final draft of that first AAPI had 47 questions and 8 requirements. Each year, as problems are identified or questions arise, modifications are made in the hope of improving the AAPI for applicants and ITDs alike.

When you prepare and submit your AAPI and other application forms, make sure you comply exactly with the instructions on the AAPI and with the procedures specified by each program. Failure to do so will indicate to the Selection Committee that you do not follow directions, and no one wants a trainee who cannot or will not follow directions. Put your name and NMS match numbers on each document and make sure that your materials are prepared carefully and attractively. This paperwork is all the Selection Committee has with which to evaluate you, and it must compete with the 80 other applications the average internship receives. If it is sloppy, unprofessional, or poorly prepared, the committee will assume that you are sloppy, unprofessional, or poorly prepared. If it is late or incomplete, it may not be reviewed at all (Mitchell, 1996).

The AAPI is a detailed but straightforward document with ample instructions. It currently is divided into five sections:

1. Background and educational information
2. Goals and interests
3. Doctoral practicum documentation
4. Test administration
5. Professional conduct

The section on goals and interests should be individually tailored to each internship to which you apply. The others remain constant from one setting to the next.

## Section 1: Background and Educational Information

This section is straightforward. The "background" subsection simply asks who you are and where you can be found.[16] Note that nowhere are you

---

[16]Some applicants have recently expressed concern over the fact that the AAPI uses your Social Security number as an identifier. Technically, a person's Social Security number should be used only by those who need it, such as employers and the IRS. In practice, it is

asked to divulge your age, ethnicity, race, marital status, gender orientation, or family status. If you wish to disclose any of this information, you can do so in your CV or in your cover letter.

The "education" subsection will overlap somewhat with your CV. It asks for details about your postsecondary education, with an emphasis on your current degree program. If you have attended more than one college or university, list them all, along with the relevant information regarding your GPA in your master's and doctoral programs and the degrees you have received. Note that it does not ask you for your GRE scores.

The most important part of the education section is your report of your progress in your doctoral program. Make sure your estimates of completion dates agree with those of your ADCT and major professor.

## Section 2: Goals and Interests

Assuming that you are academically eligible for internship, this is the single most important section of your application. You have four 500-word statements in which you can convince the Internship Selection Committees that they should invite you for an interview.

You should prepare these essays on your own.[17] They are your personal answers and they should reflect what you want to say. Be positive, realistic, and professional. Keep each of your answers within the 500-word limit. Although the current AAPI has four different essays, your goals for internship and what you have to offer the program should drive all your responses. By the time the members of the Internship Selection Committees have read your essays, they should have a good understanding of who you are, the type of training you are seeking, what you will contribute to their program, and how well you fit with their setting.

Later, after you have drafted your essays, ask your "coach" or other people you trust to review them to see if they express what it was you were trying to communicate. One successful applicant wrote, "I was at my best when I simply composed what I believed and what I thought would interest a committee without anyone's advice. Only after this did I ask a few trusted people to read and edit my essays."

---

common for educational institutions to use it as an identifier, and you may well find that it is listed on your transcript. You can refuse to divulge it, but internships are also free to pass over your application. Until NMS match numbers are assigned in time for applicants to use them as identifiers, internships need more than names as identifiers. I remember the chaos that resulted when two unrelated applicants with the same names applied to the same setting. Some of the second applicant's materials got filed in the first applicant's folder, so her application was not reviewed because it appeared incomplete. (Moreover, as one applicant on the APPIC listserv quipped, if someone assumes your identity, they may have to assume all your student loans and credit card debt as well.)

[17]Some readers have suggested that I prepare model personal statements for you. That would, of course, defeat the purpose. ITDs also read this book and they would soon learn to spot a "Megargee-model personal statement" and mark you down for using it.

122 Megargee's Guide to Obtaining a Psychology Internship

In the present version of the AAPI, the first required essay is an auto-biographical statement. This is meant to be a personal statement, not a rehash of your CV. As the directions state, "It is entirely up to you to decide what information you wish to provide along with the format in which to present it." If you want to do it in the form of a sonnet or a one-act play, you can. This essay is the nearest thing to a projective test that you will find on the AAPI. Its content gives the Selection Committee an idea of who you are that goes beyond the more structured questions on the AAPI, and its grammar, spelling, and style give the Committee a chance to evaluate how well you write.

Take the time to think through this question and what you want to communicate. Put yourself in the role of a member of the Selection Committee and ask yourself what you would want to learn about applicants from these essays. Instead of writing in broad generalities, be specific. If you choose to discuss your theoretical orientation, Mitchell (1996) suggested that instead of using a vague label such as "cognitive behavioral," you instead specify what that orientation means to you and how it influences the way you approach a case. Mitchell also advised referring to significant life events that influenced you and your choice of career. One of my students, for example, wrote about how growing up with a developmentally disabled sister guided her choice of research areas. Do not, however, use a personal statement as a confessional. I have read biographical statements that began, "It was only after I accepted the fact that I am an alcoholic and that I had ruined the lives of my family that I realized I had been chosen by God to save others by becoming a clinical psychologist." I am rarely eager to hire such people.

The second question addresses the issue of multicultural diversity. Later in the application you have an opportunity to report how many different types of patients you have seen clinically. In this section, you are to describe your experience in more general terms and reflect on how you incorporate your awareness of diversity issues into your clinical work, including both assessments and treatment approaches. Unlike the previous essay, you can use the same basic diversity statement on all your applications.

The third question in Section 2 concerns your research. Before you paste in a summary of your dissertation proposal, read the question carefully. It asks about your *goals* and *interests*, not for minute details or findings from particular studies.

In describing your research goals, be specific; something more definite than "making the world a better place" is in order. At the same time, remember you are describing the forest, not a specific tree or a leaf thereon. You might begin by discussing the research questions you are posing in your dissertation. Why are they important to you? Then look beyond your dissertation and describe your postdoctoral research agenda. What

Preparing Your Internship Applications **123**

are your long-terms goals? What will it take for you to accomplish them? In the process, you can refer to the previous studies you have already completed.

In discussing your research, keep in mind what each individual setting has to offer. Each Selection Committee reading your essay will be concerned with how well your research objectives match the opportunities available at their specific site. How will an internship in their setting help further your research goals? If an internship affords opportunities for predoctoral or postdoctoral research that relates to your goals and interests, point this out. One of my students, for example, had a strong interest in combat-related PTSD, a condition for which there are relatively few opportunities for research at our university. She applied to VA medical centers which offered her opportunities to pursue this line of research, and, naturally, she discussed this in her answers to this question. She was accepted at a major VA medical center, where she continued to do postdoctoral PTSD research after completing her internship.

The fourth required 500-word statement addresses the issue that is foremost in the Selection Committees' minds when selecting predoctoral interns. "How do you envision our internship site meeting your training goals and interests?" In other words, "How does what our internship has to offer meet your needs and goals?" and "How does what you have to offer us correspond to what we are seeking in a predoctoral intern?"

Your first task in answering this question is to define your training goals and integrate them with the training you have already received. Mitchell (1996, p. 91) noted that "an application is . . . weakened when a candidate fails to identify specific goals for the internship year." Satisfying a degree requirement is not an adequate training goal. Why should Selection Committees bother to interview candidates or rank them high if the candidates themselves appear clueless about the type of training they hope to receive on internship?

Once you have defined your goals, perhaps with the assistance of the list of priorities you previously formulated, you should ask yourself how each individual internship's training program will help you meet them. This means that you should write individualized essays for each and every site to which you apply. You should indicate your understanding of what it is each site has to offer and articulate how these specific attributes mesh with your skills and training needs. Your answer should show that you have done your homework, studied the characteristics of that particular training center, and given careful thought to how the training they offer fits with your particular attributes and needs. Be specific in referring to opportunities at each internship.

These essays may be short, but they are important. Review the internship brochures and the information in the *Directory*. Make notes. Think about your answer and outline the main points you wish to make. Ask

124 Megargee's Guide to Obtaining a Psychology Internship

yourself, "If this were the only site I could go to, what would I like most about it?"

Mitchell (1996) advised that you be honest and resist the temptation to give the internship what you think it wants to hear. She noted, "Selection Committees eye with suspicion the applicant who claims that their training site is perfect given his or her career goals, yet nothing in his or her previous work or practicum experience confirms this stated interest" (p. 91). Or as one of my students less elegantly remarked, "Don't suck up too much." If you take this advice to heart and prepare carefully-thought-out individual essays for each internship site, your application will make a much better impression on the selection staff than those of students who paste the same standard response on to every application.

In addition to the statements required in the AAPI, you may discover that some of the internships to which you plan to apply require other essays in addition to or in place of the standard AAPI application form. Some ask for as many as four additional essays. Frequent topics include:

- Why do you want to attend our internship?[18]
- What do you plan to be doing after you get your degree?
- Please list your short-term and long-term career goals in psychology.
- Describe your interpersonal strengths and weaknesses.
- Describe the clinical strengths you would bring to us.
- Describe the clinical skill areas in which you feel you lack adequate experience and that you should emphasize during internship training.

Applicants have also reported being asked to write a 1500-word autobiographical essay, describe three contributions they will have made to the field of psychology by the year 2020, discuss how their former and present practicum supervisors would have described them, and indicate how they would like their internship supervisors to describe them.

Why the additional essays or questionnaires? In some cases it is simply habit or inertia. The internship has always required these forms or essays, and no one got around to changing the requirements when the AAPI was introduced.

Some programs sincerely want the additional information. Since the AAPI does not ask about your theoretical orientation, some settings might feel it is necessary to have you discuss your theoretical orientation and how it influences your assessments and treatment approaches.

And, finally, some programs deliberately require extremely complicated and time-consuming application forms simply as a test of motivation, a way to screen out anyone who is not a serious applicant.

---

[18]A recent applicant advises checking with the internship when an essay topic, like this one, is similar to one of the required AAPI essays. When she called and inquired, she was told the essay she had written for the AAPI was sufficient.

Remember that essays and personal statements are evaluated on the basis of style and literacy as well as actual content. Writing is an important part of any psychologist's job, and these compositions show raters whether you can write clearly and cogently. Make sure you revise and edit these essays, and check them carefully for grammar, style, and spelling.

After reading dozens of similar responses, reviewers take note when one turns up that has some originality or humor. Late one night, a student who had been preparing applications all day encountered a form that asked him to "list his strengths." He impulsively wrote down, "I have never been arrested," and went on to the next item. After he had mailed the applications, he regretted his flip answer and figured he could write off that placement. To his surprise, when he interviewed, everyone at the agency was eager to meet the one intern applicant with a sense of humor, and he was treated like visiting royalty. (Of course, if you all start using his response, it won't appear original anymore.)

Keep copies of your essays and notes. Set up a folder for each internship and file them in the folder along with other application materials and the internship's brochure or Web site information. Later, when you visit internships, take the folder with you and review these materials before you interview.

## Section 3: Doctoral Practicum Documentation

This is where you document the clinical experience that you have accumulated in practicum and nonpracticum settings. Your ADCT is the ultimate authority on what constitutes practicum hours in your program. In my opinion, a practicum is a clinical placement arranged by your training program where you receive regularly scheduled supervision and where your supervisor makes periodic evaluations of your progress and reports them to your training program. Clinical work in other settings should be reported in the subsection entitled "Other Clinical Experiences."

The AAPI has detailed instructions on how to complete this section. Read the directions carefully, paying special attention to the operational definitions of such terms as "clock hours" and "clients." As I noted earlier, clock hours are the actual amount of time you spent in activities such as (a) actually treating clients, (b) support activities such as chart review, (c) receiving supervision, and (d) other activities such as assessment, teaching, consultation, and outreach services.

With regard to therapy, you must break down the number of clock hours you spent in various types of treatment, such as individual, group, career counseling, family, and couples. Whether you spend an hour with 1 person in individual treatment or with 12 people in group treatment, it is still 1 clock hour. If you have spent a significant amount of time admin-

**126**     Megargee's Guide to Obtaining a Psychology Internship

istering some form of treatment that does not fit neatly into these categories, I suggest that you add this category to the list and define it in a footnote.

The definition of clients also gets tricky. The AAPI makes a distinction between "clients" and "patients" as you move from reporting the *amount* of experience you have had to describing the *nature* of that experience. When you report on the number of clients you treated with various types of interventions, a "client" may be an individual, a couple, a family, or a group. Later, when you are describing the demographic characteristics of the various *patients* you have treated, you count every person, regardless of whether you saw them individually, as part of a family, or in a group. Moreover, if a patient fits more than one category, as, for example, a visually impaired, elderly, gay, Pacific Islander, you can count him more than once. This is why you need to maintain such detailed records.

With regard to supervision, you need to report the number of clock hours you spent receiving (a) regularly scheduled, individual, one-on-one face-to-face supervision of specific cases with a designated supervisor; (b) case-focused group supervision in which one or more fellow students are present; and (c) supervision received from peers and case consultations outside the regular supervisory session. Didactic instruction does not count as supervision. For example, if I am going over an assessment report with a student, and I digress for 15 minutes to tell her about how I derived the MMPI-2 Overcontrolled Hostility (O-H) scale, that 15 minutes of didactic instruction should not be included in the report of the number of clock hours of case-based supervision she received.

As experience with the AAPI grows and more feedback is received from applicants and Selection Committees, this section of the AAPI will continue to evolve, so make sure you have the latest definitions and policies. If you have questions, go to the APPIC Web site and consult the FAQ (Frequently Asked Questions) file. If you do not find the answer there, post an inquiry on the APPIC internship listserv, or send an e-mail inquiry to the APPIC official who is monitoring the application process that year. Don't be surprised if you get different answers from different authorities.

After you have read the instructions and clarified any questions, begin by cleaning up your database. Go through your daily log to see if all your various activities have been transferred into your spreadsheet or data retrieval system. If not, do so now. Next check your spreadsheet and make sure the information therein is complete. Does each entry indicate the type of setting and whether it was a practicum or nonpracticum position? Is it clear whether each hour was devoted to therapy, support activities, supervision, or some other specified clinical activity? Can you identify which cases were for treatment and which for assessment? Are the eth-

Preparing Your Internship Applications **127**

nic, demographic, and diagnostic characteristics of the various people you have seen recorded? Once your database has been cleaned up and edited, you can begin the sorts and data retrievals you need to respond to the questions in Section 3.

By the time you are applying to internship, you will probably have acquired additional clinical experience in paid placements or other non-practicum settings. Collate all this information separately from the practicum data and report it in the section titled "Other Clinical Experiences." You are free to organize this section any way you like. If you are in a traditional clinical training program, I suggest that you use the same categories you employed for the practicum data. Simply copy the subheadings and paste them into the "Other" section. If you are in a school or counseling program, you may find that the AAPI categories do not adequately reflect the nature of your experience. If that is the case, you may choose to use a different scheme. The important thing to remember is that the purpose of the AAPI is to help you describe the nature and the extent of your professional training.

## Section 4: Test Administration

An earlier version of the AAPI listed no less than 47 different tests and asked applicants to report their experience with each. The current AAPI lists 10 adult and 7 children's tests and asks (a) how many of each you have administered and scored and (b) how many you have interpreted and written reports on. Practice administrations do not count, nor do tests you may have been given to score or interpret as class assignments. In addition, it asks how many "carefully supervised integrated psychological reports" involving at least three sources of data you have written regarding (a) adult clients and (b) children and/or adolescents. Note that in this section you are not restricted to instruments administered in practicum settings.

After you have reported on your experience with the listed tests, you can add other assessment instruments to the list. Even though they are technically not "tests," I would also include clinical interviews, both structured and unstructured.

Don't overlook the heading, "Integrated Report Writing." The ITDs interviewed by Stedman et al. (2000) emphasized the importance they place on the number of supervised integrated psychological reports you have prepared, and most reported that few applicants had sufficient experience writing integrated test-based reports (Stedman et al., in press, under review). Instead of just recording numbers, I suggest you prepare a paragraph describing your experience administering and interpreting test batteries in various settings.

**128**    Megargee's Guide to Obtaining a Psychology Internship

## Section 5: Professional Conduct

The final section of the AAPI requires you to report any ethical complaints or disciplinary actions that have been filed against you. You are also asked to report whether you have ever been convicted of any crimes other than minor traffic violations.

If you answer "yes" to any of these questions, you are asked to attach an explanation regarding the circumstances. You should do so. As a general rule in such matters, covering up has worse consequences than acknowledging such difficulties and explaining what happened. Making false statements on an application form is itself a criminal offense in most jurisdictions, and the statement you must sign at the end of the AAPI gives the agency broad powers to investigate you and your behavior and to dismiss you without incurring any liability if they decide that you concealed or misrepresented any salient facts.

## Verification of Internship Eligibility and Readiness Form

As I noted earlier, this form is to be completed by your ADCT and filed separately from your applications. Even if a training program does not specifically request the verification form, you are expected to file one. You fill out the first section and take the form to your ADCT, who completes the form, signs it, and, usually, includes it with your letter of recommendation. Again, allow plenty of time. Do not expect your ADCT to sign off on this form the day before it is due at the internship.

The first question requires your ADCT to certify that when you submit your internship rankings to NMS you will have completed all the departmental requirements for going on internship; that is, that you have no outstanding coursework, exams, or other requirements that could prevent you from attending the program with which you are matched. This certification is essential. All the ITDs I have talked to agree that if there are any outstanding requirements that could conceivably prevent you from going on internship, it is unlikely you will be matched. Indeed, if your ADCT does not regard you as ready, your application may never get reviewed.

Your ADCT is also asked to report whether you are in good standing with your program, whether any ethical or other complaints have been filed against you, how far along you are in your degree program, how many clock hours of practicum you have completed, and how they were allocated with regard to therapy, support, additional experience, and supervision. All this information should agree with what you report in your AAPI. If it does not, you need to clear up any discrepancies before the AAPI and eligibility form are filed.

Next, your ADCT must indicate where you stand with regard to completing your degree requirements, including your dissertation. This will no doubt be done in conjunction with your major professor. The further along you are, the more favorably your application will be considered. No internship wants to risk training an "ABD" who never completes the dissertation requirement, and many, perhaps most, prefer interns who have completed their dissertations.

The last part of the eligibility and readiness form consists of 5 Likert-type scales on which your ADCT evaluates your personal and professional readiness for internship. If you do not get a strong positive evaluation on all 5, it sends a strong warning to the internship that is likely to doom your candidacy. This is why it is essential that you obtain your ADCT's support before applying.

## Letters of Recommendation

Opinions vary on the importance of letters. Surveys of ITD decision making consistently rank letters as being among the most important criteria (Lopez, Oehlert & Moberly, 1996; Stedman et al., 1981), but others maintain they are of little value (May, Rice, & Birckhead, 1990). Most letters are overwhelmingly positive, prompting some writers to ask whatever happened to the lower 90% of the student population (May et al., 1990; Miller & Van Rybroek, 1988). May, Rice, and Birckhead (1990, p. 39) concluded, "training directors will only see letters as informative if they 'damn with faint praise.' Letters are apparently used more often to lower an applicant's ranking than as a general discrimination factor," and a recent survey by Lonigan (1994) confirmed that negative letters are weighted heavily.

In my opinion, the more work that goes into preparing a letter of recommendation, the more likely it is to contribute to the decision-making process. I spend a great deal of time on composing each letter. I begin by reviewing the student's transcript, CV, academic folder, and my notes of my interviews with the applicant regarding internship. I read all the letters of recommendation sent by undergraduate mentors prior to admission to our program, and the quarterly ratings made by clinical supervisors, noting quotations I can use in my letter.

I then integrate all this information into a three- or four-page summary of the candidate's individual characteristics. This is descriptive rather than evaluative, although I do my best to put things in a positive light. For example, if a candidate has been in the program for a decade or two, I emphasize his maturity and experience, whereas one who is applying early and has relatively few hours is praised for her youthful energy and drive. If there are deficits, I acknowledge them and try to explain what the problem was. ITDs can forgive candidates for some bad grades if they know they were ill or going through a divorce at the time and the prob-

**130**     Megargee's Guide to Obtaining a Psychology Internship

lem is now resolved. Whenever possible, I try to include concrete behavioral examples to illustrate points made in my evaluation. ITDs often report that they find these individualized letters to be helpful in evaluating candidates, especially when they are attempting to compare several applicants from our program. Since our candidates appear to do pretty well, these frank appraisals evidently do not hurt their chances, perhaps because the information is accurate and placed in context.

## Whom to Solicit for Letters

You should submit at least three letters of recommendation. One should be from your major professor, one or more should be from current or recent clinical supervisors, and one must be from your ADCT. Only solicit letters from people with appropriate professional credentials who are in a position to evaluate your skills as a psychologist and who will write you a strong letter. Character references from clergy or civic leaders have no place in an internship application. Before listing anyone as a reference, make sure you ask his or her permission. If someone does not feel comfortable in recommending you, or is going to be away when the letters are due, it is better to find out early and obtain other references. I suggest that you meet with potential letter writers to discuss your goals and accomplishments. Provide each with a copy of your CV and a complete list of addresses, due dates, and instructions on how the letters are to be prepared. Some settings want references sent directly to the internship program, while others prefer that recommenders seal their letters in envelopes, sign the back, and give them to you so they can be included along with your AAPI, CV, and other materials in one big packet. Allow plenty of time and give your recommenders a due date at least a week in advance of the internship's deadline.[19] Just like you, faculty members and supervisors often leave such chores until the last minute.

Your major professor's letter should focus on your academic qualifications and research. In addition to all the other good things about you that your major professor discusses, there must be a statement that you will definitely finish your dissertation and obtain your doctoral degree in the foreseeable future. No one wants an intern who will be an "ABD."

The second letter should be from someone who is familiar with your clinical work and who has supervised you recently rather than in the distant past. If you have had recent experience in a couple of different settings, or if one person supervises your assessments and another your therapy, it is a good idea to have letters from both. Similarly, if you have

---

[19]Although you may use an overnight mail service such as Federal Express, you should not expect the people writing your letters to incur this added expense, especially when you may be only one of several people for whom they are preparing letters of recommendation.

had specialized training in some area such as neuropsychological assessment, a letter from a supervisor describing your competence in this area is helpful.

It used to be necessary that the third letter came from the ADCT. This letter constituted the program's formal endorsement of your application and it certified that you are in good standing academically and clinically prepared for internship. This is now accomplished by the verification form signed by the ADCT, so you can have someone else prepare the third letter if you choose. However, I still recommend your ADCT unless he or she has little knowledge of your qualifications.

## *Other Letters*

Opinions vary on whether you should submit more than the required number of letters. I feel that it is better to have too many letters than too few. In addition to the three "must" letters, it is wise to solicit a fourth "wild card" letter as well, preferably from a clinical supervisor who thinks you are terrific. This letter can help balance a perfunctory ADCT letter or one from someone who for some reason "damns you with faint praise." It can also fill in if one of the others is late arriving. Some programs may not evaluate any folders until there are at least three letters; your "wild card" letter will allow it to go forward without delay.

You may be applying to some places where someone on your faculty has a "special relationship" with someone. Perhaps they were colleagues some place, or maybe one of your faculty members was the ITD's major professor. If so, it may help to have that faculty member write or call his or her friend on your behalf. Check first with your ADCT, and do not ask a faculty member to make a special appeal on your behalf unless you are very interested in that setting. If, after such a call, you do not rank that internship, it will be embarrassing for both your faculty member and his or her friend.

## Work Samples

Unless you are required to submit a clinical work sample, I would not do so. A clinician can always find something to criticize in someone else's work sample. If there is a perceived flaw, you will get marked down. If it is flawless, they will assume your supervisor is responsible. Either way, it is a no-win situation. Many ITDs agree that work samples may do you more harm than good.

If you are asked for a work sample, try to ascertain if it is *required*. If it is not, you are probably better off without it. I was surprised to learn from one ITD whose hospital supposedly requires a work sample that appli-

**132**   Megargee's Guide to Obtaining a Psychology Internship

cants who do not submit one are not penalized. In fact, he noted, it seemed to work the other way—the students who *did* submit work samples tended to draw more negative ratings from faculty because the clinical faculty had something concrete to criticize! I have raised this issue with other directors and they concur.

If a work sample is definitely required, by all means prepare one. Many settings will not review an "incomplete" application. Use a case that you actually saw and for which you personally administered, scored, and interpreted the tests. One of my students sent samples from two different settings, explaining to the internship that they represent the approaches and styles of different supervisors and placements. She maintained that this demonstrated her flexibility and responsiveness to supervision.

A request for a work sample can raise ethical issues regarding confidentiality and informed consent. Obviously all materials must be disguised to protect the client's identity. This means changing not only the client's name, but also other identifiers such as birth date, case number, and the names of the clinic and the supervisor. You should also get the client's permission to share these materials with a third party. Some students request permission from clients they worked with previously. In the case of assessments, a safer course of action is to perform an evaluation expressly for your application, using a legally competent volunteer who has had the purpose of the assessment explained, given informed consent, and signed a release that will allow you to share the data and the report, suitably disguised, with internship selection personnel. Not only will this permit you to select a battery that will best highlight your skills, but it should also enable you to avoid some of the ethical difficulties associated with seeking an after-the-fact release from a client you have previously evaluated.

If you do submit a work sample, attach an explanation of why you chose this particular work sample, the circumstances under which it was obtained, and what it illustrates about your work.

## Cover Letters

Although no agency will list this as a requirement, by all means include a one-page cover letter. This cover letter will be the first thing the reviewers read, and it is vital to making a good first impression. The cover letter gives you a chance to emphasize the points you are trying to make in your resume and personal statement. Indicate who you are, what position you are applying for, what is included in your application, whose letters of reference they can expect to receive, and, in a couple of sentences, why you are applying to this particular program and why they should select *you*. This is one sure way to make your application stand out

Preparing Your Internship Applications **133**

from all the rest, especially since many of your competitors won't bother to send *any* cover letter. If a setting requests a "statement of interest," you can incorporate this into your cover letter, in which case it will be somewhat longer.

It is much easier to submit the same cover letter and personal statement to all your internships. It is also less effective. Adapt your cover letters and personal statements to each individual internship, indicating the specific people and programs that attract you and why you feel there is a good match between your abilities and needs and what the program offers. Of course, it requires a lot more work to individualize your applications, but everyone wants a hardworking intern.

Remember, most Selection Committees are faced with the task of selecting a small number of outstanding and congenial people from a large number of applicants, most of whom are qualified. Unless an application catches their attention from the start, there is little incentive to wade through it all or to invite the applicant for an interview. Raters are most likely to notice applicants who have done their homework and whose letters and personal statements show that they are familiar with the program and how it meshes with their qualifications. Many internships will decide who to interview based only on your application materials. If you don't make the cut, you don't get invited for an interview.

### Unrequested Materials

Determine each internship's policy about submitting unrequested materials such as reprints, prospectuses, or copies of term papers. If you have a published reprint, I would definitely include it, but I would hesitate at a typewritten preprint that makes the folder bulky, and I would not include academic papers unless specifically told to do so.

## ☐ Submitting Your Applications

Finally, you have all your application materials completed. For each application you should have an individualized cover letter, a copy of your CV, completed application forms, personal statements or essays, work samples if required, and any other material you are submitting such as reprints. You may also have sealed letters of recommendation and any additional forms or questionnaires that the various internships may require. Make copies of everything and file the copies in a separate folder for each internship, along with the internship's brochure. Plan on taking the folder along with you to internship interviews so you can review what you said the night before your interview.

**134**    Megargee's Guide to Obtaining a Psychology Internship

Next, assemble each individual application. Make sure that each is complete and correct, accurate and attractive. Make certain that you have the right materials in each application and that each document has your name on it. If you have prepared individualized cover letters, essays, and personal statements, as I have advised, make sure they are going to the correct place. It will not help your cause if the extremely behavioral internship gets the letter in which you express your interest in dynamic psychology and learning more about Rorschach interpretation, while the analytic institute receives the statement indicating you hope to become a radical behaviorist. Similarly, double-check your addresses and make sure the name of the training director matches the internship, and the address on the envelope matches the one inside. Finally, don't forget to sign the letters and the AAPI.

While it is important that you include everything and address them correctly, do not get obsessive. One year a fierce debate broke out on the APPIC internship listserv board over whether applicants should staple or clip their materials together. Some advocated binding them, while others sarcastically suggested gluing, clipping, stapling, and binding everything. After dozens of exchanges, reason finally prevailed; several APPIC Board members posted messages swearing that it really did not make any difference and the Great Paper Clip Debate finally ended.

## Deadlines and Due Dates

It is important that you submit your application by the date the internship stipulates. Sometimes you will find different due dates in the program's *Directory* listing, their brochure, and their Web site. To be on the safe side, be guided by the earliest date. If your packet is complete except for one of your letter writers, send it in with a note that you will send Prof. Tortoise's letter along later. Don't hold up the whole packet on the basis of one missing item. As Mitchell (1996) wrote:

> Given that 60 or 70 equally qualified candidates may be vying for four intern slots, applications that are incomplete or that are not completed until after the deadline may not be considered at all. . . . [W]hen these parts of the application [that the applicant has control over] are not sent in a timely manner, it conveys disorganization, lack of follow-through, or a lack of serious interest in the internship site. (p. 90)

Some applicants inquire as to whether a deadline means it should be sent by the specified date or received by the internship on that date. Since we are dealing with internship applications and not absentee election ballots mailed from overseas, there are no uniform rules specifying what a deadline means. There is no APPIC police forcing internships to review all the applications submitted by the deadline or prohibiting them from

Preparing Your Internship Applications **135**

considering those that arrive later. The internships individually set their deadlines, and they can follow them or not as they see fit.

My advice is to submit your applications as soon as you can for three reasons:

1. If you send your application in early, you do not have to worry about missing the deadline and you can save yourself the expense of overnight courier service.
2. Some internships are currently advising applicants that if they want to interview, they should submit their application *before* the deadline.
3. I have found that there is a primacy effect when I review applications. When I have over 100 application folders to evaluate, I have found I do a much more thorough job on the first 25 or so. By the time I have read 50 or more, my motivation has diminished and it is harder to impress me.

## Submitting Your Applications

If you plan to post your applications, take them personally to the Post Office, have them weighed, put on the correct postage, and send them off using Priority Mail at least a week before the deadline. If you have a phobia about using "snail mail," use a private overnight carrier such as Federal Express. The Postal Service's overnight mail service too often takes longer than overnight.

Some settings permit you to file applications by fax or as e-mail attachments. If you choose to do so, I recommend following up with hard copy by post or overnight carrier. I feel that hard copy on good-quality bond paper makes a better impression. Moreover, electronic letters sometimes get lost in cyberspace; I recall one November when a late-season hurricane left us without power for 8 days. We had no faxes, no e-mail, and fallen trees blocked the road to the Post Office. I was glad my recommendation letters were all in the mail.

If all has gone according to schedule, you should have all your applications submitted by the middle of November. For the next couple of weeks, there is not much to do on the internship front. Use the time to catch up on your academic work and get reacquainted with your friends and family. Take a few days off for rest and relaxation. Get some exercise. And don't forget that flu shot.[20]

---

[20]After you have mailed off all your applications, you may find that you made a typographical error on something. Some students panic and send corrections to all their internships. In my opinion, this just calls attention to the glitch and adds to the internship's workload. I would only send out a correction if the error involves vital information such as your phone number.

**136**    Megargee's Guide to Obtaining a Psychology Internship

# ☐ Following Up

It is *your* responsibility to ascertain that your application has been received by the internship facility and is complete. (Some programs will request that you include a stamped, self-addressed postcard for this purpose.) After a reasonable time has passed to allow the applications to be logged in and filed, check to make sure your application is complete and that all your letters of recommendation have been received.

Don't get annoyed if the internship staff is not able to give you an immediate answer as to whether or not some vital document has been received. APPIC recently estimated that overall, approximately 44,000 applications were submitted. If each application involves at least seven documents (cover letter, transcript, application form, CV, and three letters), that means that well over 300,000 documents have to be logged into databases and filed during a 2-month period that includes the Thanksgiving, Christmas, and Chanukah holidays. Moreover, you are not the only person calling. This is why so many ITDs and their staffs get so hassled every winter. If they can't find something right away, don't get hysterical. If you make yourself truly obnoxious to the harried clerical staff, someone may make sure that your folder really does get lost and that it stays lost. It is one way to make sure you won't be bothering them all next year.

When you get an answer, if your folders are complete, tell them that you hope to interview and start working on your travel plans. If you are told your folder is incomplete, don't panic. Perhaps the training center has misfiled something. This is especially likely if you have recently changed your name. Your academic transcript will probably have your former name, while you are using your new name. If you use a hyphenated name, such as "Eggs-Benedict," have them look under "B" as well as "E." Similarly, if you have an Hispanic name such as "Guillermo Huevos Rancheros" and you go by "Huevos," see if some material has been filed under "Rancheros." An Asiatic name such as "Egg Foo Young" could lead to materials being filed under "E," "F," or "Y" depending on how knowledgeable the clerk is with regard to Eastern customs. Finally, if you have a fairly common name, such as "Jim Smith," it is possible that more than one person with your name has applied, and some of your material may be in the other person's folder. You may be glad that they asked you for your Social Security number.

Assuming the missing material cannot be located, take steps to resubmit it. You should have copies of all the material you submitted. If a letter is missing, find out if it was ever written or mailed; if so, have a duplicate copy faxed. If not, get on the party's case.

You may be told that it is too late and that nothing more will be accepted. Send it anyway, then ask your ADCT to call the ITD or, failing that, call the ITD yourself. Messages like this are usually the result of overzealousness or misunderstanding on the part of a lower echelon clerical person. ITDs, on the other hand, do not wish to offend any university training programs unnecessarily. If even this does not work, thank the powers that be that you have discovered how rigid and autocratic that place is. You certainly would not have enjoyed interning there! Remember, you agreed back in the beginning of this book that no internship is worth pursuing as if it were the Holy Grail. Moreover, you have just saved yourself some travel money. To save more, proceed to the next chapter.

# 7
CHAPTER

# Traveling to Internships:
# How to Survive and Stay Solvent

Your next step is visiting the internships to which you have applied and interviewing. I am a firm believer in the importance of the on-site interview. Although it may not be required, I feel it greatly enhances your chances of being accepted. Moreover, interviewing in person affords you an opportunity to evaluate a setting and its personnel before deciding if you want to spend a year of your life training there. Chapter 8 deals with all aspects of the interview process. This chapter focuses on travel; if you cannot afford the trip or if you get stranded en route to the internship, all the interview skills you have acquired will be wasted.

Travel is the biggest single expense associated with applying for internships. It can also be a major hassle. The purpose of this chapter is to help you save time and money traveling to internship sites and to maximize your chances of actually getting to your intended destination on or about the time you planned, with your luggage in your possession and with your health and your temper intact. This, despite the fact that you will be traveling at the worst time of the year from the standpoint of airfares, weather, and crowds.

Researching this book, I traveled to internships all over the country . . . from Miami to Boston to Seattle to Los Angeles and points in between. In the process, I learned a great deal about traveling to internships, mostly the hard way. Based on this experience, in this chapter I will offer a great deal of advice about traveling to internships. Unfortunately, this will also make me sound like your mother. However, if you want to save money, avoid hassles, and stay healthy on the road, heat up a cup of chicken soup, find a comfortable chair, and get out your highlighter.

# ☐ Join the Club(s)

If you don't already belong, join the frequent traveler programs of the airlines you are likely to be using, the AAA automobile club, the "preferred renter programs" of the major automobile rental companies, and the "honored guest" programs of the major hotel chains. The AAA charges an annual fee; most of the others are free.

## Airlines

The main purpose of the airlines' frequent traveler programs is to build customer loyalty by reinforcing you for flying with them. The more you fly, the more "frequent traveler miles" you earn; these "miles" can later be redeemed for upgrades or free travel.

The basic mileage credits are just the beginning. Promotions occur that will award you double or triple mileage if you travel through certain cities, fly at certain times, stay at certain hotels, or pay for your travel with certain credit cards. In addition to rewarding you with free travel coupons after you accumulate enough miles, the frequent traveler programs also entitle you to reduced rates or upgrades at cooperating hotels and car rental agencies. Their on-line bulletins and monthly publications also announce special discounts and bargains that might help you save money. So, if you are traveling by air, you might as well take advantage of the freebies. The mileage credits I accumulated while researching this book helped me obtain free round-trip tickets to London for my entire family, including our five grown children.

## Automobiles

The AAA automobile clubs do more than provide emergency road service. They will give you free tour books listing selected hotels and motels and their rates in the places you will visit. They will also supply you with free state and city maps that will help you find your way from the airport to the training center. A AAA card entitles you to discounts at major car rental agencies and many hotels. They also provide travelers' checks free of surcharge. Each year, APPIC , too, negotiates discounts with one or more car rental companies. The APPIC Web site will tell you what discounts are available the year you apply.

**140** Megargee's Guide to Obtaining a Psychology Internship

The major car rental firms such as Avis and Hertz have preferred renter "club" cards. There is no charge for joining; you simply fill out an application with credit information and a profile of your preferences in automobiles, insurance coverage, and the like. You have a special toll free "800" number to call for reservations, and you no longer have to wait in line to fill out a lengthy rental agreement at the airport. When you arrive, your car should be waiting for you with the paperwork completed. Although you do not accumulate "miles" the way you do with airlines, from time to time you will receive coupons that entitle you to an upgrade or some special package.

## Hotels and Motels

Most hotel and motel chains also have their own travel clubs. Some charge an annual fee and others assess a one-time initiation fee, but most are free. If it is free, sign up. If there is a fee, it probably is not worth the price.

Compared with the airlines' programs, the hotel and motel preferred guest programs take considerable time (and expense) before you build up enough credits to qualify for an award such as a free weekend. Their main value is that they typically entitle you to certain perks such as an "800" number for improved reservation service, a special check-in line, discounts, a free breakfast, a room upgrade, or a morning paper.

## ☐ Saving Money on Air Travel

Air travel costs can vary wildly. If you ask five people sitting in the coach section of a plane what they paid for their flight, you are likely to get five different answers. The overhead involved in air travel—salaries, gate rentals, insurance, aircraft, advertising—is so high that once the airline gets a plane in the air, the distance it flies is a negligible aspect of the total cost. APPIC typically negotiates discounts for applicants flying to and from interviews. Before you start seeking a flight, access the APPIC Web site and see what they have arranged.

Airfares are driven by the need for the airlines to fill as many seats as possible over the entire system. Full or empty, they have to maintain their schedules, so they offer discounts to fill the empty seats on the less popular flights, while charging the highest fares possible on the heavily subscribed routes. This leads to some strange paradoxes. Gavzer (1992) reported that on one flight from San Francisco to Dallas, a very popular route, the fare was $360, but a flight from San Francisco to Kansas City, changing planes in Dallas, was only $195. If you booked the Kansas City flight and got off at Dallas, you could save $165. Or you may discover that

Traveling to Internships: How to Survive and Stay Solvent **141**

the whole is greater than the sum of its parts. Gavzer also reported that when a direct full-fare ticket from Los Angeles to Dallas cost $330, by taking the cheapest available flights from LA to Albuquerque ($95) and from Albuquerque to Dallas ($92), you could make the trip for $187, thus saving $143.

So how do you find these travel bargains? Travel agents can save you a great deal of time and effort, but they may not save you much money. They work on a commission, and the more time they spend saving you money, the less they earn. A good agent who values your repeat business and enjoys finding you a bargain can work with you to take full advantage of differential fares and discount rates, but do not expect that every agent will automatically give you that level of service.

If you call the airlines yourself, using your toll-free frequent traveler number, do not assume that the price you are being quoted is definitive, or even correct. Not only do different airlines have different rates subject to different restrictions, but booking agents differ in their knowledge of the system and their willingness to ferret out bargains. Each flight has only a limited number of discounted seats available, and, of course, full-fare passengers have first priority for any available seats, so the availability of bargain fares varies. You may be told on Monday that a low fare is unavailable, but if you book at a higher rate, don't expect anyone to notify you if there is a cancellation on Wednesday and the lower rate you initially requested becomes available.

Booking agents can make mistakes computing fares. A newspaper did a study in which they called agents and general managers at several different airlines inquiring about the cost of certain flights. They reported that the rates quoted differed substantially, not only among carriers, but also among agents computing fares for a particular flight. In short, if you do not like the rate you are being quoted, hang up and try again later. You may get quoted a lower price. If so, take it. Once you have made your reservation, your fare is locked in, even if the booking agent made a mistake.

If you choose to book by phone, you will often do better if you call after regular business hours. During the day, the airlines' booking agents are very busy. Their calls are monitored, and they are evaluated by how many calls they can handle in an hour. That is why you typically have to wait "on hold" until an agent is available. In the wee hours of the morning, however, there is little traffic, and the bored agents can spend much more time working with you. My wife and I have obtained some incredible travel bargains, such as $198 for a round trip from Miami to London, during these conversations at 2:00 or 3:00 a.m.

A third alternative is to use your computer to seek out the best fares and book your flights. It is not uncommon for airlines to post special discounted fares on their Web sites that are not available elsewhere. Web

142 Megargee's Guide to Obtaining a Psychology Internship

sites and "dot com" companies come and go, but there will probably be sites which will allow you to compare the prices offered by all the airlines flying the route you specify. Some current sites allow you to specify a price and see if a carrier will accept it. Obviously, the more flexible you are with regard to dates, flight times, and itineraries, the better the price you can obtain. Unfortunately that can be the sticking point. If you have specific interview appointments and have to be in certain cities at certain times, you will have less flexibility in seeking optimal fares.

Whether you use your computer, call the airlines, or use a travel agent, be prepared to invest a fair amount of time and effort in planning your trip if you are going to obtain the lowest prices. Some guidelines that may help:

1. As a general rule, you can save a great deal by booking early and paying promptly, but you often must pay a stiff penalty if you cancel or make any changes in your reservation.
2. Most business travelers return home for the weekend. To attract the discretionary traveler, airlines typically offer deep discounts on trips that extend over a Saturday night.
3. Airfares are often excessive in cities served by only one or two carriers or where the economy dictates there will be a high proportion of business travelers. It may save you money to fly to a different city and drive an hour or two. Try inserting nearby alternatives cities and see what fares come up. One applicant wrote me that by flying out of Washington, DC instead of his home airport of Norfolk, VA, he reduced the costs of flights to Boston and Chicago from over $1,000 to $278.
4. Regardless of the number of seats sold, transcontinental airlines have to get the planes they flew to the West Coast during the day back to the East Coast by the next morning, in spite of the 3-hour time zone differential. In order to fill otherwise empty seats, they often offer reduced "night owl" or "red eye" fares on overnight flights from West to East.

## ☐ Getting There Is Half the Hassle

The combination of high holiday volume and poor weather make December and January bad months to travel. Unfortunately, that's when you usually must interview. Do not schedule tight connections in hub cities, and keep your luggage in your possession. If you must check some luggage, keep essential items such as your interview notes, medications, toiletries, and a change of clothes with you in a carry-on bag. Do not wear casual clothes such as warm-up suits or jeans while flying unless you are prepared to interview in that outfit.

## Avoiding Delays

A "delay" occurs when a flight leaves the gate more than 15 minutes after its scheduled departure time. If your plane sits on the taxi way for 45 minutes waiting to take off, it does not count as a delay. Nevertheless, 25% of the flights in the United States are officially delayed.

The later in the day you fly, the more likely it is you will encounter delays. Recent Department of Transportation statistics for the Atlanta hub showed that between 7:00 a.m. and 8:00 a.m., 94% of the departures and 92% of the arrivals were on time. However, in the evening, only 70% of the departures and 62% of the arrivals were on time (Maxa, 2000). Smaller airports handle fewer flights and have fewer delays. Moral: To minimize delays, book the earliest flights you possibly can and choose smaller airports.

It is also better to fly nonstop to your destination. The more landings, take-offs, and plane changes, the more chances there are for things to go wrong. When booking, don't confuse "direct" with "nonstop." Direct flights involve one or more intermediate stops.

## Cancellations

Flights are canceled for many reasons including weather, mechanical conditions, labor troubles, and the convenience of the airline. Make sure the airline has your phone number so they can notify you of cancellations.

Your best defense against cancellations is to arrive at the airport and check in at the gate early, at least 45 minutes before your flight is scheduled to depart. Airlines often know several hours in advance that a flight will have to be canceled. If you arrive early, you will be the first to learn if your flight has been canceled and you can beat the rush in getting transferred to an alternate flight.

Although electronic tickets ("e-tickets") are convenient and can't get lost, airline computers can't talk to each other, so it is better to have a paper ticket if you have to change carriers (Maxa, 2000). If you have a paper ticket, the agent only has to sign and stamp it and you are on your way. If you have an electronic ticket, however, the agent has to go into the computer, retrieve your record, and issue you a paper ticket that other airlines will accept. By the time that has been done, someone else may have snagged the seat you were trying for.

## Switching Flights

Knowledgeable travelers advise booking an alternate flight at the first sign of delay. Sometimes a flight's departure is delayed interminably, sup-

**144**    Megargee's Guide to Obtaining a Psychology Internship

posedly to correct mechanical problems. This can be a subterfuge. An airline that has two partly filled flights going to the same city an hour or two apart may be tempted to board the first flight, delay its departure for an hour, then transfer the passengers to the second plane so they can fly one full flight instead. To accomplish this, they string along the passengers already seated on the first flight by assuring them the difficulty will be corrected momentarily. Eventually they announce that the "bad news" is the problem can't be corrected but the "good news" is they have another flight to the same city that is just about to depart and they have room for almost everyone on this other flight. Everyone then scrambles off the first plane and engages in a foot race to the second in order to be one of the "lucky" passengers who secures a seat. If you do make the alternative flight, it is a Fundamental Law of Nature that any luggage you checked will not.

Of course, sometimes there actually is a mechanical problem. If it is 10 or 15 minutes after the scheduled departure time and the passengers are all seated but the door is still open, try to find out what is going on. Perhaps, looking out the window, you see that some mechanics have disassembled one of the engines and are quizzically scratching their heads as they gaze at the parts scattered over the tarmac. Maybe the flight attendants are sitting down and working on their nails.

In either case, if it is important that you get to your destination on time, consider switching to another flight. Use your cellular phone or one on the aircraft to call your travel agent or other airlines to see if they have seats available on their flights to your destination.[21] If they do, book the flight, take your luggage, get your ticket back from the agent at the desk, and go catch your new flight. (Phoning is faster and more efficient than debarking, going to the other gate, and standing in a long line for a seat that may not be available.)

In the event your destination city is socked in by weather or the delay is caused by a "gate hold" at your destination, changing planes won't help. However, a cellular phone can still come in handy. When a flight that normally serves dinner was held at the gate well past the normal meal time, one ravenous passenger called Domino's and had a large pizza delivered to his seat on the plane.

---

[21]Experienced air travelers carry a copy of the *Official Airline Guides North American Pocket Flight Guide (OAG)*, which is published monthly and is available in major airports. For every destination in North America, it lists every flight on every airline from every city. If you are on the ground in Los Angeles waiting for your flight to O'Hare to depart, consult the *OAG*. You will see there are about five dozen other flights going from "LAX" to "ORD" every day. The people you see grabbing their luggage and heading for the door when a mechanical problem is announced are hurrying to get on one of these other flights.

# Overbooking

Airlines often overbook at peak seasons, such as December, and at prime times, such as late afternoon. When more people with reservations show up than the computer predicted, they are in what they refer to as an "oversold condition." More prosaically, it means someone is going to get "bumped."

To avoid being bumped, select your seats when you buy your tickets, and get your boarding passes issued at the time of ticketing. Take your ticket, your boarding pass, and a photo identification and check in *at the gate* at least 45 minutes before your flight is scheduled to depart. It is the folks arriving at the last minute who have not had their boarding passes stamped who are most likely to be stranded.

Before bumping anyone, the agent will announce that the flight is oversold and ask for people to volunteer to take a later flight in exchange for compensation. The amount of compensation is negotiable, but at the very least they should offer you a free round trip ticket anywhere in the system that is good for a year. One student on his way home volunteered and was given a free unrestricted round trip ticket for anywhere in the United States and a seat on another carrier's flight departing an hour later. As luck would have it, his original flight developed mechanical difficulties and he arrived at his destination several hours sooner than the rest of the passengers. If you want to volunteer, move fast. There are often more than enough volunteers.

If you are bumped involuntarily, you are entitled to compensation and you may also be able to negotiate other perks.[22] The airline will usually notify people waiting to meet you at your destination, either by telex or by letting you use the phone. If the next flight out is after a normal mealtime, ask for a free meal ticket so you can have lunch or dinner at their expense. Most airlines have clubs or VIP rooms. If you ask, the gate attendant may give you a card allowing you to wait there. If you have to spend the night, you should ask for lodging at a nearby hotel and meal checks for dinner and breakfast.

# Dealing With Gate Agents

Nice clothes, a polite manner, and a frequent traveler card may also help you get better treatment from harassed ticket clerks if your flight is can-

---

[22]Detailed advice about coping with air travel and your rights as an airline passenger can be found in the booklet *Fly-Rights: A Consumer Guide to Air Travel*, published by the Consumer Information Center, Pueblo, CO 81009. You can purchase it for $1.75 (including postage) or download a copy from their Web site, www.dot.gov/airconsumer/flyrights. Take it with you when you fly. It tells you how to cope with all sorts of crises ranging from getting bumped to lost luggage.

**146** Megargee's Guide to Obtaining a Psychology Internship

celed and you have to be rerouted (as occurred to me on three out of four flights while visiting interns one miserable December). Remember to keep on your person a list of the names and phone numbers of the people you are supposed to see so you can notify them when your plane is canceled or delayed.

While the airlines are obliged to provide meals and lodging if you are bumped, this may not apply if the flight has to be canceled, especially if the cancellation is due to weather. Under Industry Rule 240, they must get you to your destination, either on an alternate flight or another airline, but there is no guarantee *when* you will get there. You will be competing with everyone else who was on your flight for a limited number of seats, and if weather has closed the airport, no one will be going anywhere until it reopens. That is why Chicago O'Hare keeps 2,100 cots on hand and has arrangements with the Red Cross to supply more. Nevertheless, every winter newspapers feature photos of stranded passengers sleeping on their luggage.

If you are late getting to the airport and miss a flight, you may have to switch to another airline that may not accept deeply discounted or complimentary tickets. Or if your airline goes bankrupt, as one seems to do most every year, other carriers may be reluctant to accept any tickets issued by the insolvent airline. Have a credit card with a high enough credit limit or enough travelers' checks to pay for a new ticket if necessary. If you charged your ticket on the bankrupt airline to a major credit card, the charge should be canceled. Otherwise you are just one more creditor (Gavzer, 1992).

Gate attendants are human, and, like all of us, they respond better to people who are polite and considerate. *They* didn't cause the overbooking, cloud the skies, or break the engine, so don't take out your frustration by berating them. Be firm, however, and if the delay is going to ruin the rest of your life, let the agent know. Although you should not get hysterical, a quavering voice and a controlled tear or two may help.

## ☐ Car Rentals

The only practical way for you to get to some internship centers in distant cities will be to fly there and rent a car at the airport. You will find that rates and amenities vary tremendously. Like the airlines, the car-rental agencies have a glut of customers during the business week and fewer on weekends. They establish their rates to encourage discretionary travelers.

To rent a car you need to have a valid driver's license and be over the minimum age established by that company. You should also have a major credit card. Otherwise, you will be required to leave a humongous cash deposit to guarantee that you will return the vehicle.

## Traveling to Internships: How to Survive and Stay Solvent   **147**

Reserve an automobile in advance, and shop for the best deal. As I noted earlier, APPIC negotiates discounts for you with some companies. If you work for a state agency or university, you may be able to get a government rate. One might assume that firms whose names emphasize their frugality (i.e., Budget, Dollar, Thrifty) would give you the best rates. That may not be true, especially when you factor in hidden costs. Check out the major firms as well. If you ask, a travel agent can usually find the best rate and reserve a car for you.

Find the package that is best suited for your needs on this particular trip. In addition to the daily cost, ask whether there is a mileage fee. If you are not driving very far, a lower daily rate with a 100-mile-a-day allotment may be best; on the other hand, if you are going to be logging a lot of miles, a higher daily rate and unlimited mileage may be more economical.

Insurance is a major factor in renting a car. Many companies make as much from the insurance as they do from the rental. If you already have auto insurance, check with your carrier. If you are covered while driving a rental car, and almost everyone is, refuse the added coverage. (Remember your AAA membership probably covers any emergency road service.)

Make sure you know the renter's policy on gasoline. Are you expected to bring the car back with the same amount of gas as you found in it, fully fueled, or what? How much will they charge you if they have to refill it? Not knowing these details can easily add $10 or $15 to your costs.

In choosing a car-rental agency, consider whether it is located at the airport or in the boondocks. The greater convenience of the airport location may offset the price differential, especially if you are on a tight schedule. Being stuck at an off-brand car-rental office waiting for their one van to take you to the airport while your plane takes off without you can ruin the best-planned trip.

Always ask if there are discounts available. Depending on the rental company you are dealing with, you may qualify for a discount (a) through APPIC, (b) by virtue of belonging to AAA or some other organization, (c) because you are flying in on a certain airline, or (d) because you are staying in a particular hotel or motel. Make sure you take along all your membership cards, any discount or upgrade coupons you have received from your airline flyer's club or AAA, and, of course, your driver's license.

As I noted earlier, renting and returning a car is much simpler if you belong to the company's preferred renter "club" and have a prearranged rental number. When you apply, you fill out an application form that lists your preferences in vehicles, insurance options, driver's license number, preferred mode of payment, discounts you may be eligible for, credit card numbers, and so on. When you arrive at the agency, your rental contract should be all ready in an envelope with your name on it. You pick it, get

**148**    Megargee's Guide to Obtaining a Psychology Internship

your keys, and drive off. If you are in a hurry when you return the car, you merely have to record the mileage, insert the papers in a time clock, and drop it in a slot. A copy of the bill will be mailed to you.

## ☐ Lodging: Reducing the "Rack Rate"

The least expensive lodging is, of course, to stay with a relative or friend. Some internship sites arrange for applicants to stay with current interns. This not only saves you money, but also gives you an excellent opportunity to learn what life is like for interns at that facility.

Realistically, unless you have a large extended family or are only applying to places close to home, you will probably have to spend some nights in hotels or motels. If you are driving to internships or if you rent a car, you will have many more options than if you are relying on public transportation. This is where the AAA tour books come in handy, because you can use their spotter maps to locate hotels in the vicinity and check the rates that are listed. Be advised, though, that the AAA book does not include all the motels in an area, and the fact that a place is not included does not necessarily mean that it is unacceptable. You can also find accommodations and make reservations on the Web. The problem with on-line reservations is that you cannot negotiate.

If you look at the hotel and motel maps for most cities, you will see that there are generally three clusters that have a high density of accommodations: (a) the "downtown" area, especially in the proximity of a civic or convention center; (b) the airport; and (c) near the exits to an Interstate or "beltway" around the city. The downtown area catering to commercial travelers on expense accounts is typically the most expensive, followed by hotels in the vicinity of the airport, especially chains such as Hyatt, Marriott, Hilton, Sofitel, and Sheraton. However, near the airport there are often smaller, less expensive places that may lack such amenities as a pool, exercise room, or a lounge. These are the motels airlines use for stranded passengers. They often have the code word "Inn" in their names, as in Comfort Inn, Days Inn, Fairfield Inn, HoJo Inn, Red Roof Inn. However, the word "Inn" is not an infallible sign, so make sure you negotiate the rates.

Least expensive, typically, are the places near an Interstate exit. Since motorists are, by definition, mobile, they can shop for bargains, and these motels must be economical to compete. If you have wheels, you can often save money by staying at one of these places on the edge of town and driving in to the medical center instead of booking a room across from the hospital.

Although everyone knows you can shop for airfares, fewer people are aware that hotel rates are very negotiable, especially at the more expen-

Traveling to Internships: How to Survive and Stay Solvent **149**

sive places. No matter where you stay, *always ask for a lower rate*. If you don't ask for it, you will not get it. Rates are very variable and may depend on who you are talking to when you make your reservation. As an experiment, some journalists called hotels asking what the rates were (Lump, Chan, Clifford, & Tinson, 2000). Within a 20-minute interval they were quoted prices for the same basic room ranging from $164 to $314!

When you book your room, ask what discounts are available. You can probably qualify for a discount on the basis of some group to which you belong. For example, AAA membership is worth a 10% discount at participating hotels and motels. If you are a state employee, such as a teaching assistant at a state university or a psychology trainee at a state hospital, try asking for the "government" or "state" rate. If the government rate does not apply, ask for an educational or student discount. You will soon learn which chains cater to which groups.

Many major medical centers have negotiated special medical or hospital visitor rates with one or more local hotels and motels. Ask the secretary who books your interview. If the secretary does not know, simply ask for a hospital rate when you make your reservation. Because I was a hospital visitor, Hilton recently charged me only $39 for a $120 room. Each hotel has only a limited number of discounted rooms, so the earlier you book, the better your chances. The nice thing about hotels, in contrast to airlines, is that you do not have to pay in advance and there is no penalty for canceling your reservation.

Other things are also negotiable. You might be able to get a free breakfast, for example, especially if you belong to the hotel chain's preferred guest program. Other perks can include a room upgrade, a complimentary cocktail, concierge service, and a morning newspaper. If you prefer a nonsmoking room or a king size bed, ask for it. If you are a woman traveling alone, mention this and ask for a secure room. Not only will this lessen the likelihood that you will be followed across the parking lot by some polyester-clad creep from the lounge, but it may also get you upgraded to a superior room at the same price.

The time to negotiate discounts and ask for perks is when you book the room, not at midnight after you have arrived, tired and disheveled, from the airport. If you are trying to get a discount, it is best to call the hotel or motel directly, rather than the 800 number. The person answering the 800 phone may not have the necessary authority. If you cannot get what you want, ask for the assistant manager. If they still will not budge, try someplace else. As a general rule, the better the hotel and the more they are geared to business travelers, the greater the discount you can get. However, the base price of the room will be higher.

Even with all these maneuvers, if the hotel is heavily booked, the best you may be able to do is the "corporate" rate. That gets you a nice room, but it is very expensive. It is better to try somewhere else, but if you must

**150**    Megargee's Guide to Obtaining a Psychology Internship

stay at that hotel, take that rate and ask to be put on standby for the lower government or educational rate. When you check in, ask the clerk if the lower rate room opened up, and you may be pleasantly surprised. Most airlines have arrangements with major hotel chains, so you may get additional frequent traveler miles when you fly in on that airline. Ask for a coupon at the desk, fill it out, and leave it with the clerk.

Whatever the rate you manage to negotiate, make sure you obtain and record a confirmation number or name. No matter what your expected arrival time, it is a good idea to guarantee your room for late arrival by providing a major credit card number. If for some reason you cannot make it, call and cancel before 6:00 p.m. or you will have to pay for your (unused) room. Make sure you get a cancellation number, and later examine your credit card bill to make sure the charge does not appear.

Like airlines, hotels sometimes overbook, especially when there is a big convention or a major sporting event in town. Also, in some states, guests are not legally required to vacate their rooms when their reservations expire. If the airports or highways are closed because of bad weather, many guests will stay on and new arrivals are out of luck, even though they have guaranteed reservations. If you arrive after all the rooms at your rate have been occupied, the desk clerk has three choices: (a) check you into a better room at the same rate if one is available; (b) get you reservations at another hotel (and have the van take you there); or (c) shrug and express regrets.

If you were a desk clerk in this situation and you were confronted with: (a) a polite, well-dressed young person who is a member of your "Honored Guest" program, (b) some smelly slob who is clad in shorts and a stained tank top, or (c) an arrogant SOB who is calling you names and pounding the counter, which one would *you* discretely signal to come back in 20 minutes and then upgrade to the Presidential Suite?

## ☐ Dressing for Travel and Interviews

Every successful salesperson knows the importance of first impressions. Social psychologists have established that we often evaluate people as soon as we see them. According to the "physical attractiveness stereotype," we are naturally inclined to attribute all sorts of positive characteristics, including greater competence, to attractive people (Dion, Bersheid, & Walster, 1972). If you want to make a positive impression when interviewing, you should be well groomed and well dressed. Your clothing need not be expensive, but it should be neat, clean, and professional.

When in doubt, dress conservatively. For women a business suit with simple jewelry and sensible shoes is best. Go easy on the makeup and perfume. Men should wear long-sleeved shirts with a tie and jacket and

## Traveling to Internships: How to Survive and Stay Solvent    **151**

polished shoes. It is okay to wear the latest style, but remember that trendy clothes go out of style as quickly as they come in. If you are building a basic wardrobe that you plan to wear for a while, it is better to stick with classic designs.

When I am going to be on the road for several days, I take at least two complete outfits that I can mix and match. A solid color navy blue business suit and a tan or light gray one in compatible fabrics provide at least four outfits as I swap jackets with slacks. If I am flying, I wear the darker clothes on the plane since, to paraphrase the bumper sticker, "spills happen." Worsted wool is always a good choice of fabric, but on a recent 28-day freighter cruise, my wife and I discovered that the new "microfibers" traveled well without wrinkling, even after we were caught in rain storms at every port of call.

Women have a greater range of colors to mix and match, such as red, black, or white with slacks or a skirt. Or consider a solid color suit and sports coat/slacks outfit for men, and suit or blazer/skirt outfit plus a business dress for women. I suggest you stick with solids when you are building your wardrobe. Patterned materials are much less versatile and hence less cost-effective.

Think of your jacket as a frame for your blouse and scarf, or shirt and tie. Only one item should be patterned. If you wear a patterned suit or jacket, keep the other items plain. If your jacket and the shirt or blouse are solid, then you can have a patterned tie or scarf. Men should stick with white or light blue shirts. Jewelry should be understated and complementary to the overall outfit. Remember, you want people to focus on you and not be distracted by excessive or clashing accoutrements. However, don't be afraid to display a little style. One recent applicant wrote that when interviewing at three "high-status" sites, she received a number of compliments from interviewers because she was the only female candidate *not* wearing a black suit.

Take along some "nice" casual clothes such as dress jeans for going out in the evening with the present interns. Remember that you will be doing a lot of walking, so take well-shined leather shoes that are attractive but comfortable. This is not the time for five inch stiletto heels (especially for the men), but don't go to the other extreme and wear running shoes or sandals. Gender-appropriate hose is a must. Be prepared for cold or inclement weather. Now is the time to invest in that tan all-weather coat with the removable lining.

Murphy's Law applies with a vengeance when it comes to traveling. Familiarity with the operation of a sewing needle and an iron (both of which will be available where you stay) may prove useful. If they aren't in the room, call Housekeeping. You can minimize difficulties by taking the time to check for loose buttons, wobbly eyeglass frames, and frayed shoelaces before you pack.

## ☐ What to Take

Prepare for internship travel as you would for a backpacking trip in the Andes. Include "emergency equipment" such as spare glasses or contacts, a sewing kit (with extra buttons), a styptic pencil, nail clipper, band aids, spare shoelaces, and extra pantyhose (and clear nail polish to repair the pantyhose) in your travel kit. You may never need them, but if you do, you will *really* need them.

Instead of loading up your luggage with large heavy bottles, just take small containers with the minimum necessary amount of each item. If you cannot find 2-oz. travel sizes, buy small plastic bottles at the nearest discount drug store and decant the appropriate amount of whatever therein. Since liquids expand and leak at altitude, squeeze the air out of them and seal them in Ziploc freezer bags. While it is good to "travel light," it is important to take everything you might need. This is not the time to conduct an empirical test of whether that new deodorant really does last 72 hours without replenishing. Which is worse, carrying along an extra four ounces or asphyxiating the Internship Selection Committee?

Is this beginning to sound like a Scout Manual? Well, as a matter of fact, I do carry a Swiss Army knife in my permanently packed travel kit; it has reattached the handle of a briefcase, repaired eyeglasses, sharpened pencils, and opened innumerable soda bottles. A mini-flashlight that stays beside my bed in case of fire also helps me find my way around a strange motel room in the dark. Don't forget a small travel alarm, and remember to reprogram it as you change time zones. If you take your cellular phone, don't forget to include the recharging apparatus.

Interviewing and travel are both stressful, so don't be surprised if your body turns on you. Even if it functions with the regularity and precision of a Swiss chronometer at home, it can go totally out of synch on the road, especially if you have jet lag to contend with. Take along whatever you use to deal with bodily emergencies such as gastrointestinal distress, allergies, headaches, hemorrhages, cramps, etc.

Before you depart, go on the Web and download detailed maps of your destination. A number of sites can plot the route from your home or the airport to the internship site. Even if you are not driving, they can be very helpful in guiding a confused cab driver who may not speak your language, especially if you speak English.

After turning South instead of North more often than I care to remember, I added a small compass to my kit. In addition to helping me orient myself when I leave an airport or a subway, it can be invaluable in finding my way around strange hospital corridors, many of which seem to have been designed with minimal spatial cues to thwart patients bent on leaving.

Don't forget to take along the material you will need for interviewing: copies of your application, including extra CVs for interviewers, and brochures issued by the centers where you will be interviewing, along with any notes you might have made about questions to ask. And of course, bring along this book with a paper clip marking Appendix 5 on questions to ask. Again, if you are flying, keep all essential items, including your interview outfit, with you in your carry-on luggage.

## ☐ Keeping in Touch

Before you depart, make arrangements for staying in touch with your home base. Other internships may call while you are off interviewing, so your friends and ADCT should know how to reach you.

Telephone answering machines or voice mail boxes can be helpful, especially those that automatically "time stamp" your messages and from which you can retrieve your calls by phone while you are on travel status. If you take a cellular phone, leave a message with its number on your telephone answering machine. Or provide callers with your e-mail address.

While answering machines are useful, do not rely on them. Tapes can get overloaded, especially if you have some "friend" or former lover who feels it is amusing to recite poetry or play music into your machine. Power outages can erase your messages. (By the way, if you have not already done so, make sure the message on your answering machine is one that won't offend ITDs.)

E-mail is a better alternative than an answering machine. Many airports and hotels now provide computers with Internet access, or you can take a laptop with a modem to access your messages while you are on the road.

## ☐ Health Tips

Diplomats and business travelers know that it is important to stay healthy while traveling. Take the time to get a good night's sleep and keep up your exercise program. It is especially important to eat healthy. When you book your flight, ask for one of the various special meals that are available on request, such as the low fat or "heart healthy" menu. The airlines provide the same special meals for coach passengers as they do for first class, and they are fresher and more appetizing as well as being healthier.

Six weeks or more before you leave for interviews, get a flu shot. Except for a test tube, which it rather resembles, an airplane is the best place

## 154     Megargee's Guide to Obtaining a Psychology Internship

in the world for exchanging airborne viruses with people from all over the world. If you are visiting hospitals, remember that they have lots of sick people and therefore more than their share of germs. If you don't pick up something while traveling, you will from one of your fellow applicants. By Groundhog Day, many of the intern applicants who didn't get their flu shots will be sick.

# The Site Visit and Interview

For many programs, the personal interview with the candidate is the most important selection criterion. Mellott et al. (1997, p. 193) wrote:

> The process of interviewing for an internship site is very similar to the dynamics involved in interviewing for a job. The internship site is looking for a good match between the prospective intern and the internship facility. One important criterion that training directors look for is a similarity between the applicant's articulated training goals and the services provided at the internship site. Other important criteria include obtaining potential interns who are personable, open, and eager to learn.... A final quality that directors of internship sites seek in their candidates is a genuine interest in their facility.

You should make every effort to go to each training center to see it for yourself and interview in person. Not only should it enhance your candidacy, but it is your single best opportunity to obtain the data *you* need to evaluate the program and its personnel. If you are going to spend a year or more at a facility, you owe it to yourself to learn all you can about the place.[23] More than one applicant has walked into a place and immediately sensed, "This is not for me." I personally find a site visit indispensable in evaluating a program.

---

[23]An exception is when a facility has rigged the situation so that you are deprived of an adequate opportunity to evaluate their program. One of my students traveled over 2,000 miles at considerable cost and personal inconvenience to sit in a cafeteria with 50 other applicants on a Saturday morning listening to the ITD read the program's brochure to them. After a brief tour of the grounds, they were sent on their way. While he was understandably indignant, he had learned enough about the program's attitude to cross it off his list.

**156**    Megargee's Guide to Obtaining a Psychology Internship

Interviewing is the most time-consuming and expensive part of the internship-seeking process. Applicants and training staffs alike often get little else accomplished during the 6- to 8-week interviewing season. The mean expenses reported in recent polls were more than $1,000 per applicant (Oehlert, Lopez, & Summerall, 1997; Thorne, 1997), and some applicants spend twice that (Fox, 1991). One student estimated that he had spent more than $2,000 to get a job that would pay him only $15,000.

## ☐ Scheduling Interviews

A decade ago, virtually every internship required an in-person or telephone interview as an essential part of the selection process. Under the old Uniform Notification policy, Selection Committees felt it was vital to assess whether applicants were likely to accept offers if they were tendered. Fox (1991, p. 34) reported, "Some programs apparently use the interview as a screening device by indicating to applicants that interviews are optional, but that willingness to appear for a personal interview will be viewed as an index of strong interest in their program."

Now that UND has been replaced by computer matching and the supply of interns exceeds the available positions, training centers' policies have become more variable. Some internships still will not consider ranking an applicant who has not had a personal, face to face interview. Many settings encourage in-person interviews, but allow telephone interviews for candidates who cannot visit the site. A few facilities refuse to interview prospective candidates, arguing that there is no empirical evidence that the interns they obtain after interviewing are superior to those they select solely on the basis of their paper credentials. They may schedule an open house when applicants can visit the facility and be briefed on its program.

Training centers' policies with regard to scheduling interviews also vary. Some centers grant interviews to all who request them; others adopt a "first come, first served" policy, scheduling interviews for the first 20, 30, 40, or whatever candidates who ask and then not allowing any more. Many internships now interview only by invitation after they have first screened the written applications. As a result of these differences, one Northeastern internship interviewed only 10 applicants for three vacancies, whereas another interviewed 95 to 100 candidates for five slots (Plante, 1987).

To add to the confusion, some internships conduct interviews whenever applicants can arrange to visit, some confine interviewing to a 2- or 3-week period, and some require all applicants to present themselves on a specific date with no exceptions permitted. The setting's Web site or brochure may indicate their interview policy and whether certain dates are set aside for interviewing.

The Site Visit and Interview    **157**

Just as each facility has its own application date, they also vary on when they conduct interviews. Sites with late due dates and ones that first screen applications typically take longer to begin interviewing. In December and January the APPIC intern listserv is filled with messages from applicants asking whether anyone has heard from one setting or another. If an internship indicates that it interviews by invitation only, by December 15 it is certainly appropriate to call and inquire regarding your status.

The internship-selection process, including interviewing, can place a great strain on a training center. The present interns are nearing the end of their first rotations and being evaluated, and the training personnel must continue to deal with their regular clinical duties throughout internship-selection season. After they have interviewed dozens of bright, well-qualified applicants, staff can be forgiven for not being enthusiastic about seeing more. Therefore, it behooves you to request a personal interview as soon as possible. Not only will it help you make more economical travel arrangements, but late callers may simply be told that there are no appointments left.

If the internships to which you have applied specify the dates they conduct interviews in their brochures, pencil them in on a calendar. This will help you avoid conflicts when you receive invitations to interview. Some students have reported being invited and then "disinvited" when they indicated that previous commitments made it impossible for them to visit on the exact day specified. Upon being told one applicant already had an interview scheduled at another site on the day for she which was invited, one ITD told her that if she was truly interested in their facility she would cancel the other appointment. However, it is not good form to accept an invitation and later try to change the date if you receive another invitation from a more preferred program.

If you are granted an interview at a distant site and have not heard from others in the vicinity, it is perfectly acceptable to call or e-mail the other facilities indicating that you will be traveling to their locale on that date and asking if it is possible to visit their program and interview there on the same trip. Most will be understanding and try to accommodate you. Others may not. Plante (1987) described the plight of one student who had to make two round trips from Kansas City to Boston to interview at two neighboring internships because one only conducted interviews in December whereas the other would only interview in January. Her cost in airfare was equivalent to 20% of the stipends offered by the internships. As Fox (1991, p. 34) remarked, "Some directors are understanding and flexible in responding to the realities of students' life circumstances, others are embarrassingly rigid and callous."

Examine each site's brochure, Web site, or listing in the APPIC *Directory* to determine whether they prefer that you contact their program by telephone, e-mail, or U.S. mail. Unless the site specifies otherwise, I recom-

**158**    Megargee's Guide to Obtaining a Psychology Internship

mend telephoning. Winiarski (1986) noted that you can begin to get a feel for a place with your first phone call. "Does the secretary greet you warmly, or are you put on hold for 30 minutes? Are you offered lodging with other interns . . . or are you told, 'See you at the office at 9:30 Monday' and then expected to fend for yourself?"

Winiarski (1986) recommended that, if possible, you arrange to visit your lowest ranked choices first. "This will benefit you in two ways. First, if you flub up some early interviews, the damage won't be as great, and you can learn from the experience. Second, you'll have more data going into the more important interviews, and therefore know more about what to look for and have better questions to ask." His advice, of course, assumes that your motivation will remain constant. If you wait too long, you may be burned out and no longer care what sort of an impression you make. Perhaps the best advice is to schedule yourself some rest days so you can recuperate between visits.

When you make an appointment for an interview, try to find out what sort of interviews you will have. Are they going to be one-on-one interviews with members of the training staff? Committee interviews in which several members of the Internship Selection Committee talk to you at the same time? Group interviews in which you and several other applicants meet with an individual staff member? Try to find out the names of the people you will be meeting so you can learn more about them before you interview. Also make sure you know the *exact* time and place where you are supposed to report and how to get there. If you are driving, ask about the availability of parking.

If your request for an interview is refused, consult your ADCT. As a student, you probably had to deal with a secretary or executive assistant, but your ADCT will have access to the ITD and can find out directly what the problem is. It may be that your folder appears incomplete. If there is a perceived problem with your application or your apparent credentials, your ADCT can find out. If there is some misperception involved, your ADCT may be able to correct it. It could be that someone simply made a mistake. One year an ITD told me that his secretary had misinterpreted something he had said and denied interviews to anyone who called after January 1. Whatever the reason for your refusal, your ADCT may be able to arrange an interview for you by dealing directly with the ITD.

Surveying 185 applicants from the 1994–1995 selection year, Constantine and Keilin (1996) reported that they had applied to an average of 9.8 sites (SD = 4.8) and obtained an average of 6.9 interviews (SD = 3.7), for a success rate of about 70%. Not getting interviews is not the kiss of death. APPIC officials note that many sites rank applicants that they did not interview. However, if you are being notified that you are no longer being considered, it might be time to use the "lifeboat list" I described in Chapter 6. Go over your application materials with your ADCT or the person acting as your coach. Is there something that may be turn-

The Site Visit and Interview 159

ing Selection Committees off? Consider submitting some additional revised applications to programs that have late due dates. One applicant had more success after she removed any mention of being married and having children from her CV.

# ☐ Preparing for the Interview

After you have submitted all your applications and before you start traveling, there will be a lull during which you can catch your breath, regroup, and get ready for the next phase. This is a good time to prepare for interviewing.

A good way to get ready is to read the advice of previous students who have been through the process and written about their experiences. I recommend the accounts by Burt (1985), Gollaher and Craig (1994), Casey Jacob (1987), and Kingsley (1985). These first-person reports by actual survivors have an authenticity that cannot be duplicated. They will help prepare you for some of the mood swings you will experience and give you the concrete practical advice that can only be provided by someone who has been through the process. One suggests that you take along some healthy snack food such as raisins or power bars in case you miss lunch. Another advises taking advantage of every opportunity to go to the bathroom because you never know if you will get another chance. A third advocates deep breathing exercises to reduce anxiety.

Their accounts are also full of "war stories" about the strange things that can happen and the peculiar people you might encounter. Fox (1991), who was an ITD before becoming an ADCT, complained about "the high-handedness, arrogance, unprofessionalism and plain rudeness which a number of our students encounter each year in their dealings with some of our colleagues in some internship programs" (p. 35). Fox is correct. I have been out there myself and experienced it firsthand, so don't think this behavior is reserved for students. As Fox noted, "We all have our bozos" (p. 35). Nevertheless, attitudes like this rankle and are an added aggravation at an already difficult time in your lives. So, during your travels, if you think you have wandered into the Twilight Zone, recall these accounts. It may not be reassuring to realize that this is reality, but at least you will know others have survived similar insanity.

After reading these accounts, consult the CareerBuilders' advice on preparing for a job interview at their Web site at www.careerbuilder.com. Also helpful are articles by ITDs on how they view the interviewing and internship selection process. I recommend the articles by Belar and Orgel (1980), Grace (1985), and Monti (1985), all of which can be found in the book edited by Dana and May (1987). Hersh and Poey (1985) have provided a convenient and concise outline of questions that ITDs may ask you and that you can ask them. They also suggested some questions you

**160**   Megargee's Guide to Obtaining a Psychology Internship

should *not* ask. In Appendices 4 and 5, I provide you with questions asked by interviewers and other questions you can ask them. Study this material, assimilate it, and then integrate it into your own personal style. This is when your support team can assist you by allowing you to role-play or practice interviewing. Take the ITD's role and interview a fellow applicant. You will find that it greatly increases your understanding of what the person on the other side of the desk is looking for.

Before visiting a site, make sure you do your homework. Review the facility's program descriptions and brochure. Note down specific questions you have regarding that particular internship. The night before each interview, one of my recent students *outlined* the brochure, noting questions in the margins, so it would be fresh in her mind the next morning. She would take the outline with its questions along with her and refer to it during the interviews.

Whatever technique you use, you need to be focused. You should go to the internship with a clear picture of what their program offers and what information you need to obtain to help you evaluate it. Staff get turned off when applicants ask questions that show they have not done their homework and are not familiar with the basic program. If you are interested in children, don't ask, "Do you have a child rotation?" If you have read the brochure, you should know that there is a child rotation. Instead inquire about what sorts of training experiences are available on the child rotation or how interns get chosen for that experience.

As you know, *Psychological Abstracts*, in both its written and computerized (PsychLit) forms, has author indices. Take the time to look up the people you will be meeting, identify some of their writings, and download abstracts of their recent publications. Not only will this help you evaluate the setting and the caliber of personnel, but you can impress the interviewer with your knowledge of his or her research. This is also a time to recall those papers presented by internship personnel that you observed at professional meetings or workshops. You don't have to be profound. Just say, "I was interested in the work you did with Dr. Fibula Fistula on peptic ulcers; have you done anything further in that area?" (Of course, be prepared to respond intelligently when you are asked, "What aspect of that study interested you?")

## ☐ Telephone Interviews

Realistically, however, you may not have the time or money to interview everywhere. This is especially true if your top priority is a particular type of internship experience, such as a children's hospital, since such facilities are scattered all across the country. Do not write off a place because it will not be possible for you to interview there in person. Although I feel that

The Site Visit and Interview **161**

telephone interviews usually help the site in selecting students more than they help students to evaluate the site, many students who have participated in telephone interviews have reported that they got a good feel for the facility. They have been accepted at very competitive programs and had good experiences at these internships.

Since you do not have to rush to another appointment as you would during a site visit, a telephone interview is more likely to be open ended with regard to time. Moreover, you can be sure you won't have to share your time with another applicant.

Prepare for a telephone interview as you would for one at the site. Make sure you will not be interrupted. Clear the area of roommates, partners, children, and animals, and eliminate distracting background noises such as the garage band practicing next door. Assemble all the materials you will need such as copies of your application, CV, information about the internship, and, most important, a list of the questions you want answered. Keep your computer accessible so you can call up information if necessary. Some students prepare and print out answers to anticipated questions and case conceptualization notes. However, don't overprepare to the point where you lose your spontaneity and end up reading canned responses.

Many students find it helps them focus if they dress as they would for a face to face job interview. Typically, the internship calls you at a designated time. Clear the line 5 minutes or so before the appointed time. I suggest using a land line rather than a portable or cellular phone because there is less chance of static. It helps to have a glass of water available in case your throat gets dry. When the call comes in, go for it just as you would in a face to face interview.

## ☐ Going to the Interview

If you are traveling to your interviews, make sure you take everything you might need with you, including copies of your notes, lists of specific questions to ask at each internship, and the internship's brochures so you can review them before starting your round of appointments. Also take a duplicate copy of your completed application forms in case a part of your application has been lost (they will say "never received"). Don't forget the 3 × 5 inch cards on the people you will probably be meeting. If you have business cards with your name and communication numbers on them, take them along too.

Always take extra copies of your resume. The internship may not be sufficiently well organized or have the resources to provide every person you see with a copy of your CV, and it is not realistic to expect that everyone has taken the time to review all the CVs in a central file cabinet,

**162** Megargee's Guide to Obtaining a Psychology Internship

especially if it is one of those "interview everybody" weekends. So bring along extra copies to give to the interviewers.

Allow yourself plenty of time to get to your first appointment. Indeed, if you get in the night before, I recommend you do a reconnaissance trip and locate exactly where it is you will be going the next morning. Count on getting lost. In a metropolitan area, more than one applicant has ended up at the wrong hospital. When I visit internships, I always have one of our present interns drive me in from the airport, and half the time *they* get lost, even though they have lived there several months. Even if you do not get lost, parking is often scarce. This may be a good time to spend a few extra dollars on a taxi; while the cab drivers usually manage to get lost too, at least you don't have to worry about the parking.

One advantage of visiting each internship is that you can observe how they deal with you and the other applicants. Some places will be very well organized. You will be given a schedule of appointments, you may be escorted around by one of the present interns, arrangements will be made to provide you with lunch, and, as you go from office to office, you will note that the people you meet have copies of your CV and have taken the time to read it. At other places, none of these nice things will happen. You may be one of a herd of applicants who is lectured to and then marched from place to place on a cursory tour. The people you meet may be harassed and act like seeing you is just one more annoyance in another difficult day. These observations can tell you a lot about a setting and its attitude toward students.

After a while, as you travel from place to place, your perceptions of the various sites will begin to blur. Immediately after visiting a site, take 20 minutes to write down your impressions while they are fresh. (Later share them with your support group.)

## ☐ Charming the Executive Assistant

By this point in your training you must have learned that every office has a key person who gets things done. Usually a woman, she may have a title ranging from "secretary" to "executive assistant." She usually has an office that controls access to that of the titular head, who is called the "Chair" or the "Director." Although the ITD may think he or she is in charge, nothing much gets done without the executive assistant's input. She is responsible for much of the work of internship selection. She is the person who makes sure that your application and supporting materials are filed correctly and that the training staff gets their ratings made. It is she who will probably answer your phone calls requesting information or making appointments.

If possible, meet this person and charm her socks off during your visit.

The Site Visit and Interview     **163**

Whatever you do, don't alienate her. The surest way to do so is by being patronizing. A friendly executive assistant can be incredibly helpful and a hostile one can misplace your folder so it never sees the light of day.

## ☐ The Interview Process

It is vital to be on time for your first appointment. If you get there early, kill time by checking through your materials, reviewing your questions, finding and using a rest room, and so on. Then arrive at the appointed time.[24]

Once you walk through the door, you are being evaluated. Gladwell (2000) recently described studies showing that untrained strangers viewing a 15-second video of a job applicant entering a room, shaking hands, and sitting down made ratings that correlated highly with those of the highly trained raters who actually interviewed the applicants. Their conclusion was that first impressions determine much of the variance in evaluations.

May et al. (1990) reported that many ITDs are as interested in intangible aspects such as rapport, a sense of humor, and flexibility as they are in your actual answers to their questions. Maintaining eye contact and shaking hands firmly may be as important as what you say.

Sites vary in how they interview applicants. Usually you will have individual interviews with members of the internship training staff and Selection Committee. In individual interviews, the interviewers are trying to assess how well you will fit in with the training site, both personally and professionally. Your task is to establish rapport, communicate interest and enthusiasm, convince the interviewer that your qualifications will be an asset to the program, and learn as much as you can about the site.

Sometimes two or more staff members may interview you. In a committee interview such as this, you will be answering questions from several different people. Maintain eye contact with the person who asked you the question. You may be asked to present a case, interpret a test protocol, or formulate a treatment plan for a hypothetical case. The group will be more interested in your approach to the problem and how well you think on your feet than in your coming up with a particular answer.

Other times you may be interviewed along with one or more other applicants. In a group interview, your task is to show how well you interact with others. You want to shine without appearing overbearing or pushy.

Regardless of the type of interview, you want to appear *confident, compe-*

---

[24]If you arrive early, you are anxious. If you arrive on time, you are compulsive. If you arrive late, you are antisocial. Since you can't win, you might as well be on time.

**164**     Megargee's Guide to Obtaining a Psychology Internship

*tent,* and *cordial.* Indeed, some repeat these "three C's" to themselves as they enter the room, and reinforce that image with appropriate body language and by sitting straight, maintaining eye contact, listening to the interviewer, and entering and leaving with a firm (but not ferocious) handshake. You do not want to appear down, disheveled, or disinterested.

## Handling Beverages

A word about coffee and other beverages. When you are touring internships, you will often find that offering a visitor coffee or some other beverage is part of the etiquette. *Don't accept.*

Whatever the beverage, it is rarely available in the interviewer's office. If you accept, the interviewer is obliged to go down the hall to wherever the beverage area is, locate a reasonably clean receptacle, and mix the beverage from whatever ingredients are at hand. The only thing you can be sure of is that it will not be the way you prefer it.

Often the coffee center is in the secretarial pool and there will be a sign indicating that coffee is $0.25. You fumble for change, the interviewer assures you that it is not necessary, and the secretaries glare at you because it is they who have to pay for the coffee supplies. Then you return to the office with 15 minutes of your allotted 30 dissipated.

So there you sit, with your cup of coffee in one hand, your portfolio for collecting handouts and reprints under one arm, and your notepad in another hand. As you reach for your pen, you suddenly realize you have one hand less than you need. So you must, gracefully of course, park something somewhere, while attending to the interviewer's every word and formulating cogent answers. What is the fate of the beverage? Well, you can always spill it. If you do, it is a toss up whether it is better to spill it on the interviewer's desk or on yourself. (See "Packing for Travel.") Or, you can hold it clutched in one hand until the interview is over.

The question then arises what to do with the cup. Do you leave it behind for the interviewer to clean up? Do you take it with you? (Hint: If ceramic cup, leave it; if Styrofoam, take it.) You then have to cope with shaking hands with the next interviewer while holding your portfolio, clipboard, pen, and coffee cup. However, you do have a ready answer to the next interviewer's question of whether you would like a cup of coffee.

Of course, it is possible that you might actually manage to consume the beverage during the interview. If so, you will proceed to the next interview wondering how to deal with (a) an empty coffee cup and (b) a full bladder. In short, unless you are being asked to join a group in a regular coffee room, for which refusing would be antisocial, skip the coffee.

A lawyer who read this told me that in law school she had been advised

The Site Visit and Interview    **165**

to always accept a beverage because failure to do so would be considered antisocial. When interviewing at a prestigious New York firm, she had a series of six consecutive half-hour interviews with male partners of the firm, each of whom offered her a cup of coffee which she dutifully consumed. By the time the last interview was completed, she was bursting at the seams. She asked the secretary for the location of the nearest rest room, was given a key, dashed to the designated door, and headed for a stall, only to discover in the worst possible way that she was in the men's room, which was being used by three of her erstwhile interviewers. She maintains that she was set up by the secretary. (See "Charming the Executive Assistant.")

## Dealing With Adversity

Although many applicants find the interview process stimulating and enjoyable, adverse things sometimes happen. If an interviewer is running late, it may throw the rest of your schedule off, annoying other people who may be waiting for you to show up. Rushing from one building to another for her next interview, one applicant went through the first EXIT door she saw, setting off an alarm. She ended up talking to Security instead of the ITD.

When bad things happen, and they will, it is important to keep cool and retain your sense of humor. Above all, don't panic. Asking directions on how to get to her next interview, one applicant to a consortium was told she was at the wrong hospital. She raced to her car and drove across town to the other hospital, only to find that she had been misdirected and had been at the right hospital in the first place. Her advice, "Stay calm and get a second opinion."

If you are having a difficult time communicating with some staff member, don't make the fundamental attribution error and assume there is something wrong with you or your application. One year I met with an ITD who was distant and preoccupied throughout our meeting. I didn't know if it was something I had said or done that put him off, or if he was just not a very friendly person. A couple of months later, when I ran into him at a meeting, he apologized. It turned out he had just come from the veterinarian's office where he had had to have his beloved dog put to sleep. His only concern at the time was to somehow get through our meeting without breaking down.

Intern applicants are typically unaware of the political infighting that may go on at some sites. Unbeknownst to you, the fact that one staff member is promoting your candidacy may alienate another staffer. Your interest in a behavioral medicine rotation may threaten the head of the adult inpatient service. The important thing is to stay focused. Don't let

**166** Megargee's Guide to Obtaining a Psychology Internship

adverse events throw you off your game. If one interview doesn't go well, hang in there and nail the next one.

The interview process is a time for mutual evaluation. You will be evaluating the personnel and the setting, and they will be evaluating you. This means *everyone,* including the current interns who may be showing you around or taking you out for pizza. The current interns will probably be asked for their impressions shortly after you leave. One applicant staying with a current intern was running late for her first appointment. She imperiously demanded that the current intern iron her blouse while she fixed her makeup. The current intern did not give the applicant a very favorable evaluation when she was later asked for her impressions.

## ☐ Questions You May Be Asked

Before you interview, you may wish to review the questions listed in Appendices 4 and 5. Be prepared to answer why you feel this internship would be good for *you.* This is a natural question and does not infringe on any APPIC rules. Instead, it provides you with an opportunity to sell yourself to the staff by focusing on your particular abilities. Use this opportunity to comment on your expectations so that you can validate them. One student applied to a facility because of its superb inpatient child/ adolescent unit; when the applicant mentioned this, she was told that it had been closed the year before. As disconcerting as this was, it would have been a lot worse to find out after being matched there.

You will no doubt be asked why you are applying for this particular internship position. Be reasonably frank. That is, do not say, "My ADCT insisted I apply to at least one 4th-rate place so that I can be sure of getting ranked somewhere." Instead focus on programmatic elements and particular personnel with whom you would like to work. This is a good opportunity to mention any favorable comments made by previous interns from your school. It not only helps remind the person that your predecessors have done well there, but finding a mutual acquaintance is often a major turning point in an interview.

You can also comment knowledgeably on the research being done by the training staff. Having previously located and read their publications, you can discuss their work with insight (and admiration). This will convince them that you are a very intelligent and discerning individual. Remember, however, that most interviewers are good at evaluating people, so don't overdo the flattery.

After reciting all the professional reasons, do not be afraid to mention other, nonprofessional, reasons why you are applying, such as climate or geography. The fact that you want to be near aged or infirm parents, or that you hope to locate in the area, are perfectly valid considerations.

The Site Visit and Interview     **167**

You may well be asked detailed questions regarding your professional experience, theoretical orientation, or preference in personality tests. You may be asked to conceptualize a case. One applicant was even shown a videotaped segment of an intake and asked by a panel of seven staff members to formulate and defend a diagnostic impression and treatment strategy.

Remember, you are applying to a *training* facility, so they should not expect you to be a fully qualified professional. Be honest about your experience, indicating what your areas of competence are and where you need additional training. Remember your self-analysis and the reasons why you applied to this particular internship.

Don't get annoyed if some of the questions cover material that is in your CV or AAPI. The interviewer simply wants to hear a sample of your professional verbiage. Can you discuss a case coherently or give the rationale for a therapeutic intervention? Underneath, the interviewer is asking, "If I send this person on a consult to Ward 22, will our service be embarrassed?" So use this as another opportunity to impress the interviewers with your ability to think clearly under stress and to formulate cogent responses. Give them a sample of what they can expect from you in a case conference if you attend that facility.

During your site visit be prepared to back up the claims you made in your application. One year I mentioned in my letter of recommendation that a non-Hispanic applicant with a Polish surname was fluent in Spanish. Sure enough, one interview was conducted entirely in Spanish.

You may be asked some questions that stump you. Take time to think through your reply. It is always better to confess to your ignorance of a topic than to try to fake expertise. Winiarski (1986) recalled that he had mentioned having a course that dealt in part with multiple personality disorders. When the interviewer asked him if he was familiar with that literature, he gulped and replied, "No, not really, just what I heard in class." The interviewer then presented Winiarski with a comprehensive review of the literature on multiple personality disorders he had just published. Winiarski noted, "My interview would have been over immediately if I had pretended knowledge I didn't have."

## Ranking Questions

As you know, APPIC rules prohibit internships, students, and academic directors from communicating information about how you rank the internships and how they rank you prior to Matching Day. There has been excellent compliance with this rule. If you are asked, simply state that APPIC rules prohibit you from disclosing ranking information. The transgressions that do occur are typically by peripheral internship personnel who are not yet aware of the "don't ask, don't tell, don't use" policy.

**168**    Megargee's Guide to Obtaining a Psychology Internship

You should note that the rules do not prohibit a discussion about how well you and the internship meet one another's needs and expectations. As long as neither party indicates whether or not they will rank one another, it is alright to explore the fit between the candidate and the setting.

## Personal or Illegal Questions

In a standard employment interview, the rules are very clear about what the interviewer can and cannot discuss with the applicant. Federal, state, and local laws prohibit asking for any information that is not related to the job for which you are applying. (The CareerBuilder Web site has a list of illegal questions and how to deal with them.)

Unfortunately, you may encounter interviewers who are either unaware of these rules or feel they do not apply to internship applicants. Some psychologists apparently feel compelled to act "psychological" and approach the interview with a clinical or diagnostic mind set. Others act as if they were in session. One applicant reported that she was asked how she had dealt with her parents' divorce, while a married woman was asked what was the worst thing her spouse would say about her.

In recent years, older applicants and candidates with family obligations have been especially subject to personal questions. A woman in her 50s was asked if she had the stamina and energy to cope with the strains of interning. (A marathon runner and Nordic ski instructor, she was probably in better shape than the interviewer.) A 36-year-old father of six was quizzed on his religious beliefs. Single mothers are often asked how they will care for their children. (See Appendix 4.)

The important thing is not to let such questions fluster you. Decide in advance how you wish to deal with them. If you want to answer, you can, but if you do you are giving information that is not job related and which may in some way hurt your chances. One woman wrote me that after submitting her applications she discovered that she was pregnant with twins. Although her mentors advised her not to disclose her pregnancy, she chose to do so during her interviews so she could assess how flexible the various sites would be in working with her to arrange her hours and so on. She matched successfully.

You are perfectly within your rights to refuse to answer by saying, "I do not see how [whatever] has any relevance to my ability to carry out my duties as an intern." However, if you refuse to answer, you run the risk of seeming to be uncooperative. One of my students was asked to report the most negative thing she could think of about her father. When she stated she thought he was a fine man who had put all of his children through college under very difficult circumstances, she was accused of resisting.

There is often a fine line between a legal and an illegal question. It is

The Site Visit and Interview    **169**

permissible for interviewers to ask applicants if they will be able to work overtime and on weekends as long as they ask *all* applicants and not just women with children. While it is not appropriate to ask if you have had any health problems recently, it is OK to ask if you will need any special accommodations to perform the duties of the position.

Another approach is to address the job-related intent behind what appears to be an inappropriate or personal question. If you are asked about your family circumstances, for example, you might respond, "I am confident that my private life will not affect my job performance." You can also point out that despite your age, family obligations, medical condition, or whatever, you have successfully completed a demanding course of graduate study in order to become eligible for internship. Indeed, it may well be that some of the "problems" the interviewer seems concerned about have taught you to manage your time and become a more mature and caring individual than someone who has not had to cope with adversity.

The bottom line is that you are not obliged to answer personal questions. The APPIC Board recently affirmed that questions about your age, marital status, family obligations, sexual orientation, religion, and disabilities are not permitted and invited applicants who felt they were being discriminated against to submit complaints to the APPIC Standards and Review Committee (ASARC). Of course, no one did. Prior to Match Day, no one wants to risk offending the Selection Committee, and afterwards most candidates simply want to forget about the whole process. (See Chapter 9.) However, given the attention that these inappropriate questions have been receiving, my guess is that APPIC members will try to do a better job of educating their interviewers about what is and is not allowed in selection interviews.

## ☐ Questions You May Ask the Interviewer

You should go into an interview prepared to ask questions as well as answer them. One of the first you might have is who you are talking to. During the interview season, many staff members may be pressed into service, even if they do not function as supervisors and have little connection with the training program. It will help you to evaluate the program if you have a clear idea of each interviewer's role in training. It may be that the person who impressed you so, either positively or negatively, is someone who has minimal contact with the interns. The way to find out how each interviewer is involved in the training program is to ask.

As part of your preparation, you should prepare *specific* questions in advance for each setting. As in any job interview, the interviewer will be more impressed by inquiries relating to professional matters, such as the

**170**    Megargee's Guide to Obtaining a Psychology Internship

nature and extent of supervision, than with questions about the number of days off or the frequency of coffee breaks. How you phrase a question can be important. The interviewer will be more impressed with your eagerness to learn if you ask how many seminars are "offered" as opposed to how many are "required." If you think certain training experiences are important, this is the time to determine whether they will be available.

Don't be afraid to ask about living conditions in the area. Rather than being considered "unprofessional," it tells the ITD that you are seriously considering what is involved in moving to this locality. One of my students was a single mother with a 10-year-old child. She was very concerned about such things as school districts, daycare facilities, and drug use in the schools. One ITD she grilled on these subjects later called to tell me how impressed he was with this woman's professional maturity, sincerity, and commitment to being a good parent. He made her an offer under UND and was truly disappointed when she chose to go to another city that she felt would be better for her son.

Whatever you do, when you are asked if you have any questions, do not say, "No." This shuts off the dialogue and suggests that you are not interested in the setting. As one exasperated ITD remarked, "It is inconceivable that a person seriously planning to spend a year of his or her life here has no questions." So even if it has been a long day, when the final interviewer asks you if you have any questions, don't reply, "No, they have all been answered." If you do this, you may spend the rest of the time staring at each other. Recall some questions from Appendix 5, or ask the interviewer where he or she interned. Obviously it was at the current site or somewhere else. If the interviewer actually interned there, you can ask how often former interns take positions on staff and launch into all the questions you normally ask current interns, as well as for comments on how life changes when you move from being an intern to a staff member. If the person interned somewhere else, you can ask how this internship compares with the place the interviewer attended. Such a comparative approach often provides new perspectives, and you can be sure the answers will not be ones you have already heard. The point is to keep up the dialogue. Ask questions that require elaboration rather than a simple "yes" or "no." Remember you are being evaluated in part on the basis of *your* interviewing skills.

Your interviews will probably be with a variety of people: staff, present interns, and the ITD. Use your interviews with different people to cross-check information and get data on different aspects of the program, such as the clientele, working conditions, the relation of psychology to psychiatry (always important at medical centers), number and nature of colloquia, and so forth. How does the staff's perception of how rotations are assigned or the balance between training and service agree with the students'? What is it that various members of the staff seek in an intern?

The Site Visit and Interview    **171**

You might also ask for additional written information about rotations or programs that goes beyond what is included in the brochure or on the Web site, especially at a consortium where there are several different agencies. Some internships will also have information pamphlets available that describe the area and its amenities. (One recent applicant referred to this display of interest as "Sucking up in a dignified manner.")

The only thing worse than asking no questions is asking a really stupid question. For most ITDs, one of the stupidest questions you can ask is for a "general description" of the program. This tells the interviewer that you did not read the information packet they went to such pains to produce. As one ITD said, "A student must be pretty dumb to come all the way here to apply for an internship when he doesn't know anything about the program."

## ☐ Evaluating the Setting

While visiting, take the opportunity to get a feel for the atmosphere of the facility: the degree of structure, friendliness, caring for the intern's experience, attitude toward clients, and all those other intangibles. Is it fast paced or laid back? Is morale high, or do people seem disgruntled and harassed? What sorts of facilities or equipment are available for interns? Will you have your own office? Your own desk in a shared office? Your own drawer in a shared desk? How about computers, audio and video recording equipment, electronic test scoring apparatuses, and specialized equipment for neuropsychological assessment or biofeedback? How do the patients' areas look to you? How do they *smell*?

If it is possible to arrange lodging with one of the current interns, by all means do so. This affords you an invaluable opportunity to get beyond the brochure and see for yourself what life is like for interns at that setting. How do the current interns get along with one another and with staff? Will you be treated as a colleague or a serf? Do the current interns have a life outside the internship, or is it all work and no play? Do they have time for any cultural activities, leisure reading, or exercise? One applicant discovered that her hostess had had to give away her cat because she had no time to care for it. How about the cost of living? Is there any affordable housing near the facility, or do the interns have to commute? If you do not get a chance to talk to the present interns, see if you can get their home phone numbers or e-mail addresses so you can communicate with them later.

If possible, check out the town. What would it be like to live there? Get a newspaper and see what the rents are like. Drive through the areas where interns typically live. Will you need to invest in a bulletproof vest if you go for a walk? At one internship I visited, every intern had his or

172    Megargee's Guide to Obtaining a Psychology Internship

her car stolen or boosted at some point during the year. In short, before you leave, make sure that you have enough information to evaluate each setting on those factors that are most important to you. Also, if others are coming with you, check out the aspects important to them. Better yet, bring them along and let them reconnoiter while you interview.

At some point, review Chapter 3, in which I discussed the aspects of the internship to consider in deciding on priorities, especially those dealing with morale, interdisciplinary relations, collegiality, quality and quantity of supervision, and the like. At that time, you constructed what amounts to a template of your ideal internship. Score how well this internship matches that template. The more accurate information you can get during your visit, the better able you will be to decide on your rankings.

# The Endgame

When you first return from interviewing, you will probably feel relaxed and confident, albeit exhausted. You got through it and you survived! You held your own in professional interactions with top psychologists away from your home base. It is a heady experience, and you will probably be eager to swap war stories with fellow applicants. Enjoy this feeling while it lasts. Get reacquainted with your family and major professor. Soon you will be entering the final stage of the internship-selection process, the "Endgame." The Endgame is the culmination of the whole seemingly interminable process that began back in August. In early February, you will rank your choices and the training centers will rank theirs. Three weeks later, you will learn the outcome. For many applicants, these feel like the longest 3 weeks of their lives.

## ☐ The Endgame in the Bad Old Days

For those of us who were involved with the internship selection process before computer matching, today's Endgame is (blessedly) anticlimactic and free of the chicanery and duplicity that abounded in the past. Before computer matching, it was to the internships' advantage to offer positions only to students who were sure to accept. As APPIC (1999c) itself acknowledged, "The previous internship selection procedure used by our profession actually encouraged and rewarded strategizing and deal-making, resulting in tremendous stress for internship applicants."

As UND approached, ITDs would often call students to "See if you have any questions" or to ask, "How is it going?" hoping the students would

**174**  Megargee's Guide to Obtaining a Psychology Internship

reveal their rankings. Even though it was against the APPIC rules, some would go farther by saying, "You are in our top group and we would love to have you join us. Where do we stand with you?" (Johnson, 1986). And a few would even tell the students they would get an offer only if they promised to accept it.

Most students had no qualms about informing their first-choice setting that it was number 1, especially if it appeared to enhance their chances of acceptance. Indeed, surveys showed that approximately 80% of the applicants "first choiced" their favorite setting, even when they were not pressured to do so (Constantine & Keilin, 1996; Thorne, 1997). But what should they tell their lower ranked choices? As a former APPIC Chair wrote, "Any statement by the candidate other than that this particular program is the first choice is usually interpreted as lack of interest. Such a response typically leads to rejection of the candidate before or on selection day" (Zimet, 1988, p. 5). A survey of applicants under UND revealed, "A number of applicants described the high degree of pressure and confusion they experienced related to this obligation to disclose, particularly in terms of their fears about whether or not they would still be considered as viable candidates by their second- or lesser-ranked sites" (Constantine & Keilin, 1996, p. 313).

Under APPIC rules, no commitments made by either party before UND were legal or binding. When asked how to respond to an inquiry from an lower ranked internship, one APPIC Chair responded, "Do what everyone else does. Lie!" Some did, committing themselves to more than one internship. Every ITD I interviewed had tales of applicants who promised to accept an offer but then reneged. One ITD told me about an applicant who had volunteered that her internship was his first choice and that he would definitely accept an offer. On Notification Day, he "unexpectedly" received an offer from a place he regarded as more prestigious, and went there instead. This individual, now a licensed psychologist, still practices in her area, but, as far as this ITD is concerned, he is an unethical person who will never, in his entire life, get any cooperation from her, whether it involves applying for a job, referring patients, asking for research subjects, or trying to place students.

ITDs who tried to follow the APPIC guidelines also had problems with UND. Because they could not be sure which candidates would accept on UND, they had to create a list of alternate candidates in case their first choices declined their offers. This sometimes led to the practice of "stringing along." One student who had voluntarily made a first-choice commitment to an internship got a call just before UND. The ITD told him that on Selection Day he should, "Just sit tight. Don't do anything foolish." He understood this to mean that he was going to get an offer. When he told his major professor, she said it sounded as if he was on their alternate list and they were stringing him along. She advised him to call his lower ranked selections and tell them he was still interested. The student de-

The Endgame    **175**

murred; he had made a first-choice commitment, the ITD was very nice, and he was sure he would get a call on UND. He did. It was the ITD saying he was sorry, all their slots were filled but that the student had been their "first alternate." When he called all his other choices, they too had filled. Stedman (1989) reported that one well-regarded program informed numerous applicants that each was "first alternate."

Everyone—applicants, internships, and academic programs alike—hated the UND system. Stedman (1983) referred to UND as "a day of fear and loathing," and surveys showed that 40% to 53% of the applicants experienced rule violations by internships, the most common being pressure to disclose their rankings (Carifio, Buckner, & Grace, 1987; Carifio & Grace, 1992; Constantine & Keilin, 1996). By 1997 there was such widespread dissatisfaction with the system that the APPIC Board adopted stringent rules prohibiting applicants and ADCTs, as well as ITDs, from soliciting or communicating ranking information. ITDs were further enjoined from using any ranking information that applicants might volunteer. Although I was skeptical that this would solve the problem (Megargee, 1997), I felt it was an important step in the right direction.

Even more effective, in my opinion, was the adoption of computer matching in the 1998–1999 selection year. The software program and algorithms that were developed eliminated any incentive for applicants or internships to cheat. Today, most internships have learned that there is no longer any advantage in knowing how students rank the various settings, and, with the overabundance of applicants, they no longer have to worry about not filling all their positions. The best strategy for applicants and ITDs alike is to submit their rankings exactly as they see them (Keilin, 2000). There is no longer any need for second guessing or game playing.

By 1999, cheating had largely been eliminated. An APPIC survey of 500 randomly selected applicants who took part in the 1999 matching program indicated that only 25 of the 344 applicants (7%) who returned the survey perceived any violations relating to disclosing ranking information. Similarly, a survey of all 576 APPIC members revealed that only 30 of the 366 ITDs (8%) who responded reported that any applicants revealed their rankings to the internships (APPIC, 1999a). At the 2000 APPIC membership meeting, the chair of the sanctions committee reported that no official complaints had been filed regarding the 1999–2000 selection process.

## ☐ · Back to the Poker Table

Eliminating the pressure tactics and cheating has made the Endgame much less stressful. This does not mean that there is no longer any game playing. Although the nature of the game is different, you still have to play your cards correctly to get the best outcome.

**176**   Megargee's Guide to Obtaining a Psychology Internship

## Writing Notes

The Endgame is an uncertain time, and for most of us uncertainty is stressful. Intern applicants can always find something to worry about, and one worry many have recently expressed is whether or not they should send "thank you" notes after interviewing.

Under UND, it was important to assure internships of your continuing interest. Thank you notes were an easy way of expressing interest without making a premature commitment. In the third edition of this book I advised:

> Your mother no doubt taught you to write "bread and butter" notes after visiting friends to thank them for their hospitality. After you return from interviewing, you should send such notes to all the places where you interviewed. (Indeed, Gollaher and Craig [1994] advised sending notes to *every individual* you talked with.) After the interviewing season is over, a major problem for Internship Training Directors is how to determine which interviewees are still interested. A friendly, albeit noncommittal, note, thanking them for their hospitality and repeating that you were impressed with the program, is a good way to communicate the fact that you are actively considering their program. In fact, ITDs who do not get a note such as this may conclude that you are not interested. If you have some remaining questions, you can use this opportunity to ask them. This will put you in a good position to begin the "Endgame." (Megargee, 1997, p. 185)

After the "don't ask, don't tell, don't use" rule was formulated, some applicants worried that sending such notes might violate the rule. One January, after most applicants had finished interviewing, a fierce debate broke out on the intern applicant listserv over whether applicants should send thank you notes to the internships they had visited. Some felt it was the right thing to do, while others feared that expressing interest in the program might be considered a rule violation that would somehow disqualify them. Eventually, some ITDs and APPIC Board members posted messages assuring nervous applicants that if they wanted to write thank you notes they could certainly do so, but it would have no effect on how they would eventually be ranked.

Under computer matching, reassuring an internship of your continuing interest is no longer an important issue. Whether or not you send a thank you note will not influence your chances of acceptance. I now recommend that you send a note to any present interns who might have afforded you hospitality by putting you up overnight or taking you to dinner. Why? Because, as your mother told you, it is the polite thing to do. I no longer suggest sending thank you notes to the ITD or others who might have interviewed you. If it makes you feel less anxious and gives you an illusion of control, by all means do so. However, make sure you do not include anything that might be construed as ranking-related information. If you want to save the time, energy, and postage, then don't.

The Endgame     **177**

## Discarding

Once you have reflected on the internships you visited and discussed your findings with friends, relatives, and advisors, review your list. Is there any internship that you definitely do not want to attend, even if it is the only setting with which you are matched? If so, discard it. You should not rank any internship you would not be willing to attend, because if you are matched there you are obligated to go.

You, too, may be discarded. APPIC used to have a rule requiring ITDs to notify applicants who would not be included in their rankings at least 10 days before Ranking Day. Many programs could not meet this deadline, so it was dropped in 1999 (Keilin, 2000). Nevertheless, a number of programs still inform candidates if they are no longer under consideration. One ADCT with 20 years' experience estimated that even superstars can expect to be rejected by 25% of their sites, although they may not be formally notified of the fact.

If you receive a rejection, do not be devastated by the news. As I stated in the beginning, rejections are inevitable, and not everyone fits a program's needs. Most will probably send out form letters or e-mails, but if they call, don't get angry or give in to the temptation to say something nasty. Instead, be gracious, and show them that you are a class act. Thank them for the information, express your disappointment, and wish them well. (I know of at least one instance in which a program that did not fill all its slots under UND made an offer to a candidate they had previously excluded.)

## Drawing New Cards

After discarding is finished, reexamine your hand. If your list has gotten too short, and you are doubtful about your chances for getting matched at the remaining institutions, you may want to draw some new cards by submitting some additional applications to those centers with late due dates on your "lifeboat list." At this stage of the game, the thought of filling out more applications and possibly going on more interviews will probably be very aversive, but, if your list is truly too short, it is better to do it now than through the Clearinghouse after Matching Day.

## Playing Your Hand

Computer matching has eliminated the need for the players to peek into each other's hands to find out their rankings. Nevertheless, it is important for applicants and internships alike to impress each other as favorably as possible. The higher you are ranked by your favorite internships, the better your chances of getting matched with one of them. By the same token, the internships hope that their top candidates rank them high.

**178**    Megargee's Guide to Obtaining a Psychology Internship

During the Endgame, you will probably be communicating with the internships on your list. Remember that every contact you have with an agency is part of the evaluation process, even when it is with the clerical staff. If you are rude or abrasive, you will be labeled as rude and abrasive. If you pester people, you will be regarded as a pest. Such people get ranked lower than those who are thoughtful and considerate.

After interviewing, you may get calls from internships. (Again, make sure you have erased any "cute" messages, ribald songs, and so forth from your machine and replaced them with something more appropriate and businesslike.) Sometimes the internship may be seeking clarification of some issue that has come up during the Selection Committee's deliberations. A site with several programs may want to know exactly which you are applying for. Or you might get a call asking if you have any additional questions. This may be a last-minute attempt to impress you or simply an effort by an ITD to maintain his or her illusion of control. These calls may come when you least expect them, so it helps to have prepared something to say so you don't stand there stammering. Some ITDs call every applicant, some call only a select few, and many make no calls, so don't read too much into them. Computer matching is a relatively new game for ITDs, and many who cut their teeth on UND are still learning how to deal with it. Not getting any calls does not mean you are doomed, and getting several does not necessarily mean that you will be ranked high by those settings.

By the same token, you should call or e-mail the internship if you have questions that you need answered. Perhaps you have not heard anything from an internship to which you applied and you want to know if you are still under consideration. Maybe you want to clarify the nature of the various programs that are offered or to inquire whether a particular slot is paid or unpaid. By all means call or e-mail and ask your question. However, you must not break the rule on asking or communicating ranking-related information. Doing so can seriously damage your chances at that internship. No one wants an intern who can't obey the rules.

Even if you don't have a burning question, you may feel the need to communicate with an internship simply to reduce your anxiety or to give yourself one last chance to impress them. Most settings will understand your anxiety, but don't overdo it. They can tell when you are creating excuses to call. As you will see next year, when you yourself are an intern, the selection process puts a tremendous strain on most training centers. In addition to caring for clients and training the present interns, they may still be interviewing prospective applicants while attempting to evaluate those whom they have already seen. Calls from anxious applicants just add to their workload. As Mitchell (1996, p. 92) warned, "When applicants call an internship site, they should keep in mind the selection of interns is just one of the many responsibilities the agency staff is deal-

The Endgame **179**

ing with. Applicants should be specific about the reason for the call and should give the agency time to respond to their phone call. . . . Candidates who make repeated phone calls may appear overly anxious and can be a source of irritation to the staff."

## ☐ Ranking Your Selections

Ascertain exactly when you must submit your rank-ordered list (ROL) of internships to the National Matching Service. Currently, it is the first Wednesday in February. Therefore, in late January you should start ranking your choices. Do not wait until the last minute. Making your choices may be more difficult than you anticipate.

Before you begin ranking your selections, read the latest matching information and the FAQs for Internship Applicants on the APPIC Web site. Sometimes additional instructions or guidelines are posted as Ranking Day approaches. Make sure you thoroughly understand the ranking procedures. (If there is any disagreement between my advice and the APPIC directions, do what APPIC says. I hope this book will be in print for a long time and inevitably there will be some changes from one year to the next.)

Once you are sure you understand the proper procedures, consult the lists of priorities you established at the beginning of your reconnaissance. Match your templates of what you are seeking in an internship with your perception of what each program offers. Visualize yourself at each internship. How would you like working in each setting? Do not worry about how they are ranking you or where you think you stand the best chance of being accepted. Base your evaluations solely on what you think is best for you.

How many internships should you rank? I would rank each and every acceptable internship to which you applied. In the 1999–2000 selection year, APPIC (2000b) reported that those applicants who successfully matched submitted an average of 7.9 rankings while those who failed to match filed an average of 4.2 rankings. You may draw your own conclusions.

In the process of establishing your final rankings, you should consult with other people. These include your ADCT and other faculty members who may have additional information about certain programs, alumni who may have interned at programs on your list, your fellow applicants, and, of course, family members and friends who may be involved in your decision.

You may discover you need more information in order to make your rankings. Maybe one of your classmates heard a rumor of a key program change at a certain site. Perhaps your ranking of another setting depends on your chances of getting a particular rotation or working with a specific

## Sites With Multiple Programs

In making your selections, remember that many sites have multiple programs, each with its own matching number. You can use the multiple program listings to indicate your preferences with regard to programs within a given site. For example, you may prefer the child track to the adult track, or the paid positions to those that are unfunded. If you do not rank one of the programs, such as an unfunded position, you cannot be matched with it.

You can also use your rankings to indicate your preference for programs across sites. If you especially want a child clinical program, and you are applying to several internships which each have a separate program number for their child tracks, you can put all the child tracks at the various programs highest on your list, followed by the other programs at these internships.

## Shuffling the Deck

Once you have obtained all the information you need, it is time to rank your choices. Do your ranking carefully; some applicants focus exclusively on their top 2 or 3 choices and pay little attention to those farther down on their list. Although most do get matched to one of their top 3 choices, in 1999–2000, 10% were matched to programs they had ranked from 5th through 10th. How you rank these programs may determine which you will attend.

It will probably be easy to sort the centers into "A," "B," and "C" lists: one or two top choices, another two or three second echelon choices, and some others that you wouldn't mind attending but that for one reason or another you find less attractive than those on your A and B lists. However, this isn't good enough. When you submit your rankings to the NMS, you must rank each and every site on your list. Moreover, in sites with multiple programs having their own individual match numbers, you must submit a rank for each program if you want to be considered for those positions.

To assist in this process, Brill, Wolkin, and McKeal (1985) recommended setting aside 20 uninterrupted minutes. Imagine yourself 30 years hence, pleased with how you have lived your life. Looking back, reflect on how you spent most of your working time. What did you do? What was most important or satisfying to you? Then ask what sorts of professional training you most need to accomplish these goals. Do the same with your personal life. Then ask yourself what programs are most likely to provide these experiences.

Another technique is to write the name and number of each program on a 3 × 5 inch card and try placing the cards in order from most preferred to least preferred. (Using cards makes it easier to shuffle the order around than it is when you are writing numbers on a list.) You will probably experience the most difficulty in the middle of the list. As you perform this exercise, you will see why I advised you that applying to 25 or 30 sites is counterproductive.

## Using a Grid

Some students find that the card method is too simple. Some facilities are better on some factors, such as location, while others are stronger on other characteristics, such as rotations. If so, go back to the list of priorities you formulated at the beginning of this process. Reconsider the list. In the light of your experience interviewing, you may want to add some categories and delete others. For example, Stedman et al. (1995) discovered that one of the factors that differentiated intern applicants' highest, middle, and lowest choices was an intangible "gut" feeling about how well they fit in with the program. If this was not one of your original categories, you might want to add it to the list. You may also have discovered that the importance of other factors has diminished. Perhaps that "significant other" that you felt you had to be near has dumped you because you have become so obsessed with internship seeking that you have been miserable company recently. If so, rejoice! You have one less factor to worry about.

Once you have your final list of categories, you can use some of the attitude-scaling techniques you learned about in social psychology to help you make a decision. Casey Jacob (1987) advised making a "grid" or spreadsheet with columns for each factor and rows for each internship. You can then evaluate each internship on each factor using 5- or 10-point, Likert-type scales. An even better procedure is to use your 3 × 5 inch cards and rank order the settings on each factor. This forces you to differentiate among the sites.

Stewart and Stewart (1996a) went one step further and advocated a formal paired-comparison technique in which you consider every possible pair of programs and choose which one of the two you prefer on each of the variables you deem important. Thus, on "Location," for example, you would compare Program A with Programs B, C, D, . . . , N, and next compare Program B with Programs C, D, . . . , N, and so forth until each program has been paired with every other program on each variable. You then tally up the number of times you chose each program and compute a score for each program on each factor. (See Stewart and

**182** Megargee's Guide to Obtaining a Psychology Internship

Stewart, 1996b, Figure 1, for a detailed example.) Although this procedure seems very tedious, the Stewarts reported that comparing ten sites on eight factors took about an hour and a half, which is less time than many students spend obsessing over their global rankings.

In Stewart and Stewarts's (1996a) paired-comparison technique, each factor was weighted equally. However, if some are more important to you than others, you can include weights that reflect this fact. So if "work prospects for spouse" is twice as important to you as "preferred rotation," you simply multiply the scores on that variable by two. Or you can do this implicitly by including several variables that represent different aspects of the same general factor. "Climate," "proximity to family," and "urban area" are all aspects of "location." There is no end to the complexity of the schemes you can use to help you evaluate the settings. However, don't obsess too much. Remember that the point of these exercises is to help you arrive at a ranking, not give you ways to defer deciding.

When you complete this exercise, you will end up with scores for each setting that you can convert to ranks. The results may surprise you. You may find that some sites rank higher or lower than you would have expected. Give them some further thought, but don't be *too* compulsive. If your favorite site ranks fifth, for example, and you still feel you like it best, then make it your first choice. How you get your rankings is not important. What *is* important is that you have all your sites ranked.

## Couples Matching

If you want to travel in tandem with someone else, APPIC has devised a special couples matching program that allows you to coordinate your matchings with those of your partner. First, you obtain special rank-order materials for couples from NMS. Then you submit a *combined* list in which you rank-order *pairs* of programs. Keilin (1998) explained:

> The new matching program . . . [allows] a couple to submit a single rank-ordered list consisting of paired internship sites. For example, a couple's first choice may be that Partner A chooses Program W and Partner B chooses Program W; second choice, Partner A chooses Program W and Partner B chooses Program Y; third choice, Partner A chooses Program Y and Partner B chooses Program Z; and so on. The matching program uses these pairings, rather than individual choices, when placing the couple in internship positions. Any two internship applicants may choose to designate themselves as a "couple" and submit a single, paired rank-ordered list of any length. (p. 602)

For the couples' matching system to work optimally, you should rank every possible outcome, including the possibility that one person or the other may remain unmatched. This can result in a long list; APPIC reported that in 1999 some couples ranked over 150 pairs of programs.

The Endgame    **183**

Recently 21 couples participated; in 19 pairs, both partners obtained internships, and one partner in each of the remaining two couples matched (APPIC, 2000c). While not perfect, the overall rate of 95% for these couples was better than the 85% enjoyed by single applicants. Eight couples were both placed in the same city, and only four were more than 150 miles apart. (APPIC noted that some couples gave high ranks to some pairs of programs "that were hundreds even thousands of miles apart.") Obviously, the more circumscribed the geographic area in which couples apply, and the more abundant the programs within that area, the greater the likelihood of them both being matched to programs in the same general vicinity. Details regarding the mechanics of couples' matching procedures and data regarding previous couples matches are available on the APPIC Web site.

## ☐ Submitting Your Rankings

Once you have sorted out your preferences, it is time to bite the bullet and complete your ROL. The selection algorithms are designed in such a way that your best chance to get the internship of your choice is to rank your selections in your preferred order (Keilin, 2000). If there is some "dream internship" that you would love to attend but fear you have no realistic chance of obtaining, go ahead and put it first. If they listed you sufficiently high, you will get your dream match. If your dream internship, or even several dream internships, do not rank you high enough for you to match there, the computer will proceed on to your next choices. You have nothing to lose and everything to gain by calling it exactly as you see it.

In recording your rankings, remember:

1. Do not rank any program you do not wish to attend. If you do, you may have to go there.
2. If you do not rank a program you cannot be matched to it. Make sure you include every program for which you want to be considered.
3. Rank the programs solely on the basis of *your* preferences. Do not engage in second guessing or game playing. Even if you think there is little if any chance of your being matched with your first choice, put it first anyhow. You may get matched, but if you do not, it cannot hurt your chances at your second, third, or lower ranked choices.
4. Make sure you have put down the correct numbers for the programs you hope to be matched to. This is not the time for clerical errors such as transposing digits. The National Matching Service Web site lists all the program numbers for each site.

Make sure you follow the current proper procedure for submitting your ROL. APPIC and NMS have experimented with various procedures. They

**184**   Megargee's Guide to Obtaining a Psychology Internship

began by using the mails and fax for submitting ROLs. They are currently using an Internet-based system for electronic submissions. However, this may change by the time you read this book. Get the latest information from the APPIC or NMS Web sites. Whatever the current procedure, follow it exactly. Since it is a Fundamental Law of Nature that things go wrong at the worst possible time, especially when computers are involved, I advise you not to wait until the last minute to submit your ROL. After all this stress and work, you do not want to be miss the deadline because of a power failure or computer virus. However, remember that once you submit your list, it is final. You cannot change your choices.

## ☐ The Endgame from the Internships' Perspective

While you are sorting your cards and deciding how to play your hand, the ITDs and their Selection Committees are doing likewise, albeit on a larger scale. Their decisions are complicated by the fact that they must often consult with consortiums and committees and consider local policies and politics in formulating their lists, as they try to satisfy as many colleagues as possible. Some will also be trying to balance their intern classes with respect to gender, ethnicity, academic program, and similar factors.

In filling out their ROLs, some internships use *global ranking*, in which they simply list all their acceptable applicants in their preferred order, just as you do with your ROL. If "Halibut Hospital" has 36 acceptable applicants, their ITD, Dr. Almondine Dover-Sole, can simply rank them from 1 to 36 and submit the entire list. (Obviously, Dr. Dover-Sole should not list anyone that Halibut is unwilling to have as an intern. If she does, and that person is matched with Halibut, then Halibut must accept him, just as he is obligated to attend Halibut.) Under global ranking, if Halibut has six slots, the six top-ranking candidates will constitute their first "tier." The next six candidates constitute their second tier, and so on. Halibut's preferences are then matched with those of the applicants to achieve the optimal fit.

When the global matching program was being developed, some ITDs expressed concern over maintaining diversity with respect to applicants' training programs. What should Dr. Dover-Sole do if Halibut's Chief Psychologist, Dr. Barry Cuda, wants no more than one student from any given university? Leaving one applicant or the other off her ROL was obviously unsatisfactory, so NMS includes an option whereby Dr. Dover-Sole can specify that no more than one student from any given school can be matched to Halibut. I have no way of knowing how many internships exercise this option.

Another way to achieve diversity is through *program-specific* or position-specific ranking. If Dr. Cuda wants equal numbers of male and female applicants, for example, Dr. Dover-Sole can request two program numbers with three slots each. On the ROL for the first "program," she will list only women, and for the second she will rank only men. (She also has the option to specify that if they run out of male applicants before all three "male" slots are filled, it is all right to fill the remaining positions with women and vice versa.) In addition to gender, Dr. Cuda might want to achieve some diversity with respect to applicants' theoretical orientation, preferred rotations, or geographical origin. To accomplish this, a facility with six positions, like Halibut, can have as many programs (i.e., match numbers) as it has positions and can submit a separate ROL for each one.

Consider the "Moosehead Medical Center." With its psychodynamic orientation, Moosehead uses a mentoring model. Moosehead has three primary supervisors or mentors and three internship positions, so the Training Director, Dr. Buck Muledeer, lets each supervisor choose the interns they would most like to supervise. After Muledeer and his two colleagues, Dr. Carrie Boux and Dr. Fawn Deux, agree on the pool of acceptable applicants, they each fill out individual ROLs for the positions they supervise. Some applicants could get listed on all three lists; others may be included on only one.

Eventually, the various internships sort out their selections and submit their ROLs to NMS. As far as you are concerned, once you have filed your ROL and the sites have submitted theirs, your fate is in the hands of the Computer Gods. In about 3 weeks, you will learn the outcome. Take the first 2 weeks to get caught up on your life. If you have children, notice how they have grown. If you have a bank account, notice how it has shrunk. Visit your job and see if you are still employed. Try to remember what it was you were doing for your dissertation. However, set aside some time the week before Matching Notification Day. There is more work for you to do then.

## ☐ How Computer Matching Works

While you are trying to reintegrate with your life, the computers in Canada are grinding away, seeking the best possible fits between the applicants and the internships programs.[25] Let us discuss computer matching.

### Why Computer Matching?

In Chapter 1, I reviewed the internship selection strategies used previously. All had the same basic flaw: sequential decision making that gave

---

[25]Actually, it is not necessary for NMS to use a computer. The matching could be done by hand, but then it would take months instead of weeks to sort out all the outcomes.

**186**  Megargee's Guide to Obtaining a Psychology Internship

one party or the other an unfair advantage. In *laissez faire*, the strategy used prior to APPIC, ITDs had the leverage because they could make an offer whenever they chose and rescind it if the student did not accept immediately. With Uniform Notification, the training center had to make a binding unilateral commitment to an applicant and then wait until the candidate decided whether to accept. In terms of my poker analogy, some players had to reveal their hands before the others did. This disparity created the differences in power and control that led some players to try to equalize the differences by "cheating."

Computer matching resolved this problem by allowing the players to make their selections independently and reveal them simultaneously to a neutral third party, the NMS, which examines their selections, seeks the best fits, and eventually advises all the players of the results. In effect, all the players show their hands at the same time, and the computer figures out who wins and who loses, just like the dealer does in a casino game. In this game, there is no advantage in knowing what cards the other players hold or how they plan to play them. The best chance for the various players to achieve the results they want is to "call them as they see them," that is, to rank their choices solely on the basis of their perceived desirability. No other strategy can accomplish their goals better (Keilin, 2000). No longer is there any incentive for the ITDs to know the students' choices, and there is no advantage to the students in "first-choicing" one or more internships.

## How the Program Works

Once all the rankings have been entered, applicants' choices are compared with those submitted by the internships.[26] Let us suppose that your first four choices all used global selection with each submitting a single ROL. You ranked them as follows on your ROL:

1. Halibut Hospital (6 slots)
2. Codliver Consortium (4 slots)
3. Septicemia School of Medicine (12 slots)
4. Moosehead Medical Center (3 slots)

When the program comes to your ROL, it will note that Halibut Hospital is your first choice and check Halibut's list to see how they rated you. If you are in their first tier, that is, you are one of their six highest-ranked

---

[26]Unlike the medical matching program, the APPIC program begins with applicants rather than institutions. The results make no difference except in the rare example of a gridlock such as the one I described in Chapter 2. The APPIC model will decide such stalemates in favor of the student, whereas the medical model resolves them in favor of the internship setting. However, APPIC estimates gridlocks occur in less than 1 in 1,000 matches.

The Endgame    **187**

applicants, you are automatically matched. You have a position at Halibut and you are dropped from further consideration by the computer program. Meanwhile, one of Halibut's slots is marked as filled.

Suppose, however, you miss the first tier at Halibut. Instead of being in the top six, you are ranked seventh. Your first-choice bid will be put on hold for a time until the computer has examined all the other applicants' rankings. If all six of the people in Halibut's first tier also rated Halibut as their first choice, they would be matched, and Halibut would be filled. When the program gets back to you, it would then note that your first choice, Halibut Hospital, is filled and would move all your other choices up a notch. The Codliver Consortium is now your #1 (remaining) pick. If you are listed in the first tier at Codliver, that is where you will be matched. If Codliver is also filled, then Septicemia becomes your first choice, and so on.

If you think about it, you can see why, under computer matching, putting a long shot in first place does not hurt your chances at your lower ranked settings. If your first choice is filled or you are not listed, your second choice is treated as your first choice. In the Year 2000 computer match, 48% of the applicants who matched obtained their first-choice position, 67% got one of their top two choices, and 79% got one of their top three (APPIC, 2000b).

Consider another scenario. Again, suppose you ranked Halibut first but they ranked you ninth. Let us suppose that in the first round Halibut filled only three slots with their first-tier selections. With applicants applying to an average of 12 or 13 places each, it would be remarkable if all six of their top tier applicants also listed Halibut first, especially if Halibut took the opportunity to try for some superstars that they had little chance of attracting. (Under computer matching, unlike Uniform Notification, Halibut can afford to rank very desirable but unlikely candidates without hurting its chances of filling.) Halibut now has three slots filled and three still vacant. Their seventh, eighth, and ninth selections are now promoted to their first tier. This time, when the computer gets back to you, it again notes that Halibut is your first choice. Since they ranked you ninth, you are now in their first tier and you are matched with Halibut. You are dropped from the program, and Halibut now has only two slots left to fill. Halibut stays in the program until all their six slots are filled or until their list is exhausted.

Program-specific matching operates just like global matching, except each "program" has its own ROL which is balanced against the ROLs from all the other programs. Suppose the Septicemia School of Medicine divided its 12 slots evenly among its four major tracks, inpatient psychiatric, behavioral medicine, neuropsychology, and child, allocating three positions to each area. In your application and interview, you would have specified which program or programs you were interested in and then filled out your ROL according to your preferences. Suppose you ranked

**188** Megargee's Guide to Obtaining a Psychology Internship

Septicemia's behavioral medicine track first, the Codliver Consortium's behavioral medicine program second, Septicemia's neuropsych track third, Codliver's neuropsych track fourth, and Halibut Hospital fifth. If you really liked Septicemia as a site but were not enthusiastic about working with adult inpatients, you might have ranked that program toward the bottom of your ROL. Having no interest in working with children, you did not include the child program on your ROL.

In this case, if you were in the first tier for Septicemia's behavioral medicine track, you would be matched to that program. If not, the process would proceed as before. If Septicemia's behavioral medicine people ranked you fourth and they were matched with only two of their top three selections, then you would be moved up to their first tier and matched to that program. However, if all three behavioral medicine positions are filled with higher ranked applicants, the program would then try to match you with your second choice, namely Codliver's behavioral medicine program and so on until you find a match.

What if you were ranked first for the Septicemia neuropsych track? No matter how badly they wanted you, since that was your third choice, you would not be matched with that program unless and until you had failed to get into your two more preferred behavioral medicine programs. And, no matter how much you like Septicemia, there is no way you could be matched with their child program because you did not include it on your ROL.

As you can see, the rankings determine the outcomes. There is none of the bargaining that occurred under the old Uniform Notification procedure in which the Septicemia ITD might have called you on Notification Day to offer you the inpatient psychiatric slot with a minor rotation in behavioral medicine as an inducement.

With thousands of applicants and positions and countless iterations, the matching process takes time. Detailed explanations of the process are available on the APPIC Web site's FAQ file. While this is going on, you need to get ready for Match Notification Day.

## ☐ Countdown to Match Day

After you have taken a week or two off from the internship rat race, it is time to prepare for Match Day. Although you hope for the best, you should prepare for the worst. Every year 15% of the applicants are not matched on Match Day. As I noted earlier, many of those who are unmatched are students from strong programs. One unmatched woman wrote me that she had interviews at 9 of the 11 sites to which she applied. In other words, it could happen to you.

The week before Match Day, reread Chapter 10, which tells you what

The Endgame **189**

to do in the event you are not matched. During the week, you should decide what you will do if you do not match and make plans to implement that strategy. You may choose to work on your dissertation and wait another year before applying again. On the other hand, you may decide that if you do not match you will continue to seek a position through the APPIC Clearinghouse. If so, you should plan to prepare a number of generic application packets so you will be ready to submit them as soon as the Clearinghouse opens on Monday.

## Learning If You Matched

Monday, February 22, 2000 . . . Match Day . . . was a day of chaos for the 528 applicants who learned that they had not been matched to an internship. As the APPIC Board (2000a) later reported, "we heard from many unmatched applicants how difficult and stressful it was to deal with all of the following in the space of a few hours: (a) the emotional aspects of learning they were unmatched, (b) consulting with family, friends, and faculty about how to proceed, and (c) preparing to apply to programs through the Clearinghouse."

A number of unmatched applicants posted letters to the Board describing the chaos that ensued as they scrambled for the 284 vacant positions that were posted in the Clearinghouse. Several suggested that the Board adopt the procedure used in medical schools whereby unmatched applicants are notified three days earlier so they have time to deal with the stress of not matching and decide what to do about it. Subsequently, the Board adopted a two-stage notification process for the 2001 match. This worked much better.

In the first stage, which is currently the Friday preceding Match Day, applicants are informed as to whether they have been matched to any program. Those who are matched can learn which program they were matched with on the following Monday. (If you are matched, do not bother calling your top choices to see if you were matched there; the internships get no feedback on their matching results until Match Notification Day.) Those who are not matched have the weekend to decide what to do.

## Match Day

Match Day is currently the Fourth Monday in February. If you obtained a match, beginning at 11:00 a.m. Eastern Standard Time,[27] you can find out

---

[27]If you are time-zone challenged, this is 10:00 a.m. Central time, 9:00 a.m. Mountain time, 8:00 a.m. Pacific time, 7:00 a.m. Alaskan time, and 6:00 a.m. Aleutian-Hawaiian time.

**190**    Megargee's Guide to Obtaining a Psychology Internship

where you are going by e-mail and the Internet.[28] If you have no e-mail or Internet access, NMS will provide you with your results by phone.

Simultaneously, the internship programs learn who was matched to them and whether or not they have any unfilled positions. Applicants and internships can now communicate freely with one another. APPIC encourages ITDs to call their newly selected interns as soon as possible after 11:00 a.m. on Match Day, so you should stay near your phone and keep the line open. After you have received your new ITD's call, you should inform your ADCT as to where you were matched. You are then free to go celebrate. However, if any of your colleagues failed to match, it would be better to go help them deal with the Clearinghouse.

## After Match Day

Within 72 hours after the close of receiving the matching results (i.e., by the following Thursday), the Training Director at your internship is supposed to send you and your ADCT letters confirming all the details of your appointment. It should specify the conditions of your appointment, including the stipend level, fringe benefits, and the dates when the internship begins and ends. If these conditions differ in any material way from what was specified in the brochure or what you expected, you and your ADCT should get in touch with the ITD and discuss the differences.

For the candidates who matched, Match Day signals, at long last, the end of the seemingly interminable internship application season. It has consumed months of your life. At last it is over, and you will be surprised how soon it fades from memory. It never failed to amaze me how applicants who were pacing in agitation the week before Notification Day assured their younger colleagues that it was a breeze when they reported their experiences at our annual internship panel discussion a week later.

For those who did not match, Match Day is when you must decide whether or not to pursue your quest of an internship for the coming year and, if so, how to go about it. This topic is covered in Chapter 10.

---

[28]Aside from where you matched, the results are confidential. You will only be told which program you are matched with. You cannot find out how you were ranked at the other programs to which you applied. Similarly, your internship will be told only that you are matched to their program; they will not know whether you ranked them first or fifteenth (Keilin, 2000).

# Dealing With Adversity

Centuries ago, the Japanese philosopher Ihara Saikaku (1642–1693) noted, "There is always something to upset the most careful of human calculations." So, too, with seeking an internship. In the course of applying for internships, everyone experiences some adversity. When I asked previous applicants to describe disasters they had experienced, I received a wide range of responses. Many concerned interviewing. Just before her first interview, one woman discovered she was pregnant with twins. A man reported the airlines lost his luggage containing his interview suit. Another became so anxious that he hyperventilated and had an asthma attack during an interview. However, except for the woman whose car was hit by an 18-wheeler as she drove home from interviewing, the worst disaster for most was discovering that they had not matched with any internships.

## ☐ Failure to Match

For those who do not match, the APPIC Clearinghouse opens at 11:00 a.m. EST on Match Day. All the positions that remain unfilled after the matching process is completed are automatically listed in the Clearinghouse unless the ITDs specified they should not be when they submitted their ROLs. After the 2000 match, the Clearinghouse included 177 programs, with a total of 284 positions available for the 528 applicants who had not matched, some of whom no doubt decided to defer applying for another year.

**192**    Megargee's Guide to Obtaining a Psychology Internship

In addition to the Clearinghouse listings, APPIC provides a Clearinghouse e-mail list service. There the training sites can post information about the positions they have available, descriptions of their program, information about the types of applicants they are seeking, instructions on how to apply for positions, and information about how they plan to select applicants for these positions. As time passes they may also post announcements of new positions that open up. ITDs are also asked to announce when positions they have previously posted are filled.

In 2000, the unmatched applicants had to decide immediately whether to wait until next year or to seek a position through the APPIC Clearinghouse or e-mail list. Few if any were prepared for the frantic scramble that followed. Once the formal matching procedure was completed, all the APPIC rules governing relations between applicants and training sites no longer applied. ITDs could make their own rules and make offers as soon as they identified an applicant that appeared competent. Some ITDs called trusted ADCTs at their favorite universities, asking if they had any unmatched students they could recommend, accepting them sight unseen on the ADCT's recommendation. Some who had indicated that applications would be accepted for the next several days awarded their slots before the deadline was up. Students who took time to investigate positions often found they had been filled before they could apply.

The weekend warning that unmatched applicants now have gives you time to decide on a strategy and make preparations in the event you do not match. I advise my students to decide what they will do in the event that they do not match and to make their basic preparations before "Fateful Friday." My best advice is to "hope for the best, but prepare for the worst."

## Preparing for Match Day

If you fail to match, you will no doubt be upset, probably devastated. If you are a graduate student in psychology, you are used to succeeding. You may not have experienced a significant failure before, and it will take some time to deal with it. Anger and depression are natural emotions. As a clinician, you know that this is not a good time to make important decisions. Therefore, before Fateful Friday, while it is still academic, you should decide whether you will attempt to get a position through the Clearinghouse in the event you do not match. Some students elect to wait a year and improve their prospects by completing their dissertations and getting additional training. Others choose to try and obtain a position through the Clearinghouse when it opens on Match Day.

If you think that you will probably continue your quest, it is a good idea to prepare your application materials in advance. Put together a generic application packet including a CV, an AAPI, a transcript, three signed letters addressed "To whom it may concern," and your ADCT's signed Internship Eligibility form. If you get bad news on Friday, you will need to make copies of these materials and have them ready to fax, e-mail, or send by next-day courier on Monday. The Clearinghouse operates like the Oklahoma Land Rush, and you cannot afford to waste time hanging around a copying service on Monday when you need to be on the phone to ITDs.

## Deciding What to Do on Fateful Friday

On the Friday preceding Match Day, find out whether you obtained a match. If you did not match, you should immediately discuss the situation with your ADCT and other mentors. Since the weekend is coming up and the Clearinghouse scramble begins Monday, you should try to confer with your advisors as soon as possible.

The first question you need to discuss is whether you should continue to seek a position this year. If you followed my advice, you have already thought about this and made a decision in the abstract. Now that the possibility of not matching has become a reality, you should seek input from your ADCT, major professor, and other advisors.

It may be that, professionally or personally, you are simply not ready to go on internship and this fact was evident to the Internship Selection Committees. If this is the case, painful as it may be, it is probably best that you did not get chosen this year. You need to concentrate on remedying whatever deficits you have so you will be ready at some future date. This may mean taking additional courses, completing your dissertation, obtaining additional practicum experience, or perhaps getting some personal therapy or counseling.

Even if you are ready for internship, your mentors may advise you to spend another year working on your academic goals and completing your dissertation while you get some additional training and, perhaps, publish a paper or two. As I noted earlier, few students get much research done while on internship, and spending another year at your academic training center will not only make you more competitive when applying for an internship next year, but also improve your chances of obtaining a good postdoctoral position the year after.

If you and your advisors agree that you should try to seek a position through the Clearinghouse, together you should review your application strategy and materials to diagnose what went wrong. Did you limit yourself to only a few sites in a restricted geographic area? Maybe you should rethink a decision not to relocate. Did you only apply to highly competitive training sites? Perhaps you need to lower your sights a little. Did you

**194**    Megargee's Guide to Obtaining a Psychology Internship

apply to programs with which you did not really fit? A survey of 318 applicants who did not match in 1999 showed that 59% blamed the internship shortfall, 42% stated they had applied to too-limited a geographic area, 41% applied to too few sites, 35% indicated they had applied to too many highly competitive sites, and 25% blamed bad luck (Keilin et al., 2000).

Review your application for things that might turn an internship off. A weak reference letter can be deadly. If one of your recommenders admitted that you occasionally get your feet wet when you walk on water or confessed that it takes you two bounds to leap a tall building, it may have been enough to cause Selection Committees to lower your ranking or even leave you off their ROL. If you or your ADCT spot a weak letter, try to obtain a stronger one for Monday.

Recently, older applicants and candidates with family obligations have had a lower match rate than those who are young and single. If this fits you, perhaps you need to remove your age or family status from your CV. A single mother who failed to match reported that after she removed any mention of her family status she obtained a position through the Clearinghouse.

However, even after you and your ADCT have considered all the possibilities, you may still be in the dark as to why you failed to match. As long as supply exceeds demand, there are going to be some good candidates who do not match, even if they had a number of interviews and received good feedback. With so many applicants currently competing for positions, there is an element of luck in the matching process, especially at large sites that receive 100 or more applications. Your luck may have been bad. If you are female, maybe an internship needed more males to balance their class, or vice versa. Maybe after screening out their unacceptable candidates, the Selection Committee ranked the rest alphabetically and your last name is Zzzzipf. Perhaps some distant sites allocated most of their positions to candidates from universities in their vicinity that they had already supervised on practicum. You know you double-checked the numbers on your ROL, but were the internships' Selection Committees equally careful?

You will never know. In fact, you cannot even find out if or how high you were ranked at the programs to which you applied. So once you have checked your materials for flaws or defects, there is no point worrying any more about what might have gone wrong. The good news is that, if you choose to participate, a whole new ball game starts fresh on Monday. There are a number of good training opportunities still available. Survey data indicate that 65% of those who failed to match nevertheless obtain positions (Keilin et al., 2000). If you are ready for internship, you have as good a chance as anyone of obtaining one of them, especially if you work harder at accessing the Clearinghouse.

## Failing to Fill From the Internship's View

Applicants are not the only ones who get upset by failing to match. Many ITDs will also become perturbed and agitated on Monday when they discover that they failed to fill all their slots. In addition to calling and writing the interns they did match with and explaining what went wrong to their Chief Psychologists, the ITDs now have to mount a search to fill their empty positions, hopefully by 5:00 p.m. All the rules are off, so they are now free to wheel and deal as they see fit. In addition to screening applications received through the Clearinghouse, many will call trusted ADCTs and ask them if they have any unmatched students.

Applicants who have been through the post-match selection process report that many ITDs seemed to be under great pressure to fill their positions as soon as possible. Keilin et al. (2000, p. 293) reported, "Many unfilled internship positions are filled very soon after match day—many within the first week. Applicants who are not placed through the APPIC Match should be prepared to act quickly to maximize their chances of obtaining an internship position." Some settings that initially stated that they would accept applications until a certain date and then review them all together later advanced the deadline or began reviewing applications and making offers as they were received. Given this perceived pressure on many ITDs, it will behoove you to make rapid decisions and get your materials to the sites you select as quickly as possible.[29]

## Preparing for the Clearinghouse

Before Monday, you should download the current Clearinghouse information posted on the APPIC Web site. Study it so you know exactly what the rules are. In addition, identify other sources of possible internships, such as the clearinghouse for university counseling center positions maintained by the Association of Counseling Center Training Agents (Lopez & Draper, 1997).

If you decide to seek a position through the APPIC Clearinghouse or e-mail list this year, you should decide on your strategy for Monday. Are you going to limit yourself to particular types of settings, such as those that are fully funded or APA approved? Or are you willing to attend almost any internship that will satisfy your degree requirements? (According to Keilin et al., 2000, 97% of the APA-approved positions are allocated through the APPIC Match, compared with only 65% of the

---

[29]A number of students have suggested a second uniform "Match Day" for applicants seeking positions through the Clearinghouse. In May, 2001, the APPIC President indicated that the Board would consider this proposal at a future meeting. If this suggestion is adopted, it might make the scramble for positions less frantic.

**196**   Megargee's Guide to Obtaining a Psychology Internship

nonaccredited positions.) What about relocating, either with or without your family? Obviously, you will have a better chance of success if you broaden the range of possible sites. Over the weekend discuss these issues with family members and others who will be influenced by these decisions so you have a clear strategy in mind by Monday.

When the Clearinghouse and the e-mail list service open Monday morning, you need to be ready to identify likely sites, check them out, and submit your applications to them as rapidly as you can. Clear your schedule for Monday and as many subsequent days as possible.

Find a setting with optimal communications facilities. You should have a computer, a printer, and a fax machine. One woman reported it was much less expensive for her to purchase a fax machine than it would have been to fax materials from a copying service or to send out multiple overnight mail packages. Ideally you should have one phone line for e-mail and accessing the Clearinghouse, another for the fax machine, and a third, which can be cellular, for calling internships and conducting phone interviews. If the computer line is hard wired rather than call-up, so much the better.

As noted above, you should have copies of your application packet ready to be sent out by overnight courier. Overnight mail is obviously slower and more expensive than fax transmission, but the internships' fax lines often get clogged as applicants attempt to transmit 30- or 40-page application packets. If you have electronic copies of your materials, using e-mail attachments to transmit applications is another good option, assuming the internship has the ability to decipher them.

Call in your support team and ask them for assistance. You will need all the help you can get. You will often be on the phone, so it helps to have others who can operate the computer or the fax machine, address envelopes and take them to the overnight mail pickup, keep animals and children at bay, and just generally make themselves useful. It also helps if you can get your ADCT to call sites on your behalf. Remember that the rules against communicating with internships disappear at 11:00 a.m. Monday. In fact, all rules disappear then.

## Accessing the Clearinghouse

When the Clearinghouse opens, you can obtain a list of all the available positions from the NMS Web site at www.natmatch.com/psychint. Although some ITDs may have chosen not to have their programs included, most of the unfilled slots will be listed. This list is not updated, since NMS has no way of knowing which positions get filled in the hours and days following Match Day. After the first day or two, if you find an interesting position on the Clearinghouse list you should check to see if it is still available. The list is removed from the NMS Web site after 10 days.

You should also subscribe to the e-mail list on which training programs will be posting availability notices. As the day(s) go on, more and more programs will post notices there. Indeed, Keilin et al. (2000) learned that only 40% of those who obtained positions after Match Day found them through the Clearinghouse. The e-mail address changes each year. You can obtain the current address from the APPIC Web site under "Clearinghouse Information."

Your next step is to scan the lists for programs that fit the parameters you decided on. If you have a printed copy of the APPIC *Directory* handy, you won't have to keep accessing the on-line *Directory* to investigate programs.

## Filing Applications

Some students blitz the list. One man wrote he mailed 88 applications, and a woman reported she had submitted over 100 by overnight mail!

Do not expect to have much time to investigate what internships have to offer. Be prepared to apply based on what you can learn from the APPIC *Directory*, the e-mail notice, and the setting's Web site, if they have one. If you wait for an internship to send you materials, you may find the position is filled before you receive them. Keilin et al. (2000) reported that of those unmatched applicants who found positions after Match Day, 40% did so in the first week.

As you identify possible places, I suggest that you submit fax or e-mail applications on one phone line while telephoning on another. If possible, speak to the ITD, explain your situation, and indicate why you think you would be a good fit. If the ITD is not free to talk at that moment, ask for an appointment for a telephone interview or suggest you call back after your materials have arrived. Then go on to the next site.

With applicants outnumbering positions two to one, one would think that the internships would proceed at a more deliberate pace, reviewing as many applications as possible before making a decision. Perhaps in the future they will, but thus far this has not been the case. Perhaps the ITDs feel ashamed of not filling all their positions and want to remedy that situation as soon as possible. Maybe they are under the false impression that there are very few well-trained applicants in the unmatched applicant pool. Whatever the reason for their behavior, until the Clearinghouse selection system operates more deliberately, it behooves you to be prepared to move quickly and effectively to secure a position.

I have tried to convey a sense of how fast-paced the Clearinghouse operation has been in the recent past. One woman wrote me that she had a phone interview scheduled for 3:00 p.m. when another ITD called at 2:55. She explained she had an interview in 5 minutes and asked if she could call the ITD back in an hour. When she called an hour later, the

**198** Megargee's Guide to Obtaining a Psychology Internship

position had been offered to someone else. Another applicant was asked to fax an internship her application. She went to a copying service and paid to have the 50-page packet sent in. When she called to see if it had been received, she was told the position had since been filled and her application would not be reviewed.

As you can see, as it is presently constituted, the post–Match Day selection scramble will require all your available time and energy. If at all possible, clear your schedule for as long as it takes. A number of applicants complained that they had previous obligations to teach classes or see clients. When they got back, many found that the positions they were working on when they left had been filled while they were gone.

As you call and communicate with ITDs, be prepared to decide immediately whether or not to accept an offer if it is conveyed. It is all right to ask for particulars, but I think it is best not to ask for time to think it over. This is a seller's market, and given the ITDs' apparent eagerness to fill their positions quickly, they are unlikely to wait for you to make up your mind.

One APPIC rule that still applies even after Match Day is that once you accept a position you are committed to attending. If, 5 minutes after you accept a position at Moosehead Medical Center, Dr. Almondine Dover-Sole of Halibut Hospital finally returns your call, you are obliged to tell her that you are no longer available.

Once you accept a position, you should write a formal letter of acceptance in which you state your understanding of the agreement that was reached. Moreover, within 72 hours the Training Director at your new internship should send you and your ADCT letters confirming all the details of your appointment. It is important that you obtain this written confirmation because, unlike the Matching Day results, there is no other record of a verbal agreement. If there is any important discrepancy between your understanding of the offer and what is stipulated in the internship's letter, you and your ADCT should contact the ITD immediately to sort out the details. For a contract to be valid, both parties must agree on the terms; the time to discuss any misunderstandings is as soon as they are perceived, not when you report to the internship the following September.

Most of the positions available on Match Day are filled within a month (Keilin et al., 2000). Additional positions will become available and be announced via e-mail over the course of the year, right up through September. Some sites get additional funding and new positions. Medical or family emergencies may prevent some matched interns from attending. So, even if you do not get a match immediately after Match Day, it is possible you may be able to obtain one later.

## ☐ Dealing With Non-APPIC Sites

Not all internships are members of APPIC. If you are considering a non-APPIC site, either because you did not match or because its location or program is particularly attractive, you should take certain precautions.

A site that is not a member of APPIC naturally does not have to abide by APPIC rules regarding either the selection process or the training afforded. If you apply to a non-APPIC program, you may get a call from the ITD before APPIC Ranking Day telling you that you have been accepted and that you have only a day or two in which to consider the offer. If the non-APPIC site is your first choice, there is no problem. If it is not, you have to decide whether or not to accept the offer without knowing the results of the APPIC Matching. Some candidates caught in this sort of dilemma have complained to the APPIC Board, but of course there is nothing the Board can do to regulate internships that are not APPIC members.

If you are considering a non-APPIC site, Mellott et al. (1997) recommend that you investigate whether the training program meets the requirements of your university and the licensing board in whatever locale you plan to practice. They advise,

> The amount and type of supervision available and the kinds of experiences that the applicant wishes to receive during this year of training should be negotiated with the agency in advance. Once the details are finalized, they should be spelled out in a contract that is signed by the applicant, their university training director, and the on-site training supervisor. Following these steps will help ensure that the site abides by the contract and provides the intern with the experience he or she needs. (p. 195)

### The Disappearing Internship

Another kind of disaster, which is fortunately extremely rare, is the disappearing internship. This topic was not covered in the first edition of this book because, until 1991, I had never heard of an internship disappearing. That year, I encountered four cases. While this is an infinitesimal fraction of the 2,700 plus internships awarded annually, it is extremely upsetting to those concerned.

Internships can disappear by acts of God, which are called "natural disasters," and by acts of humans, which logic demands we term "unnatural disasters." The unnatural disasters are more common. We will not draw any theological or philosophical conclusions from this, but simply report on the unnatural kind first.

In 1991, Dr. Kathie Larsen, who was then Chair of APPIC, reported to

**200** Megargee's Guide to Obtaining a Psychology Internship

the membership, "As a number of states are in dire financial straits, training budgets have sometimes been a target of budget cuts. In three cases which came to our attention this summer, internship programs had funding withdrawn or frozen, months after they made offers to interns on calling day" (Larsen, 1991, p. 1). Larsen reported that APPIC intervention was successful in restoring the stipends in two of these cases. The third program was not a member of APPIC and declined intervention. Moreover, Larsen noted, "The attorneys for this program maintained that acceptance letters specifying dates and the stipend amounts were necessary for the offers made on calling day to be considered binding. The program had not written such letters" (p. 1).

There are several instructive lessons to be drawn from Larsen's (1991) comments:

1. If at all possible, go to an APPIC internship;
2. Insist on receiving a formal letter or contract from the ITD specifying the conditions of the appointment, as required by the APPIC regulations; and
3. If you are later told your position is frozen, or if the conditions of employment do not conform to those stipulated in your letter, notify APPIC and ask for their assistance.

If something like this should occur, you will find that the internship's ITD and the training faculty will be on your side and will do whatever they can to assist you. They want you as an intern, and they will be utterly appalled and abashed at any abrogation of their good faith agreement by bureaucrats or administrators. They should welcome the APPIC intervention and anything else that can be done to restore the original agreement.

Apart from some budgetary problem, could an internship change its mind after you have been matched with them? No. Matching is binding on the training program just as it is on you. Once you have received your letter, you have an enforceable contract. The only possible circumstance that I can imagine whereby an internship might be able to rescind an offer is if they discovered you submitted a false or fraudulent application. What would constitute fraud? Misrepresenting your education or employment history, forging a transcript or letter of recommendation, or concealing a felony conviction on your AAPI. These are the sorts of things that could conceivably lead an internship to reconsider and prevail in the event of a lawsuit (Hollander, 1990). If you have honestly supplied all the information required, then the internship's acceptance letter makes it a "done deal."

But what about natural disasters? Well, these do occur. Hurricanes, tornadoes, floods, and other natural disasters can strike internship facilities just like anything else. However, even such catastrophes can sometimes work out for the best. One year under UND, one of my students seemed to have nothing but bad luck. A thoroughly congenial chap, "hard luck Sam" had excellent credentials and superb letters. He should have had no difficulties, but unfortunately his first choice was a VA medical center that receives well over 100 applications. Admission there always requires good luck, and Sam's seemed in short supply. The ITD was most supportive and told Sam that he had been one of the first alternates; there were simply not enough slots available to make him an offer.

Sam was disappointed, but he accepted a position at his second choice, another VA medical center, and made the best of it. Some months later Sam called me in a panic. As he and his family were packing to move, he had received a call from his internship; there had been an earthquake and much of the institution had been badly damaged. The patients were being transferred elsewhere, and the facility was being shut down.

I called the ITD at Sam's first choice and told her about his latest hard luck. I reminded her of all the positive things she had said about Sam and asked if it would be possible for her to have Sam transferred to her program along with his stipend. It took some doing, but eventually it was all worked out. Thanks to the natural disaster, Sam ended up at his first choice, where he had a superb year.

## ☐ Dealing with Rule Violations: The APPIC Standards and Review Committee

In previous editions of this book, I had to devote an entire chapter to rules violations. In it, I described the nature and extent of various rules violations and then discussed in detail how applicants could file formal complaints against internships that broke the rules. In preparing this edition, I debated with myself whether to even discuss the topic. This in itself speaks volumes about the degree to which computer matching has eliminated most of the illegal behavior that previously plagued the internship selection process.

After the 1997 internship-selection season ended, Carl Zimet, the Chair of the APPIC Standards and Review Committee (ASARC), announced that it had been an "epic" year for allegations of selection rule violations by APPIC members. Complaints had reached an all-time high. Three years later, at the 2000 APPIC business meeting, Zimet reported that no complaints had been filed with ASARC.

The ASARC complaint process is set forth in detail in the APPIC *Directory*. It was devised by lawyers to ensure due process, and, as you might suspect, it is lengthy and involved. Complainants are urged to attempt to resolve their problems informally. Those unable or unwilling to do so must file a written complaint on a form provided in the *Directory*. The

202    Megargee's Guide to Obtaining a Psychology Internship

complaint then goes to the parties accused of the rule violation for their written response. Eventually the ASARC Board appoints a case coordinator who collects statements from all parties and makes a recommendation to the ASARC Board which may dismiss the case or make a recommendation for some sort of sanctions to the full APPIC Board.

Even in the days of UND, when the air was filled with accusations of misconduct, few formal complaints were filed. Students and their ADCTs feared repercussions if they brought charges against an internship. Even if they did pursue a grievance, the process was so time consuming that Notification Day would have come and gone before the matter was finally adjudicated.

Under UND, the vast majority of the informal and formal complaints focused on efforts by ITDs to induce candidates to reveal their rankings, and the mendacity of applicants who "first-choiced" more than one setting (Megargee, 1997). Today the most pervasive informal complaint concerns ITDs asking overly personal questions in interviews and a perceived pattern of discrimination against some older applicants with family obligations. None of the students with whom I have corresponded has filed a formal complaint with ASARC regarding these behaviors, but, based on how ASARC has handled other issues over the years, I doubt if a formal complaint would get very far. ASARC can only deal with violations of APPIC rules, and APPIC rules don't specifically address these behaviors.

Fortunately APPIC's intern applicant listserv now provides a forum for students to air their grievances. There they can receive a sympathetic hearing from the APPIC Board members who monitor the bulletin board without the need for formal complaints and legal proceedings. As we have seen, students' constructive criticism of the timing of the failure-to-match notification process led the Board to adopt the policy, suggested by some students, of notifying people who failed to match three days prior to opening the Clearinghouse. I expect that applicants' complaints about inappropriate interview questions and possible age discrimination will probably lead the Board to educate its members regarding such practices. Prevention is better than punishment.

## ☐ The Bottom Line

Applying for internships is stressful no matter what the ground rules are. Whether it is the Uniform Notification poker game or the Computer Match roulette wheel, don't let the selection strategy bother you. No matter what matching procedure is employed, it is in your best interest to be ranked as high as possible by the internship of your choice.

Although applying for internships is challenging, you should be able to cope with it successfully now that you understand what it is all about.

Remember that everybody concerned is seeking the optimal match between interns and programs in order to achieve the best possible educational experience for all involved. Many applicants experience needless anxiety because of unrealistic expectancies. Put aside any irrational concerns, and you will be able to cope with the real issues effectively.

No matter what sort of internship you decide is best for you, you want to make the best possible impression. First, make sure you are ready for internship. Develop your skills and credentials to the utmost. Take the right courses, work hard, get good grades, and earn outstanding recommendations. Read on your own, and develop your knowledge of all things clinical. Do well in a variety of practicum settings; be the person who is responsive to supervision, who can be relied on to keep cool in a crisis, and who cheerfully handles his or her share of the tough tasks. Produce quality research and get it published. Have a dissertation project approved and in progress. Above all, be honest, responsible, and ethical. In short, do everything you can to be the kind of student you will want to supervise in the years to come.

Once you have established your qualifications, review your priorities and preferences, investigate the various internships, and select those that best meet your needs. Then go for it. Make the best possible presentation via your CV, AAPI, letters, and interviews. In your site visits, obtain the information you need to make your decision, follow the rules, and be honest and forthright with the internship faculties. Work with your ADCT, discuss your options with the internship ITDs, and convince the programs that you have what it takes to succeed.

If you are well prepared to go on internship, choose your sites well, and play your cards as I have suggested, the odds are that you will obtain an internship that is good for you. Don't discard your application materials—next year you will probably need them when you apply for a postdoctoral fellowship or a supervised clinical position leading to licensure.

Continue to enhance your skills and credentials. As you will soon discover, the present oversupply of psychologists is not limited to internships. It also extends to the marketplace, especially for those who want to devote their careers to psychotherapy (Dixon & Thorne, 2000; Robiner & Crew, 2000). Remember to view yourself as a product that you will have to sell (Spruill, 1997). Since HMOs are not convinced that Ph.D.s or Psy.D.s in psychology practice psychotherapy any better than master's-level licensed social workers or counselors, it is difficult for doctoral-level clinical or counseling psychologists to justify charging higher fees. As a result, many psychologists who have specialized in the practice of psychotherapy have fallen on hard times.

As you prepare for internship, keep the issue of supply and demand in mind, and prepare yourself to fill a less crowded niche in the market-

**204** Megargee's Guide to Obtaining a Psychology Internship

place. My personal opinion is that more psychologists ought to return to their roots and focus on assessment and research. However, I am biased because that has been my career path. If you want to specialize in an area that has less competition from master's-level practitioners, consider behavioral medicine, pediatric psychology, neuropsychological assessment, psychopharmacology, and forensic psychology.

Whatever your goals, I hope you get what you are looking for and that this book has helped.

# APPENDIX 1

## Useful Web Sites for Internship Applicants

*Air travel advice:* www.dot.gov/airconsumer/flyrights.htm. Access this site to download *Fly Rights: A Consumer Guide to Air Travel*. This pamphlet provides detailed consumer information on all aspects of air travel, including your rights if your flight is canceled, delayed, or overbooked or your luggage disappears.

*American Psychological Association, Association of Psychology Graduate Students (APAGS):* www.apa.org/apags/homepage. Information and listservs for psychology graduate students. APAGS conducts internship workshops and produces a workbook for internship applicants.

*Association of Psychology Postdoctoral and Internship Centers (APPIC):* www.appic.org/. The organization that regulates the internship selection process. Use this site to access the on-line APPIC *Directory* of psychology internships and to obtain application forms, information about the internship selection process, and reports on results of matching in previous years. Sign up for the APPIC MATCH NEWS and join the intern applicant listserv.

*CareerBuilders:* www.careerbuilders.com/gh_int_htg_illegal.html. This site discusses illegal interview questions and how to deal with them. There are links to other sites which provide general information on interviewing for job seekers.

*Government forms:* www.fillform.gsa.gov. Download the free software from this site and you can fill out those pesky federal employment application forms on your computer.

**205**

## 206  Useful Web Sites for Internship Applicants

*National Matching Service (NMS):* www.natmatch.com/psychint. Access this site to obtain your match number information about how to submit your rankings, and to eventually learn where you matched.

*West Virginia University, Department of Psychology:* www.as.wvu.edu./psyc. Access this site to download Herschell and McNeil's (2000) forms for keeping track of practicum hours.

# APPENDIX 2

# Availability of Internship Positions by Region and State

**Region 1: East coast, Northern section**

| State | No. of agencies APA accredited | No. of agencies Not accredited | Funded positions Full time | Funded positions Part time | Mean full stipend | No. of applications | Mean no. of applications per position |
|---|---|---|---|---|---|---|---|
| Connecticut | 7 | 1 | 48 | 0 | 16,700 | 712 | 14.8 |
| Delaware | 2 | 0 | 7 | 0 | 17,500 | 191 | 27.3 |
| Massachusetts | 20 | 3 | 112 | 5 | 15,900 | 2,237 | 19.0 |
| Maine | 2 | 0 | 6 | 0 | 19,100 | 99 | 16.5 |
| New Hampshire | 4 | 0 | 16 | 0 | 14,000 | 318 | 19.9 |
| New Jersery | 10 | 3 | 54 | 0 | 15,400 | 1,020 | 18.9 |
| New York | 52 | 9 | 313 | 11 | 16,900 | 6,330 | 19.5 |
| Pennsylvania | 18 | 1 | 83 | 0 | 16,700 | 1,681 | 20.3 |
| Rhode Island | 1 | 0 | 18 | 0 | 17,200 | 282 | 15.6 |
| Vermont | 1 | 1 | 7 | 0 | 16,500 | 68 | 9.7 |
| Total | 117 | 18 | 664 | 16 | 16,530 | 12,938 | 18.2 |

**Region 2: East coast: Southern section**

| State | No. of agencies APA accredited | No. of agencies Not accredited | Funded positions Full time | Funded positions Part time | Mean full stipend | No. of applications | Mean no. of applications per position |
|---|---|---|---|---|---|---|---|
| District of Columbia | 8 | 1 | 32 | 0 | 19,200 | 939 | 26.8 |
| Georgia | 9 | 2 | 34 | 0 | 19,700 | 865 | 23.4 |
| Maryland | 13 | 2 | 72 | 0 | 21,200 | 1,420 | 19.2 |
| North Carolina | 6 | 1 | 37 | 0 | 17,330 | 727 | 19.6 |
| South Carolina | 3 | 0 | 21 | 0 | 16,500 | 340 | 16.2 |
| Virginia | 14 | 0 | 53 | 0 | 19,800 | 1,009 | 19.0 |
| Total | 53 | 6 | 249 | 0 | 19,469 | 5,300 | 20.7 |

# 208 Availability of Internship Positions by Region and State

### Region 3: Eastern central

| State | No. of agencies APA accredited | Not accredited | Funded positions Full time | Part time | Mean full stipend | No. of applications | Mean no. of applications per position |
|---|---|---|---|---|---|---|---|
| Alabama | 2 | 1 | 15 | 0 | 15,500 | 137 | 9.1 |
| Florida | 16 | 14 | 147 | 0 | 13,800 | 2,363 | 13.5 |
| Michigan | 14 | 5 | 66 | 5 | 16,100 | 1,015 | 13.2 |
| Mississippi | 2 | 2 | 19 | 0 | 18,200 | 217 | 11.4 |
| Ohio | 13 | 3 | 79 | 0 | 17,300 | 1,092 | 13.8 |
| Tennessee | 7 | 4 | 47 | 2 | 15,600 | 753 | 15.4 |
| West Virginia | 3 | 0 | 9 | 0 | 16,000 | 151 | 16.8 |
| Total | 57 | 29 | 382 | 7 | 15,480 | 5,728 | 13.3 |

### Region 4: Northern central

| State | No. of agencies APA accredited | Not accredited | Funded positions Full time | Part time | Mean full stipend | No. of applications | Mean no. of applications per position |
|---|---|---|---|---|---|---|---|
| Illinois | 25 | 15 | 159 | 0 | 15,700 | 3,293 | 20.2 |
| Indiana | 11 | 4 | 54 | 1 | 15,900 | 989 | 18.0 |
| Iowa | 4 | 1 | 15 | 0 | 16,900 | 296 | 19.7 |
| Kentucky | 5 | 1 | 20 | 0 | 19,800 | 442 | 22.1 |
| Minnesota | 9 | 2 | 39 | 0 | 16,900 | 666 | 15.9 |
| Wisconsin | 7 | 5 | 43 | 2 | 15,400 | 758 | 17.6 |
| Total | 61 | 28 | 330 | 3 | 16,138 | 6,444 | 18.9 |

### Region 5: Western central

| State | No. of agencies APA accredited | Not accredited | Funded positions Full time | Part time | Mean full stipend | No. of applications | Mean no. of applications per position |
|---|---|---|---|---|---|---|---|
| Arkansas | 2 | 1 | 10 | 0 | 19,100 | 88 | 8.8 |
| Kansas | 5 | 1 | 26 | 0 | 16,600 | 339 | 13.0 |
| Louisiana | 5 | 0 | 18 | 0 | 16,800 | 366 | 20.3 |
| Missouri | 9 | 3 | 55 | 0 | 17,700 | 265 | 12.6 |
| Nebraska | 2 | 0 | 28 | 0 | 22,600 | 158 | 5.6 |
| Oklahoma | 3 | 0 | 21 | 2 | 14,900 | 194 | 8.4 |
| South Dakota | 1 | 0 | 3 | 0 | 18,500 | 56 | 18.7 |
| Texas | 19 | 5 | 122 | 0 | 19,500 | 1,735 | 14.1 |
| Total | 46 | 10 | 283 | 2 | 18,653 | 3,201 | 12.7 |

## Availability of Internship Positions by Region and State    **209**

**Region 6: West coast and Mountain**

| State | No. of agencies APA accredited | Not accredited | Funded positions Full time | Part time | Mean full stipend | No. of appli- cations | Mean no. of applications per position |
|---|---|---|---|---|---|---|---|
| Arizona | 5 | 2 | 25 | 0 | 16,300 | 571 | 22.8 |
| California | 35 | 2 | 256 | 15 | 15,800 | 4,802 | 16.0 |
| Colorado | 8 | 3 | 42 | 2 | 14,700 | 796 | 18.1 |
| Hawaii | 3 | 0 | 12 | 0 | 23,700 | 113 | 9.4 |
| Montana | 1 | 0 | 3 | 0 | 16,200 | 70 | 23.3 |
| New Mexico | 2 | 0 | 11 | 0 | 16,600 | 189 | 17.2 |
| Nevada | 1 | 0 | 3 | 0 | 18,000 | 57 | 19.0 |
| Oregon | 5 | 2 | 32 | 0 | 15,500 | 406 | 12.7 |
| Utah | 5 | 5 | 35 | 1 | 16,400 | 387 | 10.8 |
| Washington | 6 | 2 | 47 | 3 | 15,400 | 712 | 14.0 |
| Wyoming | 2 | 1 | 9 | 0 | 16,200 | 135 | 15.0 |
| Total | 73 | 17 | 475 | 21 | 16,800 | 8,238 | 16.0 |

# APPENDIX 3

## A Sample Curriculum Vitai

**Curriculum Vitae**
**Rosa Thorne**
(Formerly Rosa Cholla)

### Addresses

*Home*: 2702 Elm Street
University City,
East Idabama 82046
(111) 222-3333
(Leave message)

*Work*: Psychology Clinic
ML 102, East Idabama
State University
University City, EI 82032
(111) 888-7777, Ext. 240

### Personal Data

*Birthplace*: Santo Loco, Costa Rojo
*Citizenship*: U.S. (naturalized 10/1/88)
*Birthdate*: 2/27/75
*Marital Status*: Married
*Ethnicity*: Hispanic
*Social Security*: 222-33-4444

### Education

2000
to
Present

Doctoral Candidate, Psychology Department
East Idabama State University
*Major*: Clinical Psychology
*Minor*: Nutrition
*Dissertation Topic*: The Influence of Grain Price Fluctuations on the Incidence of Post-Traumatic Stress Disorder Among Midwestern Farmers (Prospectus Defended: July 4, 2000)
*Major Professor*: B. J. Mentor, Ph.D.

A Sample Curriculum Vitae    **211**

*Comprehensive Examination*: Passed, December 25, 1999
Areas of Concentration: Psychopathology, Food psychology

1998    Master of Science, Psychology Department
East Idabama State University
*Major*: Clinical Psychology
*Major Professor*: Elsie Bordenkau, Ph.D.
*Thesis Title*: *Personality Changes Resulting from Pesticide Exposure in Rural Children*

1996    Bachelor of Science, *magna cum laude*
Horatio Alger College
Collegetown, East Idabama
*Major*: Psychology
*Minor*: Home Economics
*Honors*: Phi Beta Kappa, Sigma Xi

## Other Educational Experiences

February 12, 1999: Advanced 8 PF Test workshop (6 hrs.)
Presented by Raymond Stenscore, Ph.D.
Sponsored by American Personality Association,
Central City, East Idabama

April 18, 1998: Eating Disorders Workshop (8 hrs.)
Presented by Duncan Donut, Ph.D.
Sponsored by East Idabama Psychology Association,
University City, EI

## Special Skills

Native fluency in Spanish.

## Professional Affiliations

East Idabama Psychology Association
Student Member
Vice President, 1999

American Association of Food Psychologists
Associate Member

**212** A Sample Curriculum Vitae

*Professional Credentials*

Licensed Food Counselor, East Idabama (License #000248)

*Supervised Clinical Experience*

June 2000   *Psychology Trainee*
to          University City Community Mental Health Center
Present     University City, EI

Duties: Outpatient-based assessment and therapy with adult, adolescent, and child populations. Client population includes a variety of developmental, anxiety, mood, personality, and organic disorders. Complete assessments performed for learning disabilities, neuropsychological, attention deficit hyperactivity and personality disorders. Therapy experience includes group, family, conjoint, and individual using an eclectic approach. (20 hrs./wk.)

*Supervisor*: Alice Sage, Ph.D., ABPP

Sept. 1999   *Crisis Management Unit Team Member*
to          East Idabama State University
Present     University City, EI

Duties: On-site intervention and evaluation of psychotic, suicidal, and homicidal crises; assess dangerousness and need for hospitalization; transport clients to psychiatric receiving facilities with a member of the East Idabama State University Police Department. (On call for 24 hours, roughly 6 days a month.)

*Supervisor*: Delilah Sampson, Ph.D.

June 1998   *Psychology Trainee*
to          East Idabama State Hospital
May 2000   Central City, EI

Duties: Inpatient-based assessment and therapy with an adult population. Responsibilities include screening admissions using objective and projective devices; intellectual and personality testing as requested by resident psychiatrists; and leading assertiveness training groups. (10 hrs./wk.)

*Supervisors*: George Thyme, Ph.D. and Mary Marjoram, Ph.D.

A Sample Curriculum Vitae    **213**

| June 1997 | *Psychology Trainee* |
| to | East Idabama State University |
| May 1998 | Campus Psychology Clinic |

Duties: Individual, family, and marital therapy involving clients with wide variety of presenting problems (including: child management, marital issues, social skill deficits, low self-esteem, substance abuse, depression, stress management, impulse and anger control, and learning disabilities). Assessments for learning disabilities, attention deficit hyperactivity disorder, behavior problems, and emotional problems. (15 hrs./wk.)

*Supervisor:* Sara Nutmeg, Ph.D.

### Teaching Experience

| Sept. 1999 | General Psychology for Honors Students |
| to | Freshman/Sophomore Level Course |
| Present | Department of Psychology, East Idabama State University |

*Duties:* Responsible for all phases of teaching including the preparation and administration of lectures, selection of reading materials and assignments, construction of examinations, and the assignment of course grades.

| Jan. 1999 | Sensation and Perception |
| to | Junior/Senior Level Course |
| May 1999 | Department of Psychology, East Idabama State University |

*Duties:* Responsible for all phases of teaching, including the preparation and administration of lectures, the selection of reading materials and assignments, the development of experiments to demonstrate sensory and perceptual principles, the construction of examinations, and the assignment of course grades.

| Sept. 1998 | Physiological Psychology |
| to | Sophomore Level Course |
| Dec. 1998 | Department of Psychology, East Idabama State University |

*Duties:* Laboratory assistant. Responsible for preparing and conducting laboratory sections, including didactic instruction, supervision of students, and grading laboratory reports.

## 214    A Sample Curriculum Vitae

### Research experience

June 1999     Dissertation in progress.
to
Present

In this study I am using a time series analysis to investigate the association of fluctuations in grain prices and the incidence of post-traumatic stress disorders among Midwestern farmers, covarying for loan interest rates, in comparison with the incidence of PTSD among service workers in the same area.

My prospectus was defended July 4, 2000 and data collection is almost complete. I anticipate defending my dissertation before leaving for internship.

June 1998     Research Assistant
to                 B. J. Mentor, Ph.D.
May 1999

I worked 10 hrs./wk on Dr. Mentor's NAA-funded epidemiological study of nutrition and stress in rural Americans. In the course of this research I administered 350 Structured Clinical Interviews and was responsible for coding demographic data.

June 1997     Masters Thesis Research
to
May 1998

As part of Prof. Elsie Bordenkau's large study on rural psychopathology, I compared the Eight Personality Factor (8 PF) profiles of 25 male and 25 female adolescent farm children who had been exposed to toxic levels of malathion and DDT as children with matched samples of suburban children from the same school. As predicted by Bovine's Dissipation theory, the exposed male children were higher than the suburban boys on scales assessing Threshia and Harvestia and lower in Sowing and Reaping. No differences were noted for the girls.

### Publications and Presentations

Thorne, R. C., & Bordenkau, E. (1989). Effects of herbicide exposure on personality factors in rural adolescents: A test of Bovine's hypotheses. *Journal of Food Psychology, 12,* 432–441.

A Sample Curriculum Vitae **215**

Thorne, R. C. (1989, May). *Environmental influences on personality development*. Paper presented at the meeting of the East Idabama Psychological Association, Central City, East Idabama.

Mentor, B. J., Bordenkau, E., & Thorne, R. C. (in press) Nutritional stresses in adolescence. Chapter to appear in C. Bovine and B. Allspice (Eds.), *Comprehensive handbook of food psychology* to be published by the East Idabama State University Press.

## References

B. J. Mentor, Ph.D.
Professor of Psychology
Psychology Department
East Idabama State University
University City, EI 82032

Alice Sage, Ph.D.
Chief Psychologist
University City Community Mental Health Center
2102 River Road
University City, EI 82066

Sigmund Spinach, Ph.D.
Director of Clinical Training
Psychology Department
East Idabama State University
University City, EI 82032

# APPENDIX 4

## Questions Interviewers Ask Intern Applicants

These last two appendices are placed at the end so you can find them easily. If you have a few minutes while you are waiting for an interview, you may want to review these questions.

Some interviewers use a fairly structured approach such as that described by Hersh and Poey (1984). They follow a formal list of topics and systematically explore your experience in various areas such as individual therapy, group therapy, inpatient, outpatient, assessment, supervision, and so on. In each area, you are asked about your past experience, orientation, work style, and areas that need improvement. Others may use the AAPI as a basis for the interview, going from topic to topic and asking you to describe each area more fully or to comment on your experiences.

The interviews my students have experienced have typically been less structured and more personal. In standard employment interviews, personal topics are off limits, but, as I noted in Chapter 8, many interviewers apparently feel that this does not apply to psychologists and inquire about personal matters. Some even go so far as to turn what should be an employment interview into an intake or treatment session. If this happens, don't let it throw you off stride.

Most interviewers are as interested in *how* you respond as they are in the actual content of your answers. It is okay to ask for a moment to think about your answer to a question and to admit that you do not know the answer. Remember that this is an interaction; listen to what the interviewer has to say.

Research shows that we often judge a person in the first few minutes, even seconds, of personal contact. Humor, flexibility, good eye contact, and a firm handshake are important. Remember the "three C's"—you want to appear confident, competent, and cordial.

**216**

Questions Interviewers Ask Intern Applicants    **217**

## ☐ General Professional Questions

- How did you become interested in psychology?
- How did you become interested in (specific professional/research interest areas)?
- What is your theoretical orientation? How does it influence how you conceptualize a case?
- What would you be doing if you were not in psychology?
- What do you see as your personal strengths and weaknesses? How do they influence your work? What have you done to deal with your shortcomings?
- What do you hope to get out of your internship?
- What are your goals after internship? In 5 years?
- List three contributions you hope to have made to psychology by the year 2020.

## ☐ Questions About Your Credentials

- What were your GRE scores? GPA?
- How many graduate programs accepted you?
- Why did you choose your training program?
- Why should we accept *you* over other equally qualified candidates?
- What do you have to contribute to us?

## ☐ Questions About Research

- What is your dissertation topic? How is your research progressing? Where do you see it going?
- How does our setting fit in with your research goals?
- How did you get interested in that topic?
- What is the clinical relevance of your research?

## ☐ Questions About Assessment

- Tell us about an instrument with which you feel competent.
- How many complete batteries have you administered, interpreted, and written up? What instruments would you include in a complete battery and why?
- What is your favorite intelligence test? Why do you prefer that to [names others]?

**218** Questions Interviewers Ask Intern Applicants

- What is your opinion of projective techniques?
- What Rorschach scoring system do you use? Why?
- What do you think of this Rorschach response?
- What is your opinion of MMPI-2? MMPI-A? The MCMI-III?
- Comment on this MMPI-2 profile.
- What is your opinion of the most recent diagnostic nomenclature? How could it be improved?
- What further assessment training or experiences do you need?
- [Interviewer described a referral question] What instruments would you administer and why?
- [Panel of seven interviewers showed applicant a brief video of a client] Provide a diagnosis and treatment strategy and indicate how you arrived at that formulation.

## ☐ Questions About Treatment

- What is your greatest strength as a therapist?
- What is your orientation in therapy? What do you think of dynamic/behavioral/etc. approaches?
- How do you conceptualize the process of therapeutic change?
- What is your opinion of empirically supported treatment approaches? With what ESTs are you familiar?
- What experience have you had with family/group/inpatient/etc. treatment?
- How do you conceptualize the process of therapeutic change?
- How do you use emotion in therapy?
- Talk about a therapy case you had. How did you conceptualize the case? What was most effective?
- Describe a case that went well. One that presented difficulties. One that presented multicultural issues.
- Have you ever been in therapy? How did this affect how you conducted therapy?
- What further therapy training or experiences do you need?

## ☐ Questions About Supervision

- What sorts of supervisors have you had?
- How would your previous supervisor describe you? Your present supervisor? How would you want your internship supervisor to describe you?
- Describe a conflict you had with a supervisor and how it was resolved.
- What type of supervision is best for you?

Questions Interviewers Ask Intern Applicants     **219**

- What were your best and worst supervision experiences?
- [For older applicants] How will you relate to supervisors who may be younger than you?

## ☐ Questions About Clients

- What sorts of clients have you worked with? Which were you most comfortable with? Effective? Least comfortable? Least effective?
- Describe your experiences with culturally diverse clients.
- Have you ever administered [specifies test] to [specifies minority group]? What problems does that pose in administration or interpretation?
- Have you worked with clients such as we have here?
- What type of client is most difficult for you to work with? What type of feelings do you have toward such cases? How do these feelings interfere with your treatment?

## ☐ Questions About Ethics

- Tell me about an ethical problem you have been faced with and how you handled it.
- [Describes situation] What are the ethical implications of this situation?

## ☐ Questions Dealing with Recruiting

- What can we do to make you want to come here?
- How do you see us as fitting with your goals?
- Are you really willing to relocate to attend this internship? How do your spouse or children feel about relocating?
- Which of your interest areas are/are not addressed by our program?
- Where else have you applied and what attracted you to these places?
- Why would someone from an "X-oriented" department want to come to a "Y-oriented" program?
- What attracts you most to our internship?
- How do you want us to remember you?

220 Questions Interviewers Ask Intern Applicants

## ☐ Purely Personal Questions (Most of Which Are Inappropriate).

- Tell me about yourself.
- What do you see as your personal strengths and weaknesses? Who are you, personally?
- Tell me about your family. Are you married? Do you plan on having children? When?
- Do you have any children? Tell me about them. What arrangements will you be making for them while you are interning?
- Will your family obligations interfere with your ability to put in the hours that this position requires?
- If you move here while your partner remains behind, how will your relationship be affected? Will you be going home most weekends?
- Would you really move here in view of your spouse's career goals?
- How will you be able to live on [our stipend]? What are your sources of support? Will you need to take a second job?
- Tell me about your family problems.
- What was the worst thing about your father? Your mother?
- How did you deal with your parents' divorce?
- What would your spouse/partner say is your worst characteristic?
- What do you do in your spare time?
- How do you deal with stress?
- How is your health? Would we have to make any special accommodations if you came here?
- [To an older applicant] Do you think you will have enough energy to complete our demanding internship?
- Are you a religious person? How does your religion affect your work?

## ☐ Other Questions

- What psychologist do you most admire? Why?
- If there was an Nobel Prize in psychology, who should be the first recipient?
- Do you think you can handle high-stress situations? Why?
- What else would you like me to know that is not apparent from your CV?
- What is your greatest weakness?
- What is the one question you hope I will not ask you?

# APPENDIX 5

## Questions Applicants Can Ask Interviewers

At some point, most interviewers will ask you what questions you have. As I emphasized in Chapter 8, you should always have some questions ready to ask. One reason you went to the time, trouble, and expense to interview at a site was so you could learn more about it. This is your chance.

Just as you may get annoyed by interviewers who ask you for information that is readily apparent from your CV or AAPI, you should not ask for material that is supplied in the internship's brochure. It is, however, OK to ask if the information in the brochure is up to date and accurate. If not, what has changed?

## ☐ Questions Regarding The Setting (Professional)

- What are you looking for in an intern?
- What interested you in my application?
- What's the main thing former interns would say about their experience here?
- What does an intern do during a typical work week?
- Do you anticipate any staff or program changes for the next year?
- What is the relation between psychology and other disciplines?
- Are interns here regarded as employees or students?
- What is the balance between service and training? Does funding for the program depend on fees generated by the interns and staff?
- How does the program here compare with where you interned?
- Does this program encourage specialization or diversification in training?
- What are the possibilities of doing research during the internship? Would you say there is a research focus here?

**221**

**222** Questions Applicants Can Ask Interviewers

- [To a present intern] What do you like most about this internship? What do you like least?
- Is this a congenial setting? How do trainees and staff get along?
- What is there about the training afforded here that makes it special?

## ☐ Questions Regarding the Setting (Personal)

- What is the cost of living here?
- Are any changes in stipends or benefits expected?
- Is daycare for children difficult to find? How are the schools in this area?
- How available are jobs in my spouse's field?
- What is the availability of affordable housing here?
- Do many interns take outside jobs during the intern year?

## ☐ Questions Regarding Rotations

- Do you anticipate any changes in the rotations being offered next year?
- How are rotations determined? Are they fixed or flexible?
- Do interns negotiate for rotations?
- What are the common presenting problems on the [insert] rotation? What is the typical duration of treatment? What is the ratio of therapy to assessment?
- [To an intern] What rotations do you regard as being truly outstanding? Which ones should you avoid?

## ☐ Questions Regarding Assessment

- Do you use a standard assessment battery?
- What is the ratio of assessment to treatment?
- What is the attitude toward projectives?
- What are the opportunities for neuropsych assessment?

## ☐ Questions Regarding Therapy

- What opportunities are there for family/group/etc. therapy?
- Are there opportunities to conduct groups on the inpatient unit? What kinds of groups are done? Supportive, problem-centered, insight-oriented?
- How many long-term clients does an intern carry?

Questions Applicants Can Ask Interviewers **223**

- Are interns expected or encouraged to have personal therapy? If so, who provides it and what are the goals?

## ☐ Questions Regarding Supervision

- How many supervisors does an intern have? How are they assigned?
- What do you as a supervisor have to offer that I might not get elsewhere?
- Is all supervision provided on site? Is supervision on an individual or group basis?
- How much and what type (audio, video, live) supervision is provided?
- What are the theoretical orientations of the supervisors? Which is predominant?

## ☐ Questions Regarding Didactics

- What types of seminars are offered? What are some typical topics?
- Who are some of the Grand Rounds speakers you have had in the last year?

## ☐ Questions Regarding the Matching Procedure

- Do you use different matching numbers for different programs?
- Do you ever take more than one student from a given university?

## ☐ Questions Regarding Future Opportunities

- Where do your interns go after finishing their internships? Where are some of your former interns now? What kinds of job opportunities are there for psychologists in this area?
- Does the internship play an active role in trying to place its graduates?

# REFERENCES

American Psychological Association. (1986). *Accreditation handbook*. Washington, DC: Author.

Association of Psychology Postdoctoral and Internship Centers. (1994). *Selection day: Internship offers and acceptances—Summary of results*. Report presented at the annual APPIC Business Meeting at the 102nd annual meeting of the American Psychological Association, Los Angeles, CA.

Association of Psychology Postdoctoral and Internship Programs. (1997, April 5). *Policy statement announced by the APPIC Board*. First APPIC Membership Meeting and Conference, Orlando, FL.

Association of Psychology Postdoctoral and Internship Programs. (1999a). *1999 matching program. Survey results—APPIC member internship training directors*. Report dated April 19, 1999, published on the APPIC Web site, pp. 1–6.

Association of Psychology Postdoctoral and Internship Programs. (1999b). *1999 matching program. Survey results—Internship applicants*. Report dated April 18, 1999, published on the APPIC Web site, pp. 1–9.

Association of Psychology Postdoctoral and Internship Programs. (1999c). *The APPIC match: Frequently asked questions for internship applicants*. Report dated June 28, 1999, published on the APPIC Web site, pp. 1–12.

Association of Psychology Postdoctoral and Internship Programs. (2000a). *APPIC match 2001 changes*. Report dated June 20, 2000, published on the APPIC Web site, pp. 1–2.

Association of Psychology Postdoctoral and Internship Programs. (2000b). *APPIC match report from the APPIC Board of Directors*. Report dated February 22, 2000, published on the APPIC Web site, pp. 1–4.

Association of Psychology Postdoctoral and Internship Programs. (2000c). *APPIC match report # 2 from the APPIC Board of Directors*. Report dated March 24, 2000, published on the APPIC Web site, pp. 1–2.

Belar, C. D., Bieliauskas, L. A., Larsen, K. G., Mensh, I. N., Poey, K., & Roehlke, A. J. (Eds.). (1987). *Proceedings of the National Conference on Internship Training in Psychology*. Washington, DC: Association of Psychology Internship Centers.

Belar, C. D., Bieliauskas, L. A., Larsen, K. G., Mensh, I. N., Poey, K., & Roehlke, A. J. (1989). The national conference on internship training in psychology. *American Psychologist, 44*, 60–65.

Belar, C., & Orgel, S. (1980). Survival guide for intern applicants. *Professional Psychology, 11*, 672–675.

Blom, B. E. (1990). Remarks from the editor. *APIC Newsletter, 15*(2), 5–7.

Blom, B. E. (1991). Remarks from the editor. *APPIC Newsletter, 16*(2), 2–3.

Brems, C., Thevenin, D. M., & Routh, D. K. (1991). The history of clinical psychology. In C. E. Walker (Ed.), *Clinical psychology: Historical and research foundations* (pp. 3–35). New York: Plenum.

## References    225

Brickley, M. (1998). Integrating an internship into a market-driven psychology practice. *Professional Psychology: Research and Practice, 29*, 390–393.

Brill, R., Wolkin, J., & McKeal, N. (1985). Strategies for selecting and securing the predoctoral internship of choice. *Professional Psychology: Research and Practice, 16*, 3–7.

Brown, R. (1996). Training in professional psychology: Are we addressing the issues? *Professional Psychology: Research and Practice, 27*, 506–507.

Burt, C. E. (1985). Reflections on interviewing for internship. *Clinical Psychologist, 38*, 91–93.

Carifio, M. S., Buckner, K., & Grace, W. C. (1987). APPIC guidelines: Are they really helpful? *Professional Psychology: Research and Practice, 18*, 407–409.

Carifio, M. S., & Grace, W. C. (1992). Ignored data on the development of psychology internships. *American Psychologist, 47*, 428.

Carlin, A. S. (1982, August). *Is there a free lunch? Experiences with unfunded interns.* Paper presented at the annual meeting of the Association of Psychology Internship Centers. Washington, DC. (Reprinted in *Internship training in professional psychology,* pp. 497–500, by R. H. Dana & W. T May, Eds., 1987, Washington, DC: Hemisphere)

Casey Jacob, M. (1987). Managing the internship application: Advice from an exhausted but content survivor. *The Counseling Psychologist, 15*, 146–155.

Chamberlain, J. (2000, February). Where are all these students coming from? *American Psychological Association Monitor,* pp. 32–33.

Clay, R. (1997, April). Concerns about internships lead APA to conduct survey. *American Psychological Association Monitor,* p. 51.

Constantine, M., & Gloria, A. (1996). Managed health care and predoctoral internship sites: Preliminary findings and implications for training programs and internship candidates. *APPIC Newsletter, 21(1)*, 4, 18.

Constantine, M., & Gloria, A. (1998). The impact of managed health care on predoctoral internship sites: A national survey. *Professional Psychology: Research and Practice, 29*, 195–199.

Constantine, M., & Keilin, W. G. (1996). Association of Psychology Postdoctoral and Internship Centers' guidelines and the internship selection process: A survey of applicants and academic and internship training directors. *Professional Psychology: Research and Practice, 27*, 308–314.

Constantine, M., Keilin, W. G., Litwinowicz, J., & Romanus, T. (1997). Notification day perceptions of unplaced internship applicants and their academic training directors: Recommendations for improving future internship selection processes. *Professional Psychology: Research and Practice, 28*, 387–392.

Dana, R. H., & May, W. T. (Eds.). (1987). *Internship training in professional psychology.* Washington, DC: Hemisphere.

Davies, R. (1987). Demise of the 3rd year internship: The changing role of the internship in graduate training. *Professional Psychology: Research and Practice, 18*, 481–484.

DeAngelis, T. (2000). School psychologists: In demand and expanding their reach. *APA Monitor, 31(8)*, 30–32.

Dion, K., Bersheid, E., & Walster, E. (1972). What is beautiful is good. *Journal of Personality and Social Psychology, 24*, 286–290.

Dixon, K. E. & Thorn, B. E. (2000). Does the internship shortage portend market saturation? 1998 placement data across the four major national training councils. *Professional Psychology: Research and Practice, 31*, 276–280.

Drummond, F. E., Rodolfa, E., & Smith, D. (1981). A survey of APA and non-APA approved internship programs. *American Psychologist, 36*, 411–414.

Durand, M. V., Blanchard, E. B., & Mindell, J. A. (1988). Training in projective testing: Survey of clinical training directors. *Professional Psychology: Research and Practice, 19*, 236–238.

Eggert, M. A., Laughlin, P. R., Hutzell, R. R., Stedman, J. M., Solway, K. S., & Carrington,

# 226 References

C. H. (1987). The psychology internship marketplace today. *Professional Psychology: Research and Practice, 18,* 165–171.

Faverman, R. K. (2000). When is a new psychologist ready for independent practice? *APA Monitor, 31*(8), 44–47.

Fox, R. E. (1991). Improvements still needed in selection process. *APIC Newsletter, 16*(2), 33–36.

Gavzer, B. (1992, June 14). Fly smart. *Parade Magazine,* pp. 4–6.

Gladwell, M. (2000, May 29). The new-boy network: What do job interviews really tell us? *New Yorker,* 68–72; 84–86.

Gollaher, K. K., & Craig, N. W. (1994). *Securing a pre-doctoral internship: A student's perspective on how to succeed in the internship application process.* Torrance, CA: NWC Enterprises.

Grace, W. C. (1985). Evaluating a prospective clinical internship: Tips for the applicant. *Professional Psychology: Research and Practice, 16,* 475–480.

Greenberg, D. J., Cradock, C., Godbole, A., & Temkin, T. (1998). Cost effectiveness of clinical training in a community mental health center. *Professional Psychology: Research and Practice, 29,* 604–608.

Guerrero, R. (2000, July). *1999 survey of internship applicants: Match outcome for APPIC internship applicants.* Unpublished technical report. Washington, DC: Research Office, American Psychological Association.

Hall, R. G., & Cantrell, P. J. (Eds.). (1996). *Directory of internship and postdoctoral programs in professional psychology, 25th Edition: 1996–1997.* Washington, DC: Association of Psychology Postdoctoral and Internship Centers.

Hall, R. G., & Hsu, J. (Eds.). (1999). *Internships and postdoctoral programs in professional psychology. APPIC Directory 28th Edition, 1999–2000.* Washington, DC: Association of Psychology Postdoctoral and Internship Centers.

Hall, R. G., & Hsu, J. (Eds.). (2000). *Internships and postdoctoral programs in professional psychology. APPIC Directory 29th Edition, 2000–2001.* Washington, DC: Association of Psychology Postdoctoral and Internship Centers.

Hecker, J. E., Fink, C. M., Levasseur, J. B., & Parker, J. D. (1995). Perspectives on practium: A survey of directors of accredited PhD programs and internships (Or, what is a practicum hour, and how many do I need?). *Professional Psychology: Research and Practice, 26,* 205–210.

Herschell, A., & McNeil, D. W. (2000). A method to track practicum hours during psychology graduate training: Easy, cheap, and necessarily obsessive. *Behavior Therapist, 23,* 58–61.

Hersh, J. B., & Poey, K. (1984). A proposed interviewing guide for intern applicants. *Professional Psychology: Research and Practice, 15,* 3–5.

Holaday, M., & McPherson, R. (1996). Standardization of APPIC predoctoral psychology internship application forms. *Professional Psychology: Research and Practice, 27,* 508–513.

Hollander, P. A. (1990). Internships and the law: Questions and answers. *APIC Newsletter, 15*(1), 56–57.

Humphreys, K. (2000). Beyond the mental health clinic. New settings and activities for clinical psychology internships. *Professional Psychology: Research and Practice, 31,* 300–304.

Johnson, M. C. (1986). The pre-doctoral internship selection process. *Professional Psychology: Research and Practice, 17,* 291–293.

Kaslow, N. (2000, August). *Report presented at the annual APPIC business meeting.* American Psychological Association Convention, Washington, DC.

Keilin, W. G. (1998). Internship selection 30 years later: An overview of the APPIC matching program. *Professional Psychology: Research and Practice, 29,* 599–603.

Keilin, W. G. (2000). Internship selection in 1999: Was the Association of Psychology Predoctoral and Internship Centers' match a success? *Professional Psychology: Research and Practice, 31,* 281–287.

Keilin, W. G., Thorne, B. E., Rodolfa, E., Constantine, M. G., & Kaslow, N. (2000). Examining the balance of internship supply and demand: 1999 Association of Psychology Postdoctoral and Internship Centers' match implications. *Professional Psychology: Research and Practice, 31,* 288–294.

Kingsley, K. (1985). Reflections on internship year. *Clinical Psychologist, 38,* 93–94.

Krieshok, T., Lopez, S. J., Somberg, D., & Cantrell, P. J. (2000). Dissertation while on internship: Obstacles and predictors of progress. *Professional Psychology: Research and Practice, 31,* 327–331.

Larsen, K. G. (1991). Chair's column. *APPIC Newsletter, 16*(2), 1–2.

Laughlin, P. R., & Worley, J. L. (1991). Role of the American Psychological Association and the Veterans Administration in the development of internships in psychology. *American Psychologist, 46,* 430–436.

Lonigan, C. J. (1994, August). *How to be right for the place that you want: Results from a survey of internship directors.* Paper presented at the "Obtaining Internships in Clinical Psychology" symposium at the 102nd annual meeting of the American Psychological Association, Los Angeles, CA.

Lopez, S. J., & Draper, K. (1997). Recent developments and more internship tips: A comment on Mellott, Arden, and Cho. *Professional Psychology: Research and Practice, 28,* 496–498.

Lopez, S., Oehlert, M., & Moberly, R. (1996). Selection criteria for American Psychological Association-accredited internship programs. A survey of training directors. *Professional Psychology: Research and Practice, 27,* 508–520.

Lump, N., Chan, D., Clifford, L., & Tinson, E. (2000, May). Get the best hotel deal. *Readers Digest,* 82–86.

May, T. M., & Dana, R. H. (1990). Issues concerning the internship selection process. *APIC Newsletter, 15*(1), 29–32.

May, T. M., Rice, K., & Birckhead, L. (1990). A current perspective on intern selection: The state of the art. *APIC Newsletter, 15*(2), 37–42.

Maxa, R. (2000, December 1). Rudy Maxa tells how to avoid most air-travel delays. *Bottom Line: Personal,* 10.

Megargee, E. I. (1997). *Megargee's guide to obtaining a psychology internship* (3rd. ed.). Washington, DC: Taylor and Francis.

Mellott, R. N., Arden, I. A., & Cho, M. E. (1997). Preparing for internship: Tips for the prospective applicant. *Professional Psychology: Research and Practice, 28,* 190–196.

Miller, R. K., & Van Rybroek, G. J. (1988). Internship letters of recommendation: Where are the other 90%? *Professional Psychology: Research and Practice, 19,* 115–117.

Mitchell, S. (1996). Getting a foot in the door: The written internship application. *Professional Psychology: Research and Practice, 27,* 90–92.

Monti, P. M. (1985). Interviewing for internships. *The Behavior Therapist, 10,* 205–206.

Ochroch, R. (1990). The need for half-time internships: Affirmative action on behalf of parents of young children. *APIC Newsletter, 15*(2), 35–37.

Oehlert, M. & Lopez, S. (1998). APA-accredited internships: An examination of the supply and demand issue.

Oehlert, M., Lopez, S., & Summerall, S. (1997). Internship application: Increased cost accompanies increased competitiveness. *Professional Psychology: Research and Practice, 28,* 595–596.

Peterson, D. R. (1985). Twenty years of practitioner training in psychology. *American Psychologist, 40,* 441–451.

Peterson, D. R. (1991). Connection and disconnection of research and practice in the education of professional psychologists. *American Psychologist, 46,* 422–429.

Petzel, T. P., & Berndt, D. (1980). APA internship selection criteria: Relative importance of academic and clinical preparation. *Professional Psychology, 11,* 792–796.

Pion, G., Kohout, J., & Wicherski, M. (2000). "Rightsizing" the workforce through training reductions: A good idea? *Professional Psychology: Research and Practice, 31,* 266–271.

## 228 References

Plante, T. G. (1987). Comments on the internship application process. *Professional Psychology: Research and Practice, 18,* 7–8.

Rabasca, L. (2000). Making the case for more school-based mental health services. *APA Monitor, 31* (8), 34–35.

Resnick, R. J. (1997). A brief history of practice—Expanded. *American Psychologist, 52,* 463–468.

Robiner, W. N., & Crew, D. P. (2000). Rightsizing the workforce of psychologists in health care: Trends from licensing boards, training programs, and managed care. *Professional Psychology: Research and Practice, 31,* 245–263.

Rossini, E., & Moretti, R. (1997). Thematic Apperception Test (TAT) interpretation: Practice recommendations from a survey of clinical psychology doctoral programs accredited by the American Psychological Association. *Professional Psychology: Research and Practice, 28,* 393–398.

Shemberg, K. M., & Leventhal, D. B. (1981). Attitudes of internship directors toward pre-internship training and clinical models. *Professional Psychology, 12,* 639–646.

Solway, K. Huntley, D. K. Stedman, J. M., Laughlin, P. R., Belar, C. D., Flynn, M. F., & Carrington, C. H. (1987). Survey on non APA-accredited internships and their interns. *Professional Psychology: Research and Practice, 18,* 176–178.

Spitzform, M., & Hamilton, S. (1976). A survey of directors from APA-approved internship programs on intern selection. *Professional Psychology, 7,* 406–410.

Spruill, J. (1997). *The business side of psychology.* Paper presented during panel discussion at the First APPIC Membership Meeting and Conference, Orlando, FL.

Spruill, J., & Pruitt, S. D. (2000). Preparing psychologists for managed care settings: Enhancing internship training programs. *Professional Psychology: Research and Practice, 31,* 305–309.

Stanford University Career Planning and Placement Center. (1988). *How to write your resume.* Stanford, CA: Author.

Stedman, J. M. (1983, March). Fear and loathing on intern selection day. *American Psychological Association Monitor.*

Stedman, J. M. (1989). The history of the APIC selection process. *APIC Newsletter, 14*(2), 35–43.

Stedman, J. M., Costello, R. M., Gaines, T., Jr., Schoenfeld, L. S., Loucks, S., & Burstein, A. G. (1981). How clinical interns are selected: A study of decision-making processes. *Professional Psychology, 12,* 415–419.

Stedman, J. M., Hatch, J. P., & Schoenfeld, L. S. (2000). Preinternship preparation in psychological testing and psychotherapy: What internship directors say they expect. *Professional Psychology: Research and Practice, 31,* 321–326.

Stedman, J. M., Hatch, J. P., & Schoenfeld, L. S. (in press). Internship directors' valuation of preinternship preparation in test-based assessment and psychotherapy. *Professional Psychology: Research and Practice.*

Stedman, J. M., Hatch, J. P., & Schoenfeld, L. S. (under review). The current status of psychological assessment training in graduate and professional schools.

Stedman, J. M., Neff, J. A., Donahoe, C. P., Kopel, K., & Hays, J. R. (1995). Applicant characterization of the most desirable internship training programs. *Professional Psychology: Research and Practice, 26,* 396–400.

Stewart, A. E., & Stewart, E. A. (1996a). A decision-making technique for choosing a psychology internship. *Professional Psychology: Research and Practice, 27,* 521–526.

Stewart, A. E., & Stewart, E. A. (1996b). Personal and practical considerations in selecting a psychology internship. *Professional Psychology: Research and Practice, 27,* 293–303.

Stricker, G. (1997, April). *Slouching toward the millennium.* Keynote address delivered at the First APPIC Membership Meeting and Conference, Orlando, FL.

Thorne, B. (1997, March 17). *Results of the CUDCP Internship Survey.* Personal communication.

Thorne, B., & Dixon, K. E. (1999). Issues of internship supply and demand: A survey of

## References   **229**

academic clinical and counseling programs. *Professional Psychology: Research and Practice, 30*, 198–202.

Tipton, R. M., Watkins, C. E., Jr., & Ritz, S. (1991). Selection, training, and career preparation of predoctoral interns in psychology. *Professional Psychology: Research and Practice, 22*, 60–67.

Winiarski, M. (1986). *Applying for internship*. Unpublished manuscript, Psychology Department, Florida State University, Tallahassee.

Zeiss, A. M., (2000). Reenvisioning internship training in clinical and counseling psychology: Developments in the Department of Veterans Affairs System. *Professional Psychology: Research and Practice, 31*, 314.

Zimet, C. N. (1988). Further comments on the internship application process. *Professional Psychology: Research and Practice, 19*, 5.

Zimet, C. N. (1990). Chair's column. *APIC Newsletter, 15*(2), 4–5.

Zimet, C. N. (1991). Chair's column. *APPIC Newsletter, 16*(1), 1–3.

# INDEX

Academic credentials, 23–25, 29
  enhancement of, 33–34
  questions about, 217
  required for eligibility, 71
  (See also Curricula vitae (CV))
Academic Directors of Clinical Training
  (ADCTs), ix
  goals of, 19–20
  projective testing expected by, 95–96
  restraints on, 13
  verification of eligibility by, 31–32,
    128–129
Accreditation:
  criteria for, 1–2
  of internship programs, 45, 51–52, 70,
    199
  required by internship programs, 71–
    73, 72(table), 74(table)
  (See also American Psychological
    Association (APA))
Accreditation Handbook (APA), 25
Aesthetics, of curriculum vitae, 111–113
Age factors, 33, 108, 194
Air travel:
  joining frequent traveler programs, 139
  obligations of airlines, 146
  saving money on, 140–142
  timing of, 142–146
  web site for, 205
  (see also Travel)
American Association for Applied
  Psychology (AAAP), 3
American Automobile Association (AAA),
  139
  discounts offered through, 149
  tour books, 148
  (see also Travel)
American Board of Examiners in
  Professional Psychology (ABPP), 2
American Psychological Association
  (APA):
  Accreditation Handbook, 25

accreditation of internship programs,
  51–52
annual meeting of, 30
Graduate Student Association's
  Internship Task Force, 119
match rate for accredited programs,
  195–196
professional training by, 3–4
Publication Manual, 106
web site for, 205
(See also Accreditation)
American Psychologist, 51, 95
Anxiety about internship, 43–45, 49
Applicants:
  eligibility requirements for, 71, 73
  expectations of Internship Training
    Director, 20–21
  first impression of, 21–22
  number of internships available to, 14–
    17, 44–45, 89, 203
  unmatched, 189–190 (See also
    Clearinghouse)
Application for Psychology Internship
  (AAPI), 28, 114
  duplicate forms for interview, 161
  submitting, 133–135
  uniformity of, 119–120
Application process:
  dissertation status and, 58, 71
  filing after Match Day, 197–198
  follow up for, 40, 136–137
  how many to send, 117–118
  personal questions, 18
  statistics on, 44–45
Arden, I.A., 114
Assessment field of psychology:
  interview questions about, 217–218
  practicum experience ranked by
    Internship Training Directors, 22
  as prospective career, 204
Association for the Advancement of
  Behavior Therapy (AABT), 30

**230**

Index **231**

Association of Counseling Center Training Agents, 195
Association of Psychology and Postdoctoral Internship Centers (APPIC), 1
creation of, 9–13
materials available on web site, 27–28
Standards and Review Committee (ASARC), 169, 201–202
web site for, 205
(See also Application for Psychology Internship (AAPI); Clearinghouse (APPIC); Directory of Internship Programs in Professional Psychology (APPIC); Verification of Internship Eligibility and Readiness form (APPIC))
Attitude-scaling techniques, 181
Auto-biographical essay, 122, 124
Automobile rental companies, 139
(see also Travel)
Availability of internship positions, 14–17, 44–45, 89, 203, 207(table)–209(table)
Awards, listed on curriculum vitae, 100, 102

Behavioral medicine, 204
Belar, C.D., 91, 159
Berndt, D., 95
Beverages, in interviews, 164–165
Blanchard, E.B., 95
Blom, B.E., 63
Boulder model, 4, 6
Brill, R., 180
Brochures about internship programs, 61, 91–92
Burt, C.E., 159

California State Psychological Association, 6
Canadian Psychological Association (CPA), 70
Cancellations, while traveling, 143
CareerBuilders:
on illegal questions, 168
on preparing for interviews, 159
web site for, 205
Casey Jacob, M., 49
on importance of preparation, 27
on interview preparation, 159
on ranking internship preferences, 181
on selecting internship programs, 66
Certification (see Licensing procedures)
Chamberlain, J., 16
Character references, 130

Child care, 63
Children's facilities, 2, 75–76
Cho, M.E., 114
Clearinghouse (APPIC), 41
access to, 196–197
e-mail list service of, 192
match reports, 14–15
preparation for, 192–194
time frame of, 197–198
Client experience:
diversity of, 122, 126
documentation of, 125–126
expectations by Internship Training Directors, 25–26
interview questions about, 219
(see also Record keeping)
Clinical experience:
included on application, 125–127
listed on curriculum vitae, 103–105
work samples from, 29
(see also Record keeping)
Clinical programs, 71–73, 72(table), 74(table)
Clothing, for travel and interviews, 150–151
Communication:
with internship programs, 177–179
with National Matching Service, 189–190
Community mental health centers (CMHCs), 2, 29, 76
Competitiveness:
anxiety about, 44–45
of internship programs, 89–90, 115–116
of non-accredited internship programs, 52, 199
between students from same institutions, 117–119
Comprehensive examinations, 71
Computer matching, 13–14, 37, 173–175, 185–188
Confidentiality, 132
Confirmation of internship selection, 11–12, 190, 198–201
Consortia, 77
Constantine, M., 7–8, 158
Contracts, 198, 200
Correctional facilities, 2, 77–78
Costs:
of applying, 46–48
of direct and indirect expenses, 47(table)
stipends and, 64–65
(See also Travel)
Council of University Directors of Clinical Psychology (CUDCP) survey of costs, 47
Counseling programs, 71–73, 72(table), 74(table)

**232** Index

Couples matching, 62, 182–183
Cover letters, 132–133
Craig, N.W., 115, 159
Credentials, interview questions about, 217
Crew, D.P., 16–17
Curricula vitae (CV), 37
  extra copies for interview, 161–162
  organization of, 110–111
  preparing, 97–110
  resumes vs., 97, 102
  samples of, 28–29, 210–215
CV (see Curricula vitae (CV))

Dana, R.H., 32, 159
Deadlines for application, 38–40, 115, 134–135
Delays, while traveling, 143
Developmentally disabled, facilities for, 2
Didactic training, 29, 54, 223
Directory of Internship Programs in Professional Psychology (APPIC), 37, 69
  accreditation status listed in, 51
  comparison of available internships, 16
  contents of, 70–73
  criteria for internships, 1–2
  half-time positions listed in, 63
  information gathering about sites, 69–70
  number of training centers in, 10
  on-line version of, 70, 91
  preferences of agencies listed in, 74(table), 90
Discarding (see Rejection)
Dissertation:
  research during internship, 58
  status required for internship eligibility, 71
Diversity, of clients, 122
Dress, for travel and interviews, 150–151
Drummond, F.E., 95
Durand, M.V., 95

East Coast region, internship programs in, 85–86, 207(table)–208(table)
Eastern Central region, internship programs in, 86, 208(table)
Education:
  including on curriculum vitae, 100–101, 109
  information for application, 120–121
Electronic tickets (e-tickets), 143
Employment:
  current, 48
  future plans for, 60–61, 170, 223
  history, 102–103, 109–110
  interview questions about, 217

Equipment available to interns, 57
Essays, for application, 121–125
Ethics:
  of internship selection, 12
  interview questions about, 219
  of providing work samples, 132
  truthfulness on application, 128
Evaluation anxiety, 44
Evaluation of internship programs, 50, 115–116
  assembling initial list of sites, 88–93
  of facilities, 57
  personal considerations, 61–67
  of prospective co-workers, 54–55
  questions to ask, 221–223
  scheduling interviews, 156–159
  of setting, 171–172
  site visit and, 155, 165–166

Facilities, 57
Faculty:
  letters of recommendation from, 130
  level of involvement in application process, 20
  as source of information, 88
  (See also Academic Directors of Clinical Training (ADCTs); Internship Training Directors (ITDs))
Family obligations, 33, 37
  anticipation of, 30–31
  couples matching, 62, 182–183
  discussing in interview, 168–169
  evaluating internships and, 61–62
  match rate and, 194
  stress of application period and, 48
  (See also Personal questions)
"Fateful Friday" (see Match Notification Day)
Financial considerations (see Costs)
First impression of applicants, 21–22, 150, 163
Forensic psychology, 204
Fox, R.E., 46, 156, 159
Funding of internship programs, 3, 5, 6, 53–54

Gainesville conference, 24–25, 90
Gavzer, B., 140–141
General hospitals, 2
Geographic considerations, 27, 37, 62–64, 68, 166–169
  circumscribed searches, 116–117
  for lodging, 148
  regional differences, 85–87, 207(table)–209(table)
  (See also Family obligations)
Gladwell, M., 163

Global matching, 184, 187
Gloria, A., 7–8
Goal setting, 44, 49–50, 95
   essays for application, 121–125
   for ranking internship preferences, 180–181
   training needs, 60
Gollaher, K.K., 115, 159
Government forms, 205
Government funding of programs, 3, 5, 6
Grace, W.C., 92, 159
Graduate education, 71, 101
Greenberg, D.J., 21
Grid, for ranking internship preferences, 180–181

Half-time internships, 63
Hall, R.G., 52
Hamilton, S., 95
Hatch, J.P., 25–26
Health care benefits, 64
Health issues, 38, 108–109, 153–154, 169
Health maintenance organizations (HMO), 2
   (See also Managed health care (MHC))
Herschell, A., 28, 104–105, 206
Hersh, J.B., 159–160
High school education, 100
Honors, listed on curriculum vitae, 100, 102
Hospitals, types of, 2, 80–83
Hotels (see Lodging)
Hsu, J., 52

Identifying data, for curriculum vitae, 99–100, 120–121
Illegal questions, 168–169
Information gathering:
   for curriculum vitae, 98
   directly from internship sites, 91
Informed consent, 132
Insurance:
   car, 147
   health, 64, 65
Integrated psychological reports, 127
Interdisciplinary relations, 58–59
Internet:
   application materials available on web sites, 27–28
   for research, 69
   for travel arrangements, 141–142
   web site addresses, 205–206
   web sites, of internship programs, 91
Internship Training Directors (ITDs), ix
   confirmation of offer from, 190
   criteria for client experience, 25–26
   criteria ranked by, 22

evaluating prospective, 54–55
goals of, 20–21
Selection Day procedure, 174–175
survey of, 4–5
Internship Training in Professional Psychology (Dana and May), 32
Interviews:
   conduct during, 163–166
   importance of on-site, 138
   open houses as alternative to, 156
   preparing for, 159–160
   questions for applicants, 216–220
   scheduling, 41, 156–159
   success rate of obtaining, 158
   telephone interviews as alternative to, 160–161
   thank you notes for, 176
   (See also Evaluation of internship programs)

Keilin, W.G., 158, 182, 195–196
Kingsley, K., 159
Krieshok, T., 58

"Laissez faire" period of selection process, 8–9
Larsen, Kathie, 199–200
Legal status of applicant, 108–109
Letters of recommendation, 130, 194
Leventhal, D.B., 4–5
Licensing procedures, 29, 51–52, 101
"Lifeboat list," 116, 158
Likert scales, 32, 129
Lodging:
   cost of, 148–150
   with current interns, 171, 176
   frequent traveler programs, 139, 140, 150
   (see also Travel)
Lonigan, C.J., 129
Lopez, S.J., 16, 96

Mail services, 135
Major professor, letter of recommendation from, 130
Managed health care (MHC), 203
   impact of, 6–8
   internship sites at health maintenance organizations (HMOs), 2
Match News (APPIC), 28
Match Notification Day, 41
   filing applications after, 197
   notification process, 189–190
   planning for, 188–189
   unmatched applicants, 189–190
   (See also Clearinghouse)

**234** Index

May, T.M., 32, 159, 163
McKeal, N., 180
McNeil, D.W., 28, 104–105, 206
Medical benefits, 64
Medical schools, 2, 78–79
Mellott, R.N., 114, 155, 199
Mentors:
    advanced students as, 27, 30
    as source of information, 88
Military internships, 2, 79–80
Mindell, J.A., 95
Minority applicants, 108
Mitchell, S., 122–124, 134, 178–179
Moberly, R., 96
Monti, P.M., 159
Morale, of interns, 65–66
Motels (see Lodging)
Mountain region, internship programs in, 87, 209(table)
Multiple applicants, from same training programs, 117
Multiple programs at sites, 180

National Conference on Internship Training, 2
National Matching Service (NMS), 14, 37
    listings of unfilled positions, 196–197
    program numbers for, 183
    rank-ordered list for, 179
    registration numbers, 54, 99
    web site for, 206
    (See also Computer matching)
National Register of Health Service Providers in Psychology, 1, 2, 51
Natural disasters, 200–201
Negative factors, about internship programs, 66–67
Negative letters of recommendation, 129
Networking:
    opportunities, 30
    with personnel from training sites, 69
Neuropsychological assessment, 204
Non-accredited programs, 71–73, 72(table), 74(table)
Nonprofit outpatient clinics, 76
Northern Central region, internship programs in, 86, 208(table)

Oehlert, M., 16, 96
Offers, of internships (see Confirmation of internship selection)
Open houses, 156
Organizational charts, of internship sites, 58–59
Orgel, S., 91–92, 159
Overbooked flights, 145

Packing, for interviews, 152–153
Paperwork, 35–37, 119
Part-time internships, 63
Pastoral counseling centers, 2
Patients vs. clients, 126
Pediatric psychology, 204
Personal information:
    characteristics of applicants, 118–119
    on curriculum vitae, 99–100, 108–109
Personal questions, 168–169, 220
    inappropriateness of, 18, 108
    used to assess applicants, 33
    (See also Family obligations)
Personnel at internship sites:
    evaluating prospective co-workers, 54–55
    interacting with clerical staff, 162–163
Peterson, D.R., 4
Petzel, T.P., 95
Physical attractiveness stereotype, 21–22, 150, 163
Placement, of interns, 60–61
Plante, T.G., 157
Poey, K., 159–160
Political infighting at sites, 59, 165–166
Politics, of selection process, 19
Practicum experience:
    choosing an internship to complement, 52–53
    documentation of, 125–127, 206
    importance of, 95
    internship program requirements for, 25–27
    listed on curriculum vitae, 103–105
    requirement for, 25–26
    (See also individual types of settings)
Predoctoral vs. postdoctoral internships, 7
Presentations, 105, 106
Prestige, of internship programs, 59–60
Private general hospitals, 80
Private psychiatric hospitals, 2, 81
Professional preparation, for internship, 23–25
Professional schools, 5–6, 72
Professional societies, 30, 34, 102
Program-specific matching, 184–185, 187
Program types required by applicants, 71–73, 72(table), 74(table)
Projective testing, 95–96, 217–218
Psychological Abstracts, 160
Psychological preparation, for internship, 23
Psychopharmacology, 204
Psychotherapy, 73
Publication Manual (APA), 106
Publications, 33–34, 106
    importance ranked by ITDs, 22
    listed in curriculum vitae, 110

Index     **235**

Quality of life, 65–66
Questions:
  for applicants to ask interviewers, 159–
    160, 169–171, 221–223
  responding to, 166–169, 216–220
  (See also Personal questions)


Rank-ordered list (ROL), 179, 182–184
Ranking internship programs, 177, 179–
  180
  disclosure and, 174–175, 179
  goal setting for, 180–181
  grid for, 181–182
  questions asked of applicants and, 167–
    168
  questions to ask interviewers, 222
  submitting rank ordered list, 183–184
Recommendation, letters of, 39–40, 129–
  131
  for Clearinghouse, 194
  importance of, 95
Reconnaissance, 68–69
  (see also Researching internship
    programs)
Record keeping:
  to aid application process, 28
  client data, 126
  for clinical experience, 104–106
  for curriculum vitae, 98–99
  forms for recording practicum
    experience, 206
  during non-accredited internships, 52
  of practicum experience, 125–127
Recruiting, interview questions about, 219
Rehabilitation hospitals, 2
Rejection, 45, 177
Rental car companies, 139–140, 146–148
  (see also Travel)
Research, academic:
  describing goals of, 122–123
  interview questions about, 217
  opportunities during internship, 57–58
  record keeping, 105–106
Research field of psychology, 204
Researching internship programs, 87–88
  identifying appropriate sites, 46, 68–70
  interview preparation and, 160
Resumes, 97, 103
  (see also Curricula vitae (CV))
Ritz, S., 75
Robiner, W.N., 16–17
Rodolfa, E., 95
Rorschach test, 73–75, 217–218
Rotations:
  availability of, 53–54
  questions to ask interviewers, 222
Rule violations, 201–202

Schoenfeld, L.S., 25–26
Scholarship section, of curriculum vitae, 110
School-based internships, 2, 71–73,
  72(table), 74(table), 81–82
Selection process by internship programs,
  8–17, 94–96
  (See also Computer matching; National
    Matching Service (NMS); Uniform
    Notification Day)
Self-evaluation for internship readiness,
  32–33, 36
Seminars:
  available at internship sites, 54, 223
  to supplement graduate programs, 29
Sending application materials, 39–40, 91,
  133–135
Service vs. training, during internship, 56
Settings, types of, 2, 73–85, 221–223
Shakow, David, 3–4
Shemberg, K.M., 4–5
Site visits, 155
  (See also Interviews)
Smith, D., 95
Solway, K. Huntley, 52
Specialization, in specific psychology
  fields, 52–53, 88, 204
Specialized skills of applicants, 29, 89–90,
  101, 109
Spitzform, M., 95
Spreadsheet software programs, 28, 104–
  105, 126–127
  (See also Record keeping)
Standards and Review Committee
  (ASARC), 169, 201–202
State hospitals, 2, 82–83
"Statement of interest," 133
Statistical summaries, of internship
  programs, 70–71
Stedman, J.M., 9, 25–26, 72, 76, 175
  on consortia, 77
  on correctional facilities, 78
  on criteria used by internship
    programs, 33
  on integrated psychological reports, 127
  on medical schools, 79
  on selection criteria, 104
  on training in testing and
    psychotherapy, 73
  on university counseling centers, 83
  on Veterans Administration medical
    centers, 85
Stewart, A.E., 49, 181–182
Stewart, E.A., 49, 181–182
Stipends, 64–65
  (See also Costs; individual types of
    settings)
Strategic preparation, for internship, 26–
  27

**236** Index

Supervision:
  interview questions about, 218–219
  questions to ask interviewers, 223
Supervisors:
  evaluating prospective, 55
  location of, 56
Supplies, for travel, 152–153
Supply and demand of internships, 14–17, 44–45, 89, 203, 207(table)–209(table)
Support group, forming a, 34–35

Teaching experience, 105
Telephone answering devices, 40, 153
Telephone interviews, 160–161
Test administration, 127
Test assessment, 26, 73
  (See also individual types of settings)
Thank you notes, 176
Thematic Apperception Test (TAT), 73–75
Theoretical orientation, 55–56
  assessing programs for, 90
  including on application, 122, 124
  (See also individual types of settings)
Time management:
  for application process, 31–32, 35–42, 114–115
  Clearinghouse and, 197–198
  estimate for direct time expenditure, 46(table)
  scheduling interviews and, 156
  for travel, 142–146
Tipton, R.M., 75, 76
  on consortia, 77
  on medical schools, 79
  on private general hospitals, 80
  on private psychiatric hospitals, 81
  on state hospitals, 82–83
  on university counseling centers, 84
  on Veterans Administration medical centers, 85
Training programs, 95
  during internship, 56, 60
  listed on curriculum vitae, 101
  required from applicants, 72(table), 74(table)
Transcripts, 32, 92–93
Transmission of application materials, 39–40, 91, 133–135
Travel:
  by air, 140–146, 205
  booking, 141–142

by car, 139
dressing for, 150–151
expenses of, 47(table)
health tips for, 154–155
lodging, 148–150, 171, 176
packing for, 152–153
planning for, 37, 138–140
web site for, 205
Treatment, interview questions about, 218

Undergraduate education, 100
Uniform Notification Day (UND), 9–13
  policy, 10
  procedure of, 173–175, 186
  (See also Computer matching)
United States Public Health Services (USPHS) fellowship program, 5
University counseling centers, 83–84

Verbal agreements, 198, 200
Verification of Internship Eligibility and Readiness form (APPIC), 24, 28, 114, 128–129
Veterans Administration (VA) medical centers, 2, 3, 84–85
Violation of rules, 201–202
Voice mail, 153
  (See also Telephone answering devices)

Watkins, C.E., Jr., 75
Web site addresses, 91, 205–206
  (See also Internet)
West Coast region, internship programs in, 87, 209(table)
West Virginia University, Department of Psychology web site, 206
Western Central region, internship programs in, 87, 208(table)
Winiarski, M., 158, 167
Withdrawn offers, 199–201
Wolkin, J., 180
Work experience (see Employment; Practicum experience)
Work samples, 29, 131–132
Written acceptance, of internship position, 42, 198, 200

Zeiss, A.M., 84
Zimet, Carl, 201